THRIVING IN THE GIG ECONOMY

FREELANCING ONLINE FOR TECH PROFESSIONALS AND ENTREPRENEURS

Adam Sinicki

Apress®

Thriving in the Gig Economy: Freelancing Online for Tech Professionals and Entrepreneurs

Adam Sinicki
Bicester, UK

ISBN-13 (pbk): 978-1-4842-4089-2 ISBN-13 (electronic): 978-1-4842-4090-8
https://doi.org/10.1007/978-1-4842-4090-8

Library of Congress Control Number: 2018962549

Managing Director, Apress Media LLC: Welmoed Spahr
Acquisitions Editor: Shiva Ramachandran
Development Editor: Laura Berendson
Coordinating Editor: Rita Fernando

Cover designed by eStudioCalamar

Distributed to the book trade worldwide by Springer Science+Business Media New York, 233 Spring Street, 6th Floor, New York, NY 10013. Phone 1-800-SPRINGER, fax (201) 348-4505, e-mail orders-ny@springer-sbm.com, or visit www.springeronline.com. Apress Media, LLC is a California LLC and the sole member (owner) is Springer Science + Business Media Finance Inc (SSBM Finance Inc). SSBM Finance Inc is a **Delaware** corporation.

For information on translations, please e-mail rights@apress.com, or visit http://www.apress.com/rights-permissions.

Apress titles may be purchased in bulk for academic, corporate, or promotional use. eBook versions and licenses are also available for most titles. For more information, reference our Print and eBook Bulk Sales web page at http://www.apress.com/bulk-sales.

Any source code or other supplementary material referenced by the author in this book is available to readers on GitHub via the book's product page, located at www.apress.com/9781484240892. For more detailed information, please visit http://www.apress.com/source-code.

Printed on acid-free paper

In loving memory of my Dad, Janusz Sinicki

Contents

About the Author. vii

Foreword. ix

Acknowledgments xi

Introduction xiii

Chapter 1:   Welcome to the Gig Economy. 1

Chapter 2:   Getting Started with the Gig Economy and
             Finding Work 13

Chapter 3:   Expanding Your Reach. 31

Chapter 4:   Choosing Your Gigs and Rates Wisely 51

Chapter 5:   Delivering Great Work 75

Chapter 6:   Communication and Collaboration 99

Chapter 7:   The Busywork of Business 123

Chapter 8:   Lifestyle Design. 151

Chapter 9:   Looking Forward. 175

Chapter 10: Setting Sail: Making the Gig Economy Work for You. 201

Index 219

About the Author

Adam Sinicki is a writer, programmer, and presenter living in Bicester, Oxfordshire, UK, where he spends a lot of his time on his laptop in the local coffee shops.

Adam has been working on a freelance basis as a programmer and SEO writer for the past eight years under the company name NQR Productions. He currently spends a lot of this time as a blogger and YouTube presenter at Android Authority, where he covers phone reviews as well as development content. Adam has also found success with numerous other projects, including his own Android app Multiscreen Multitasking, which had over 30,000 paid downloads across its various iterations and came as preloaded software on over 60,000 handsets in India. He also provided the code for Coldfusion's Voxis Launcher.

This is Adam's second book with Apress, the first being *Learn Unity for Android Game Development* (2017).

If you'd like to read more of Adam's work, he also discusses tech, online business, and his other passions for fitness, psychology, and self-development over at his blog: The Bioneer (www.thebioneer.com) and YouTube channel (www.youtube.com/thebioneer). The latter now has over 50,000 subscribers. You can also find him on Instagram (www.instagram.com/thebioneer) and Twitter (www.twitter.com/thebioneer). Stop by and say hi!

When Adam's not working, he enjoys reading comics, working out, playing video games, and relaxing at home with his wife Hannah. They are currently expecting their first baby.

Foreword

I first met Adam Sinicki back in July of 2013. Adam was a subscriber of my YouTube channel ColdFusion. He reached out to me explaining how he had written apps for Android and asked me if I wanted to work on one with him. This was the start of a long-standing project that we both took great joy and excitement in. The result was an Android application called Voxis, essentially a homescreen replacement for Android. The app transformed the look of one's phone to a modern, sleek design with the click of a button. Previously this task took hours of customization and downloading separate apps.

Adam had previously already coded an app of his own, Multiscreen Multitasking, which was very forward-looking for 2013 (this was years before floating chat-heads in Facebook or anything of that nature). Adam was great to work with, friendly, and was always keen to try out new ideas.

From the start we did most of our work remotely and, amazingly, we both worked from home. Adam from London, England, and I from Perth, Australia. Through the wonders of online collaborative technology, we were able to design, implement, release, and market the app (through my YouTube channel).

The completed end-to-end pipeline of the Voxis project highlights the brave new world we live in when it comes to the gig economy. For the first time in history, work can be done from anywhere and by anyone with an Internet connection and a computer! With freelancing websites becoming popular, there are more opportunities than ever before for self-managed work.

Dagogo Altraide, Founder of ColdFusion Studios,
www.youtube.com/user/coldfustion

Acknowledgments

This book would not have been possible without the love and support of my wonderful wife, Hannah Sinicki. She is my best friend and my rock.

I'd also like tip my hat to the people who inspired me to set up my own business in the first place: my dad Janusz Sinicki, Uncle Z, and granddad Bernard Hunt. Also, Tony Stark.

I should also thank my good friend Matthew Tutt, who introduced me to the world of making money online (and who once held the number one spot on Google for that precise search term!). I likely wouldn't have ended up in this job if it wasn't for all his help!

A shout out to Chris "Goof" Hanlon. Because it has become a tradition, not because he has done anything particularly useful.

Plenty of other people got their acknowledgements in the last book . . .

Introduction

The Internet gives us the power to access the world's information in an instant, to leverage incredibly powerful tools located across the world, and to collaborate as teams distributed remotely. We can create things that would previously have been impossible for a single person, and we can communicate our ideas with millions of people at a time.

We are only just tapping into the full potential that all this offers—even as newer tools and innovations expand the possibilities even further.

The gig economy has emerged as a natural outcome of this change. With more freedom to work when and how we choose, more of us are now opting to forego conventional 9-5 jobs and to start deciding for ourselves how we want to shape our careers.

Why spend hours every week commuting into an office, only to be given a fraction of the value you have provided to the client or customer? Why feel forced to choose just one career, or to let someone else decide on your working hours and wages? Why work on projects you have no interest in?

By offering services on a "per gig" basis, we free ourselves to select the kind of work that best serves our goals. We can use this to accelerate our careers and create a star-studded portfolio, or we can use it to design a lifestyle that lets us spend more time doing the things we love—with the people we love.

And more exciting still, by doing this, we become pioneers of a brave new world.

If you are a tech professional, then you are uniquely equipped to do this, and to enjoy all the benefits that the lifestyle has to offer. That said, anyone with a little entrepreneurial spirit and familiarity with digital tools will be able to make the gig economy work for them. Programmers, security specialists, web designers, video editors, Internet marketers, writers, editors, photographers, musicians, coaches . . . all these professions are starting to find new ways of working online. And while this book is particularly tailored to tech professionals, the same tips, rules, and ideas can be applied in any industry and reach any goal.

Whether you choose to run a business full time providing services to clients on a case-by-case basis or choose to create a "side hustle," there are amazing opportunities here for all.

And this book will provide you with all the information, tips, tools, encouragement, and motivation to get out there and make it happen. You will learn not only how to find clients willing to pay for your services, create a business and file taxes, and use the most common tools to deliver work and get paid, but also how to stay focused and productive when working without a boss, transition to this new way of working without taking unnecessary risks, and develop yourself further and grow your personal brand.

We will also explore how the gig economy is likely to change and develop with the introduction of newer technologies—and how you can prepare for those changes.

It is exceedingly likely that this type of work will become increasingly commonplace. Fewer and fewer people are now remaining in single jobs their entire lives, and many of us are becoming "digital polymaths" with multiple skills to offer. Internet speeds are getting faster, and tools are getting smarter.

But by taking this leap early on, we can reap amazing benefits right now and give ourselves important footholds in this emerging market—the "fourth industrial revolution." Keep reading if you want to become an early adopter of this new and exciting way of life.

Welcome to the Gig Economy

An Exciting Opportunity for Tech Professionals and Entrepreneurs

If knowledge is indeed power, then you have at your disposal the most powerful tool in the history of mankind.

I have heard many writers bemoan the fact that technology has not impacted the world in the ways depicted in so many science fiction films. There are no flying cars and very few silver jump suits.

And yet, in my view, the many ways that technology has actually changed the world are actually even *more* interesting. For example, the Internet has changed how we communicate with one another, how we entertain ourselves, and how we work. Nobody could have predicted it.

Today, more and more people are working online, and more and more businesses are working remotely. There are more opportunities than ever before for professionals—especially within the technology industry—to further their careers and work how, when, and where they want. The world is just catching up to these new possibilities, but it is safe to say that they are going to fundamentally change our way of life.

© Adam Sinicki 2019
A. Sinicki, *Thriving in the Gig Economy*, https://doi.org/10.1007/978-1-4842-4090-8_1

In fact, they already can. And if you act fast, you can get a foothold in an emerging marketing and gain a significant advantage over the competition.

This is your chance to become a pioneer. To work in a manner that wasn't possible even just a few years ago. To design the lifestyle that you want, to create opportunities that you never imagined, and to earn a solid and stable income in the process; all thanks to the transformative power of technology.

By working "gigs" online, you can earn a little side income, or you can completely change your lifestyle and remove the shackles of 9-to-5 office work. You can join the many "digital nomads" who travel the world while working online, or you can elevate your own rising star and design your dream job.

Who needs flying cars?

Whatever your ambition, the Web can make it happen. You'll discover how in this book.

The Gig Economy

The "gig economy" is one term that can be used to describe the manner of working just introduced. But it is also a rather broad term, so perhaps it would be useful to define precisely what we mean when we use it.

"Gig economy" is broadly used in this book to refer to the abundance of short-term work and contracts. This is driven by companies that hire staff for individual projects and pay them on a per-job or hourly basis, rather than offering them a full-term employment contract. This often applies to food delivery, taxi services, and even skilled labor such as programming and engineering.

Unfortunately, this type of agreement often benefits those companies far more than it benefits the freelancers that work with them. In short, those taxi and food delivery gigs come with all the disadvantages of working for a single organization (it becomes harder to juggle other work, you are given minimal flexibility as to which jobs you take on and when etc.) and all the disadvantages of being self-employed (no contract, no fixed wage, no health insurance, no sick pay).

Thus, the term "gig economy" often comes with negative connotations as a result; similar to "zero-hour contracts." But the gig economy can *also* refer to the trend of taking on online gigs. In this context, it refers to freelancers who advertise their skills on sites like Upwork, PeoplePerHour, and Fiverr (indeed, jobs advertised on Fiverr are referred to as "gigs" by the company's own terminology). The concept is the same: the individual will be paid per job or per fixed, short-term contract.

It can also mean working in an office, but even that has more advantages when it is skilled work that we are talking about. No longer are you an easily replaceable cog in a machine, but a valuable superstar who is choosing where to spend their time.

This is the precise same type of agreement, but now the power lies in the hands of the freelancer. It's up to you to choose which jobs you take on, the contracts you want to negotiate, and how (and ideally where) you actually complete the work. When you work online it is far easier to juggle multiple clients, and to decide which jobs to take on. This is where freelancing gives you the flexibility and freedom to work how *you* want, to increase your profits, and to enjoy even greater stability.

Companies are increasingly looking for professionals to complete short jobs for them, and the Web has given us the tools to make that more convenient than ever. The goal is not to let those companies use this to take advantage of us, but rather to use it to *our* advantage.

Many people will still object to the idea of freelancing, believing that it is inherently less stable and secure. But as you read through this book, you will learn that this doesn't have to be the case; you can have your cake and eat it too.

So, from this point onward, the "gig economy" refers specifically to online work catering to tech professionals (and others outside the tech industry to a slightly lesser extent) who want to work on a freelance basis with no strings.

The Benefits of Freelancing: Who Is This For?

Freelancing through online gigs in the tech industry (and other fields) brings with it a huge range of different advantages. Of course, it's not for everyone, though, so it's best at this point that you understand what you're getting into … before you decide to swallow that red pill and change your perception of reality irrevocably.

Note that the freelancing option doesn't have to be a binary, either-or kind of thing. You can just as well work online as a freelancer in your spare time to make some money on the side. If you like the sounds of some of these points but are put off by others, then you *do* have the option to go half in. You can pick and choose. And that's a big part of the appeal! I'll be discussing that option more later in this book.

What Freelancing Does for You

So, why freelance? This section describes some of the highly significant ways in which freelancing and entering the gig economy can transform your life for the better.

Time Flexibility

Have a friend who brags that their organization offers them flextime? Ha! Flextime is nothing to you as a freelancer!

If you want to work four-hour days and are willing to take the cut in income that comes with that, then that's your call. If you want to finish work early one day "just because," then most of the time you can. If you want to work an extra hour a day and stop working Mondays, then that's an option too—that's what I do!

There are limits to this flexibility. of course. If you continually shirk on your deadlines, then people are going to stop working with you. And if your contract requires you to be online during certain hours, then you can't pack in early without telling anyone. But if you're smart in your planning (which this book will help you with), then you'll be able to choose a work schedule that you enjoy.

And, of course, that means you can choose to prioritize other things in your life. I am never more appreciative that I work for myself than when my wife needs me to pick her up from work early because she's unwell. Being a freelancer lets me be there for the people I love.

Or maybe you just want to spend more time skiing, or working out, or building a side business. Freelancing gives you more freedom, time, and energy to "do you."

Note   Working gigs is ideal for "bootstrapping" a new business idea, as will be discussed in Chapter 9.

Notice how Bruce Wayne doesn't have a super-demanding 9-to-5 day job? Or Peter Parker? Or Clark Kent? Do you want to be Batman? Or stressed-out Joe?

Freedom of Location

If you're the kind of person who doesn't like being micromanaged, who gets frustrated that they have to stick to a certain dress code, and who would much rather take their lunch break when it suits them, then you'll likely enjoy the gig economy.

By working remotely via the Web, you'll have the freedom to operate from a home office if you so choose, which means that you can enjoy all of the creature comforts and luxuries of being in your own environment. That also means there's no need for a commute—the value of which cannot be stressed enough. Imagine your current working day without a 20- to 90-minute slog each way during rush hour. And without the cost of fuel or train tickets!

If you follow this through to its logical conclusion, then it leads you to some exciting possibilities as embodied by "digital nomads" who travel the world while working from a laptop (more on this later). That may not appeal to you, but there are other options. When I lived in Bournemouth, a seaside town on the southern coast of England, I would regularly take a stroll down to the beach and sit with a cocktail (fruit cocktail—I was working!) and watch the world go by. Today I often work in libraries and coffee shops in Oxford and London.

In his book *Guns, Germs, and Steel* (W.W. Norton, 1997), author Jared Diamond explains how those tribes that were most geographically blessed were eventually the ones able to grow into developed civilizations. With the gig economy, geography need no longer be a limiting factor.

Work You Enjoy

When you work online or work short-term gigs, you'll gain the flexibility to take on the jobs that you want, to work with the people and organizations you want, and to stop working when you want.

Love coding but not a fan of collaboration? Then just pick and choose those types of jobs.

Enjoy web design but hate marketing and "communication overhead" (I hear you)? Then find an agency.

This is a learning process for sure, and to begin with you won't be able to afford to be picky. But with time, you'll be able to pick and choose the kind of work that appeals to you and turn down the rest. That's the kind of thing that gets you fired in conventional employment.

Set Your Own Fee

When you work gigs, you get to set your own fee, although there is normally a bit of a trade-off here between this point and the others (e.g., do you do work less and earn less, or do you take on more work that you don't enjoy as much?).

Ultimately, though, you can decide how much money you need to earn and then set that as your target. While it might be hard to negotiate the rate of pay you want at first, you will *always* have the option to put in more hours, and sometimes that is going to be handy. Boiler broken at a time when you *really* can't afford to have it fixed? Then just calculate how many more jobs you need to accept and find a way to make that work around your other commitments.

Want to treat yourself to a meal out guilt-free? Then just do a bit of work one Saturday. The option is always there.

Productivity

Believe it or not, chances are that you can be *hugely* more productive when you're self-employed.

When you work for a big organization, you are on their time. They are paying for you to be available between the hours of 9 and 5 (typically). But are they necessarily getting the best work out of you in that time? The answer for many businesses is no: they'll have you answering the phone, responding to e-mails, attending meetings, doing menial errands, and so forth. All of these little jobs serve predominantly as distractions from the main bulk of your work: the skilled, value-creating work that you were originally hired to do.

Imagine how much more work you could accomplish in eight hours if you didn't have all those frustrating distractions and if you could work in an uninterrupted state of flow, the psychological state of intense focus, first described by Mihaly Csikszentmihalyi in *Flow: The Psychology of Optimal Experience* (Harper Perennial Modern Classics, 2008) and subsequently applied specifically to working productively in Cal Newport's *Deep Work: Rules for Focused Success in a Distracted World* (Grand Central Publishing, 2016).

You now have two options: do twice the *actual* work and double your income (and your career progression) OR clock off at 4 p.m. and call it a day. And I'll talk to you about how to get better at stints of intense concentration later in this book.

Stability

I also believe that, in many ways, being self-employed is actually a *more* stable and reliable way to earn money versus working for an employer.

Think about it: If you are employed by just one company and that company goes under, you're out of a job. No more income. The same goes if you get let go.

But if you have ten ongoing clients, what are the chances that *all of them* are going to up and leave you at the very same time? Very slim, one would hope.

Not only that, but more and more people are going to be turning to freelancers as word gets out. Why would a company limit itself to the local pool of talent when it could go online and find *the very best in the business* to do the job? Why would a company spend resources and office space on a permanent member of staff when it can get the same work done with no overhead, no administration, and no commitment?

And smaller consumer services will also benefit from the same things. Why would someone choose to get their services from a large, faceless corporation—where they will pay more overhead and struggle to ever get in touch with the top brass—when they could work directly with a more affordable individual, someone who has earned their trust through a blog and who will be ready to answer questions immediately?

This topic is discussed in more detail in the book *Race Against the Machine* (Digital Frontier Press, 2011), by Erik Brynjolfsson and Andrew McAfee, where it is described as the "great restructuring." Brynjolfsson and McAfee, by the way, suggest that the people who will thrive in this new business economy will be those that are able to work with "intelligent machines." That's you!

This is simply future-proofing. More and more jobs will become outsourced. If you're already a freelancer, then you will be ready, you will have a foothold in the market, and you will have the competitive advantage.

Your Own Business (And Personal Development)

When you work freelance, you run your own business. It might not feel like it, because you're not the CEO of a big corporation barking out orders and speaking to boards of directors. But nevertheless, you will be a sole proprietor (sole trader), or you will own a limited liability company (limited business). You may have your own company name and trademark, or you might have a "personal brand."

Either way, thinking about yourself as a "business" not only is crucial to your success, but will also make the entire process all the more rewarding. You'll be building lists of clients and contacts, managing relationships, developing new skills (R&D), investing in equipment and training courses, and promoting yourself. The only difference is that now *all* of those things will be benefiting you directly. You won't get "thank you" and a bigger Christmas bonus when you bring in a massive new job/client: you'll reap 100% of the profit.

If you're currently working for an company and feeling underappreciated, then becoming your own business is the perfect tonic.

What Freelancing Isn't (The Downsides)

While I am always the first to reel off the virtues of freelancing to anyone who asks (and a lot of people who don't), there are also some important considerations to take into account. It's not all sunshine and roses, and this section points out some of the things to keep in mind when deciding if this lifestyle is right for you.

You Need Discipline

If you're going to freelance, then you *need* to be disciplined. That means you need to be able to shut the world out and go to town on that website backend/search engine optimization (SEO) content. It means you need to be able to avoid the temptation to take breaks whenever you feel like it, and it means you need to be able to stay self-motivated in order to meet deadlines.

If you can't imagine working from home without being tempted to give up and play computer games, then perhaps this lifestyle isn't for you. With that said, though, note that this discipline is something that can be practiced and that will improve with time.

What's *just as important* in terms of discipline is that you take the time off when you *aren't* working. This will ensure you're at your most productive when you return to work and it will also prevent you from making yourself ill or alienating friends and family!

Other People

This is a vague heading, sure, but other people create all kinds of problems for you as a freelancer.

First off, you will find that you often have a hard time trying to describe to other people what exactly it is you do. When you tell people you're self-employed, they'll very often assume what you *really* mean is that you are unemployed (as does the delivery guy, presumably, after the fourth parcel you accept in your pajamas at 11 a.m.).

I spent the first four years of self-employment being asked when I would "get a real job." Once people started seeing my name on big websites and learned of my business trips abroad, they finally stopped.

The other problem is that people can't quite get their head around the fact that you're not available for calls and to run errands. If you work from home, then you'll find that people call you during work hours and are offended if you aren't free to answer or chat.

The problem is that you'll want to take advantage of your flexibility, and when you do, other people may assume that you have unlimited flexibility. Sometimes you *will* be free to meet up during the day and work later in the evening instead. But if you do it once, people may not realize you can't always do it (without getting very behind on sleep or work).

Oh, and the next time that someone asks you "what you do," expect it to be a long conversation!

Lack of Other People

Now I'm being purposefully contrary. But the point I'm making is that you will be working on your own much of the time. That means a lot of isolation, and for some people, being part of a "team" is one of the big perks of work.

For that reason, this type of career is arguably better suited to introverts. That said, when the time comes to speak with a client in person, it can help to be a bit more extroverted (there is such thing as an ambivert!).

If you feel you will suffer as a result of not being around co-workers, then you need to make sure that you make up for it by jam-packing your free time with social alternatives. I used to work in London sometimes and meet my wife or cousin for lunch, for instance.

Ultimately in my view, I'd rather spend more time with people I care about than people I have been made to work with. But again, this comes down to personal preference.

Admin

There is also a fair amount of admin and "fiddly stuff" to contend with when setting up any business. While a sole proprietor has less to worry about than a limited liability company, you do still need to consider things like filing tax returns, logging your expenses and income, dealing with clients, investing in marketing (maybe including trademarks), and more. You'll need to sign up to websites, and you may wish to create your own business website.

All this *can* be a headache and it is often a considerable "barrier to entry." In other words, if you're not 100% sure about working as a freelancer, potential admin tasks may be enough to deter you from diving in. The good news is that you can take these responsibilities on slowly and eventually automate or outsource a great deal of them.

Risk

One of my goals in this book is to demonstrate to you that being an online freelancer can be just as stable as being employed. In fact, it can actually be *more* stable in some cases—as I said earlier. But in the interests of balance, let's consider risk.

At the end of the day, you won't be employed. You won't have a long-term contract. There is no guarantee that the work will keep coming. That's a *shift* in the way we have been brought up to view work, and for some, that's bound to incite just a little anxiety.

All risk can be mitigated, and I do believe you'll see that as we proceed through this book. BUT you do need just a *little* courage in order to strike out on your own. Depending on how you're wired, that risk might be seen as a positive thing.

The game is afoot!

What You Will Learn

If you've read all the preceding potential downsides of freelance work and you're still with me, then congratulations! You may just be cut out for the gig economy after all.

And this book is going to serve as your ignition and your roadmap. The aim is to help you see the possibilities, to help you set up a working business model, and then to navigate the *many* pitfalls along the way to fulfill your vision.

Topics covered will include:

- The types of work you can sell

- Where to sell that work

- How to promote yourself

- How to distinguish a good client from a bad one

- How to negotiate the best rates

- How to juggle a massive workload

- How to manage your money

- How to do gigs "on the side" to supplement your income

- How to learn online to increase your skill set

- How to transition to full-time freelancing

- How to set up an online business

- How to grow, scale, and develop your business

- How to handle admin, taxes, and so on

- How to optimize your work/life balance and take full advantage of the flexibility you are now afforded

- How the gig economy will grow and develop into the future

Plus, the usual vague "and much more."

Chapter Summary

So, in this chapter, we explored the compelling reasons to consider entering the gig economy, especially as a tech entrepreneur. I hope it has inspired you while at the same time preparing you for the reality of being self-sufficient in this way.

In the next chapter, we'll be looking at the steps you need to take to make this lifestyle a reality. You'll learn where to find clients and how your relationships with them will tend to work. This chapter was the why; next up comes the how.

Getting Started with the Gig Economy and Finding Work

What to Sell and How to Sell It

Hopefully, I've set the scene for the gig economy sufficiently in Chapter 1 and you're now feeling psyched to get started. And probably a little anxious. A little anxiety is good; it keeps you focused.

But it's all still rather conceptual and abstract at this point. So enough with the aspirational talk; let's get practical! In this chapter, you're going to learn the nuts and bolts of selling your skills online. What you can sell, where you can sell it, and so forth.

© Adam Sinicki 2019
A. Sinicki, *Thriving in the Gig Economy*, https://doi.org/10.1007/978-1-4842-4090-8_2

What Are You Going to Sell?

Maybe you came into this with a business model in mind. Maybe you're going to turn your current job into a freelance gig. Or maybe you have a passion that you want to turn into a profitable business.

But on the other hand, you might just know you want *out* but have no idea how to get there.

The good news is that there are *lots* of services you can sell online, and chances are that there's at least *something* you can offer. This book is aimed specifically at technology entrepreneurs, and if you are a coder, a web developer, an Internet marketer, or anyone else with basic computer skills, then you're going to have *tons* of options.

But if you're not any of those things, then don't worry—this book is for you as well, and there are plenty more options. This section provides some ideas to whet your appetite. You don't need to read all of this section; just glance over and see what sticks out to you.

Tech Skills That Sell Well Online

While you can sell pretty much anything under the sun—and you'll see just how true this is in a moment—the reality is that certain skills are more suitable for selling online than others. This is owing not only to demand, but also factors such as value, time, and marketability. Here are some great places to start.

Programming

Programming is perhaps *the* best skill you can sell online. It is *particularly* skill-based and it's something that's in high demand. Countless businesses are looking for programmers to develop apps, to work on in-house software, and to manage their websites.

All types of coders are in demand online, though some languages are in greater demand than others, of course. Python is often up there as one of the most sought-after languages, as is Java. Knowing C and C++ is great for game development, while using C# and having a familiarity with Unity or Unreal will also help in this regard. Likewise, specific skills pertaining to Android development or iOS can also be beneficial.

The holy grail is the "full-stack developer." This is someone that can handle everything necessary to build a fully functioning, interactive website or web app with a back end, user profiles, and other features. In other words, you'll need HTML and CSS for web design, along with something like PHP for the back end, MySQL, and so forth.

That said, other key areas that are increasingly important for developers include cloud computing, big data analysis, artificial intelligence (AI), and machine learning. These are areas that are increasingly up and coming, and it's important that you keep your ear to the ground for other opportunities.

The key is to market yourself correctly. If you call yourself a programmer and simply list the languages you're confident in (and the ones you're a bit shaky on), you'll face a lot of competition and get a lot of job offers that aren't quite right for you.

But if you market yourself as a games developer who works with Unity and C#, then you're going to stand out from the crowd and get a lot more specific work offered. Other ideas that will get more attention than "programmer" are "full-stack developer for web applications" and "virtual reality developer," for example.

Alternatively, become an "Android app developer." This way, you're not offering to collaborate on projects or create libraries and methods—rather, you're offering a complete package for a specific type of program.

You can even offer "refactoring"—or offer to port iOS apps to Android. Look at your skills and think about the work you'd like to do . . . then let your imagination go to town.

IT

This is a much broader term, but *any* kind of IT skill can be sold online or on a freelance basis.

Tech support is something that can be offered remotely thanks to remote desktop viewer tools like Splashtop Remote and TeamViewer. And often just talking someone through the problem over the phone is more than enough.

Better yet is once again to specialize in one of the currently "hot" trending areas. IT security is *huge* right now thanks to numerous high-profile data breaches, and if you can offer to secure a company's network or website, you'll have no difficulty getting work.

Many of these services will ultimately be consultant roles. Though if you're looking for slightly meatier contracts, you could also find yourself in the position of a project manager overseeing the implementation of a new piece of software or new security policies.

Web Design

Web design is a concept. The best web designers should be familiar with popular CMSs (content management systems) like WordPress, but should also have the necessary HTML, CSS, and PHP skills (and more) in order to tackle more ambitious projects. You'll also need to be able to create professional-looking designs, which will mean learning software such as Adobe Illustrator and Photoshop. If you don't know a raster file from a vector file, then you have some learning to do—a lot of people mistakenly think they have all the necessary web development skills without fully understanding the market.

That said, you can always break this down and be more focused. If you are able to use WordPress and know how to buy a URL and set up a new hosting account, then you might offer "simple" web design this way (or even use something like Squarespace if you are code-phobic). Likewise, you could just offer logo design.

And if you only have half the skills you need to design a website, you could always outsource the bits you *can't* do or find a partner who will handle that aspect.

3D Modeling

3D modeling is a *very* valuable skill that often goes overlooked. This is a specialist skill that's in demand, and if you can do it, you'll be able to offer everything from 3D logo designs and video openers, to prototyping through 3D printing and creating models for computer games.

Internet Marketing/SEO

Internet marketing and SEO are *still* big business, although the game has changed a lot since the early days.

Again, you can get as broad or as granular as you like here: you could offer SEO specifically, social media marketing, or *Instagram* marketing. You could use your social media skills to become an "online agent for athletes."

OR you could offer an entire Internet marketing service. This could be bespoke, starting with a "marketing strategy" consultation, resulting in a tailor-made package with content writing, link building, and more.

Writing

Writing is a "tech job" in as much as it is actually a form of Internet marketing, specifically referred to as "content marketing." If you want to be an online copywriter, then you're largely going to be working for companies that need that content to boost their discoverability on Google. In other words, you need to know the basics of SEO and how to get the client to the top of the SERPs (meaning Search Engine Results Pages). This is writing but with a dose of "tech understanding" for good measure.

Likewise, selling writing becomes a lot easier if you have a specialty or expertise. Such as ... I don't know ... maybe tech? As a programmer, I've been able to find a lot of work writing tutorials, courses, and even the previous book I wrote for Apress: *Learn Unity for Android Game Development.*

Video Editing

Video editing is a skill that is in increasing demand thanks to the popularity of video marketing, YouTube, and online courses. If you are familiar with (or can familiarize yourself with) Adobe Premiere Pro, VEGAS Pro, or Apple Final Cut Pro, then you'll find there are lots of gigs out there for you.

VAS

A VAS is a virtual assistant service. This is basically an outfit that will complete all the jobs that a company or individual doesn't have time for, whether that's collecting contacts or performing "outreach" (contacting blogs or clients to work with in the future). Essentially, any non-skilled job that doesn't require you to be physically present can be performed by you as a VAS.

Very often we imagine VAS companies as being based in India and speaking broken English. However, that is not always the case, and there's nothing stopping you from fulfilling these services in a more "premium" fashion for busy executives and small startups.

Non-Tech-Related Jobs

Not a techie? Or want to try your hand at something different? Most of the skills you'll learn in this book can equally apply to other types of work, so there's no need to limit yourself. These ideas are for wayward friends who want out of their 9-to-5 jobs:

- *Business consulting*: Consulting can take pretty much any form. If you have business experience, then why not try helping startups get off the ground?

- *Writing*: This is one of the jobs that the *most* people will be able to do with minimal experience - as long as you can write well enough, there are companies that need the copy and content. I mentioned writing already in the context of the tech expert, but you can also write for blogs in a more casual sense, offer copywriting for businesses (that means copy for websites, adverts, press releases, etc.), or even write for magazines.

- *Composer:* YouTubers, game developers, video makers, and more are looking for tunes to add to their creations. If you can use software like FL Studio, then you can provide those beats.

- *Voiceover/presenter:* From video marketing and explainer videos, to video games and online courses - they all need a VO.

- *Proofreading:* Where there is a need for content and copy, there is also a need for proofreading.

- *Photography:* This is also great for passive income if you put your photos up on a stock photos site.

- *Videography:* Video marketing is big online, and being able to help create those videos with high production values puts you in high demand.

- *Data entry/analysis:* This is another job that a company may wish to outsource in order to reduce admin and overhead.

- *Law:* Law services can be provided remotely to businesses or B2C.

- *Translator:* If you're a polyglot, then you're laughing! This is a highly in-demand role, owing to the multi-lingual nature of the web.

- *Coaching:* Career guidance, personal training, counseling… as long as you have the skills[1] you can teach others.

- *Art:* Many artists now use Instagram to sell commissioned and non-commissioned works.

- *Catching fish:* This is just to point out the literally *endless* number of possibilities. I have a friend who actually offered this service through a website to landowners with overpopulated bodies of water. He didn't charge for the job, but instead sold the fish he caught to restaurants. The job you do doesn't even need to be online or remote if you market using a website!

---

[1]Often it is possible to acquire certification in personal training, coaching, career counseling, and similar services with minimal work. Consider then that your transition to working for yourself doesn't necessarily have to mean continuing with your current field of expertise. You can invest in some learning and development and try out a whole new role that you've been interested in!

Combining Jobs

Can't choose from all the preceding options and the many more ideas that may now be swimming through your mind?

Great: then take on several!

There is literally nothing stopping you from providing multiple different services and thereby rounding out your résumé more while keeping your work much more varied and less predictable. The friend who caught fish also provided SEO services *and* taught English to Spanish expats. Whoever called him that day would define the work he was doing next. There is nothing stopping you from doing the same thing if that idea appeals to you.

More Ways to Sell Your Skill

Think outside the box a little as well when thinking about how you are going to "package" your skills. For instance, if you are a developer, then creating software for companies and individuals is just one avenue.

Other options might include

- Teaching others to code/coaching
- Writing articles/news about programming
- Consulting
- Upgrading software/fixing bugs
- Maintaining and running software on a recurring basis
- Overseeing large software engineering projects
- Checking programming

Any of these could help you to stand out from the competition, to leverage other skills in your arsenal, and to potentially develop a better workflow to suit your lifestyle.

Likewise, if you are an online fitness coach, then consider that this is something you can write about, teach to others, and so forth.

Ways to Be More Specific

Likewise, think about ways that you might market yourself to be more specific and thereby choose the type of projects you work on. For instance, you could be a game developer who works primarily with Unity. Or how about a web developer specializing in websites for estate agents? What about a writer who only writes about fitness?

Why Companies Need Freelance Coders

My hope is that this book will be useful for anyone who is interested in selling their skills online. But it is *particularly* aimed at programmers and tech professionals. Here's the good news: your skills have never been more in demand.

Here is a snippet from an e-mail I recently received from a real tech company:

> *Our little company is growing, and we need help making [PRODUCT] more stable and feature rich. Problem is, there is a massive talent shortage of software engineers at the moment. Even the recruiters and big companies are struggling to find people round here. If you know a software developer, would you do us a massive favor and forward this on to them?*

Now is a good time to be a programmer or any other kind of tech professional if you want to work online. Right now, companies are crying out for individuals with coding and IT skills who have the flexibility to take on short jobs and work remotely. And it's only likely to continue. Often this is referred to as "the future jobs market," but as you will see, the future is *now*.

In order to better fulfill this need as a freelancer, it helps to understand *why* this is the case and to understand specifically what it is that these companies are looking for (or who). By getting inside the minds of your clients, you can better cater to their needs.

So, who is the prototypical "buyer persona" for—let's say—an app developer?

When a Company Needs an App

Let's say that an average, middle-sized company needs an app. Maybe it's a restaurant chain that wants an app for people to order their food from. Maybe it's a publishing company that wants to showcase their books and provide digital downloads through a mobile storefront. Maybe it's a toy manufacturer who wants to add extra value by providing an app that will control said toy.

Whatever the case, the company now has a few choices:

- Hire a team of developers or a single developer who can cater to the company's needs
- Try and tackle the problem with existing staff
- Outsource the process to a third-party company or agency
- Look for a local employee willing to work a fixed-term contract
- Look for a freelance app developer online

The final option is *by far* the most appealing choice for the company.

Why is this?

Well, the first option would mean spending a lot of money and doing a lot of admin. It would entail paying sick leave, paying tax, possibly providing health insurance, filling out lots of documents, and finding desk space. Then there's the fact that the company would be drawing from a local pool of talent that is statistically much less likely to be able to offer the precise skills and experience that the company is looking for.

More to the point, if a company needs a single, basic app, then it's not likely to require much maintenance or updating. In other words, if they hire an in-house employee or team, then what do those workers do the *rest* of the time?

Outsourcing to a third-party development company/agency is a good option too—except it will inevitably be more expensive, as that company has *far* more overhead.

By going online, a company can find a talented individual with the *precise* skills that the company needs for its project, hire them for a relatively low fee, and avoid any commitment or complicated administration.

Where to Find Work

Once you've decided what service it is that you want to sell, the next step is to find people to sell it to. The ideal scenario is that people are going to come to you and your reputation will do the talking. Later on in this book, I'll detail how you can get to that point and set up a website to act as a portfolio.

But if you're hoping to quit your job, or you're looking to make more money on the side, then you probably can't afford to "build it and [hope] they will come."

Unless you have been fortunate enough to take clients with you when you left your last employment (and are not barred from doing so by a noncompete agreement), you're going to have to get proactive about how you find your gigs. Fortunately, there are several platforms out there that make that possible.

And the best place to start for many people will be with freelancing sites.

Freelancing Sites

Here are just a few of the better-known freelancing sites on the Web:

- Upwork (www.upwork.com)
- PeoplePerHour (www.peopleperhour.com)
- Freelancer (www.freelancer.com)
- Constant Content (www.constant-content.com)

- Fiverr (www.fiverr.com)

- Guru (www.guru.com)

- 99Designs (https://99designs.com)

- Toptal (www.toptal.com)

- College Recruiter (www.collegerecruiter.com)

These are sites that are specifically designed for people looking to sell their skills online and for companies looking to outsource projects and work. Let's look at several in more detail.

Upwork

Upwork (formerly Elance-oDesk) is currently the largest and most well-known of the freelance websites and can serve as a useful "blueprint" for what to expect on any of these platforms.

To get started on Upwork as a freelancer, you first need to sign up and create an account at www.upwork.com. From there, you fill out a profile by adding your profile image, your skills and areas of expertise, and a portfolio including images of work you've completed. You'll also be able to take online tests in order to verify your abilities. For instance, there are short tests you can take to demonstrate your spelling or to demonstrate your capabilities with any of a huge variety of programming languages and tools. Here are just a few examples of the tests available at the time of writing:

- English Spelling Test (US Version/UK Version)

- Email Etiquette Certification

- PHP Test

- Call Center Skills Test

- JavaScript Test

- Internet Marketing Test

- Android Programming Test

- WordPress Test

While completing these tests will take a little time, it will also make you a more appealing prospect for potential clients—so it is worth the investment. The same goes for uploading screenshots and photos of completed work.

You'll also set an hourly rate, though of course this will be negotiable when you begin speaking with the clients.

Once you've set up your profile and bulked it out as much as possible, you can then either wait to be contacted (which does happen occasionally) or do a search for relevant jobs and "Submit a Proposal."

Upwork is free for the most basic account, but you'll need to pay $10/month (currently) if you want to upgrade to a Plus account. This will—among other things—give you more "connects," allowing you to contact more people about potential work. Of course, Upwork also charges a commission, which unfortunately falls to the freelancer to pay (currently 20% for the first $500 with each client, 10% for the next $10,000, and 5% for lifetime billings).

Upwork is a great tool and a lot of people have had success with it. Personally, I find it has one of the more involved processes for finding new work and for completing that work. There's also a "Work Diary" that counts your keystrokes and takes screenshots of your screen (six times an hour), among other things. You can forego this if you agree to fixed-price jobs, which are based on "milestones," but that will be largely at the client's discretion. And you need to think about how opting out is going to look to the client—especially when the competition is happy to use these tracking tools. If the tracker didn't exist, then it would be fine. But the fact that it *does* exist means it looks strange if you refuse to use it. It also means that the market generally is more predisposed to working per hour rather than per job. And as we'll see later, this is often a less flexible and profitable way to work.

In short, Upwork feels (to me at least) like it benefits the client more than the freelancer. And it forces you to work within its parameters to such an extent that you can actually end up losing some of the very flexibility that might have attracted you to freelance work in the first place.

PeoplePerHour

PeoplePerHour (www.peopleperhour.com) is a lesser-known platform but actually a superior one in my personal experience, especially if you are based outside of the United States. A friend of mine has gotten some high-paying and long-term clients from here, and I have likewise had serious job offers despite putting in barely any time.

PeoplePerHour charges 15% for the first $280 earned and 3.5% thereafter—considerably less than Upwork. That said, there are some admin fees and other hidden costs and the site doesn't do the best job of communicating these in a clear way (which always leaves a bit of a bad taste).

The best part is that PeoplePerHour has no time tracker. While some clients see this as a bad thing, I hope you've already realized that this is very *good* news for us freelancers. And really, clients should see it this way too. If someone delivers the work they agreed, then do you really need to spy on their computer use for the entire day? Would you *rather* they dragged their heels or got the work done as quickly and efficiently as possible?

Freelancer

Freelancer (www.freelancer.com) is yet another option, which charges 3% or thereabouts for each payment and for jobs awarded.

Freelancer does offer a desktop tracking app, which is recommended for building trust with employers. According to Freelancer, the tracking app increases average earnings by "up to 300%"—though I would treat that statistic like a bag of chips ... with a large pinch of salt!

The good news is that because the tracking app isn't built into the site itself, it's somewhat less mandatory than it is on Upwork. But it's still there and it's still something that a client can push for. And to many freelancers, that's a problem.

Other Options

Freelancer also offers "Contests," which gives you the chance to submit your work and get paid if it is deemed to be the best submission by the job creator. This system has its pros and cons and is something you might occasionally attempt—especially if you have supreme confidence in the quality of your work or you're desperately struggling to find clients.

This manner of working is actually particularly popular when it comes to design jobs. **99Designs** (https://99designs.com) is a site built entirely around this premise, for instance, and was actually used by Tim Ferriss when designing the cover for *The 4-Hour Workweek* (Vermilion, 2009).

Fiverr (www.fiverr.com) is another freelancing site that offers a slightly different format. As the name suggests, this site is all about selling individual gigs for a fiver. These range from the standard (copywriting, programming, design, etc.) to the bizarre (singing "happy birthday" dressed as Marilyn Monroe). The reason I mention it here is that it is now possible to list jobs for any price and the reputation is gradually changing. Fiverr makes the process of finding work and getting paid very easy, and the market is slightly less saturated for tech professionals.

Unfortunately, Fiverr takes a 20% cut, and then you'll have to pay PayPal's fees on top of that. But if you factor these issues into your pricing, then it can be another useful tool in your arsenal thanks to its unique setup. We'll be discussing this more later on.

There are industry-specific options too. There is **Constant Content** (www.constant-content.com) for copywriters, for instance, or **Crowdspring** (www.crowdspring.com) and **Cad Crowd** (www.cadcrowd.com) for those with 3D modeling skills. Or what about **College Recruiter** (www.collegerecruiter.com), which is specifically aimed at college students looking to pay their way through their studies?

Rent-a-coder (www.rent-a-coder.com) is a site where you can rent gardeners. Psyche! It's actually a site for renting coders. Likewise, you can also find jobs for coders over at **Stack Overflow** (https://stackoverflow.com).

For those in various other commercial industries, you can find sites that will list professionals in your line of work. There are online indexes filled with therapists and coaches, artists and musicians, narrators and agents . . . you name it! Get on those sites and create a profile.

Then there's **Toptal** (www.toptal.com) for those with the truly impressive portfolios and skill sets. The site only accepts 3% of applicants and includes an intense screening process, including tests and interviews. Of course, the prices you charge and the quality of work you find should reflect that. Something to aim for!

Look, I could go on all day and make an entire book comparing all these different platforms, the sign-up processes, and the pros and cons of each. I'm not going to, however, because a) any information I share here will quickly become outdated, and b) you can get the precise same thing from a quick Google search.

What works best for you will depend on your workflow, the type of clients you're looking for, your level of expertise, and more. Once you sign up, the process is *largely* the same.

How to Succeed on Freelancing Sites

Finding the freelancing sites to sell your services on is only the first challenge. More important is working out how to thrive in those environments!

Here are some key pointers that will help you out.

Be Specific

Rather than creating a profile that emphasizes your skills as a developer, instead try to emphasize your *particular* area of expertise. Maybe you're an iOS app developer. Maybe you're a Unity game developer. Either way, it's easier to stand out and be the best in a smaller crowd. Not only that, but the *type* of work you receive in this way is likely to be better suited to your particular skill set (meaning that you can complete it more quickly—more on this later!).

Consider the advice that you are given when applying to "conventional" jobs with a résumé and cover letter: alter both to better fit each opportunity, rather than repeatedly sending out the same résumé to everyone. On

Upwork or Freelancer, you only have one résumé, which is your profile. But it still follows that you'll have more work if you can make yourself the perfect match for a certain type of role. If you really can't decide the kind of work you want to prioritize, then consider setting up two different profiles on two different sites!

Consider Your Profile Photo

When hiring someone online, often companies face the challenge of putting their trust in someone they've never met before and never *will* meet. The best thing you can do to mitigate that is to choose a profile photo that looks professional and friendly. This should be a high-quality head shot, ideally against a white or non-distinct background.

Start Small

Another tip is to know your limitations and to gradually build up to higher rates and bigger jobs. In other words, if you list your services at a huge amount per hour or per gig, then you need to be able to back that up with a great portfolio and lots of positive reviews.

Be Liquid

Sites like Fiverr will allow you to change your prices as often as you like. This then gives you the opportunity to react to your current workload. If you have a lot of jobs lined up, then you can increase your rates. If you are experiencing a bit of a dry spell, then you can lower them. There will inevitably be busier and quieter periods, so be ready to react to the changing market.

Add a Video

Some sites will give you the opportunity to add a video. Where this option is available, it is very much worth considering. Not only can a video help your profile to stand out, but it can also increase trust and familiarity and make you appear more professional. Creating a video with high production values takes skill in itself. This is not something that a kid living in their mom's basement will be able to accomplish and it gives you the opportunity to be much more persuasive and charismatic than you can be in writing.

Listing Skills

Many freelancing sites encourage freelancers to list their skills, which is what allows clients to try and find those professionals whose repertoire best suits their needs. It's important that you list the correct skills here, in order to achieve that honed profile that we've already discussed. Also important is to avoid adding *too many* skills in that case, which can potentially lead to your message being lost. This is particularly true if you have skills that are vastly different. At one point I tried to list myself as a software developer, writer, and fitness model! Unsurprisingly, I didn't get many takers. Try to avoid having many more than ten "core skills" and really make those ten count.

Try to list front and center those top few skills that you really want to promote and then back this up with a selection of "soft skills." That means things like communication, teamwork, and time keeping. Likewise, it can be useful to express a familiarity with particular tools that you often use in your line of work. This might mean collaboration software like Slack or Asana. For a software engineer, it might mean demonstrating experience with GitHub or Firebase. Remember though, if your skills list is starting to look crowded, you can always move some of these from this section and allude to them in your overview or your descriptions of previous work.

Experience and Proof

Anyone can create a profile and fill it with expertise and experience—and employers are wary of that fact. Your job then is to try and back up everything you claim by offering some kind of evidence. That might take the form of customer reviews and testimonials to back up just how "easy and pleasant" you are to work with. Or it might mean offering photographic evidence/screenshots in order to show that you really did have a hand in that project. Qualifications are also excellent—ideally with scans of your certificates. Likewise, you should also list any full-time positions you've held in other organizations. And all of this should be on top of any of the tests offered by the freelancing site you're using.

Again, this is why it's a good idea to start out with lower rates: so you can build up those reviews that will then help you to land the bigger fish. And this will also help you to gain a portfolio of great projects. Of course, there are other ways you can do this too—such as working on open source community projects or doing volunteer work—and we will discuss these options later in this book.

Don't forget the other types of clout and experience you might have too. For instance, if you have a very large social media reach, then this demonstrates technical expertise and business knowledge. Not to mention it's something that your clients might want to get a piece of (meaning you can increase your rates).

Write Well (Or Get Help!)

Most of the freelancing platforms have a section where you write an overview or introduction. This is where you sell yourself and summarize what you are looking for and why clients should hire you. In future chapters, we'll discuss the basics of persuasive writing for marketing your talents, but for now consider the following tips:

- Be *crystal clear* about what you offer and the kind of work you're looking for—no jargon or buzzwords. If your reader doesn't know whether you cater to them after the first two sentences, it is game over.

- Know your "target persona," which is the ideal client for your project. Don't try to appeal to everyone.

- Describe your most impressive credentials early on.

- Communicate your trustworthiness, professional attitude, and great service. People are still nervous about hiring online contractors. Put their mind at ease and make it sound as simple as possible.

- Consider the end goal of your clients and how your specific skill set will help them to reach it.

- Push for them to get in touch even if they don't want to hire you yet. You could say: "If you have any questions or don't see what you're looking for, then don't hesitate to get in touch!". Contact is easier to sell and nearly as valuable.

Of course, it's also very important to ensure that your profile is well written. That means good grammar, good vocabulary, and clear communication. If you aren't confident in your written English, then get someone who is a grammar whiz to take a look at your profile before you submit it to a website.

Digital Marketing

If you're familiar with digital marketing and SEO, then you'll understand the role of keywords. Keywords are phrases that people search for regularly that are identified and targeted by businesses hoping to reach the top of Google Search results (or similar). In other words, if you wanted to sell hats, you might try to get your site to rank high for the phrase "buy hats online." Those are your keywords.

Most freelancing sites have a kind of search engine built in. This is how specific profiles are selected and returned when clients search for the jobs they need to have performed. For instance, someone looking for an Android programmer might search for "Android programmer." This is another reason to go narrow:

because the more niche your skill set, the less competition you will face in the search results.

To increase your chances of getting to the top of the search results, you need to ensure that you use that specific phrase frequently throughout your profile: not only as a listed skill but also in your write-up. Overdoing this is a mistake though, as it can come across as forced and manipulative and ultimately result in your profile being penalized. The key once again is to make sure that your profile is focused which will ensure your profile comes up naturally when employers look for someone with your skills and experience. Keep keywords in the back of your mind while writing but don't force the issue.

Likewise, consider the other elements influencing the algorithms that underpin these systems. Normally, being more interactive with other users will boost your visibility, as will those positive reviews.

Experiment

In Internet marketing, there is a technique called split testing or A/B testing. This means creating two slightly different versions of the same sales letter or page and then seeing which performs best. You then adopt whichever version leads to greater profit.

While it won't be terribly scientific, you can do something similar yourself by making small changes to your profile and then seeing what brings in the most work.

Winning Bids

Remember that not all the work you find on Upwork or PeoplePerHour is just going to land at your feet. Sometimes it will be you who needs to go out and *find* the work by applying to job listings. This will often mean writing proposals that demonstrate why you're the perfect fit for the project. Keep these short and to the point, demonstrate that you have properly read and understood the task, and provide a link to your samples. Communicate in a professional and friendly manner and don't undervalue yourself in order to try and win the bid. We'll be talking about how to price your services in Chapter 4.

Chapter Summary

In this chapter my aim was to show you how to start finding clients, as well as helping you to get inside the minds of the kinds of businesses and individuals you might end up working with. I hope you now understand how the gig economy *works*.

In Chapter 3, we'll be taking this concept further and looking at how you can go beyond these conventional methods in order to cast your net farther and wider—and to find higher-paying clients in the process.

Expanding Your Reach

Thinking Outside the Box, Creating a Website, and More

While freelancing platforms are the obvious choice for those looking to get started with freelancing (hence the name), they are but *one* option. And actually, thinking outside the box can help you to find untapped opportunities and avoid direct competition.

In fact, I tend to avoid these types of platforms where possible. They are mostly too rigid for my liking, even going as far as to prevent you from exchanging contact details with your clients. Of course, from the platforms' perspective, you can understand why they don't want you to make deals on the side, and of course there are ways around it, but it's still frustrating. Isn't the point of working for yourself to *avoid* arbitrary rules and restrictions?

So, what other options do you have? I'll start this chapter by describing the preferred methods that have worked for me and for others I know. Many of these have led to some very big opportunities that wouldn't have been possible had I restricted myself only to freelancing platforms. From there, we'll explore a host of other optionos that will be suitable for small to large operations.

© Adam Sinicki 2019
A. Sinicki, *Thriving in the Gig Economy*, https://doi.org/10.1007/978-1-4842-4090-8_3

Forums

When I first decided I wanted to work online, I had the bright idea of heading over to **Digital Point Forums** (http://forums.digitalpoint.com) and posting an ad to sell my skills there. Digital Point is a site for webmasters and Internet marketers. It is where people who run online businesses can exchange tips and advice, as well as sell their skills and digital assets.

I posted to Digital Point once and for the next two years I had a steady stream of clients! One of those clients is still with me today, over eight years since I originally posted!

Two other very similar sites that do the exact same thing and that I have posted on are **Warrior Forum** (www.warriorforum.com) and **Black Hat World** (www.blackhatworld.com). These sites generally now require you to pay if you want to post an ad, but it's a one-off fee of around $30 in most cases, and from there you have free reign to manage your clients *however* you see fit with no further commitment. It's considerably better in that sense.

If you're a web designer, if you create plug-ins or WordPress themes, if you're an Internet marketer, if you are a copywriter, probably even if you're an app developer ... there is a market for all those skills on these websites. And if you post a great ad (which we'll be getting to in the next chapter), you'll often find this is enough to bring a steady stream of reliable work.

Now of course there are still downsides. For one, you'll often be selling to less "established" clients. That's a polite way of saying that many of these clients are trying to make a quick buck on Google by making cheap, spam-filled websites. That's not great for your portfolio and it doesn't pay all that well. This is especially true because a lot of these clients aren't all that concerned about quality and will often be happy to pay a pittance for writers who speak English as a second language. Badly. Or programmers who basically just steal code.

There is a very real risk here that you end up getting paid .50 cents per 100 words, writing about insurance. Or churning out low-quality websites for $50 a pop.

But this comes down to how you market yourself. There *are* serious players here that are willing to pay more and that are looking to offer something of value. And more to the point, if you're looking to quickly start bringing in cash—this is a great way to do it. From there, you can gain the skills and experience you need and "bootstrap" yourself to greater heights. Again, all of that is coming up in this book.

If you're willing to start from the bottom, then you can use this strategy to have money in your PayPal account by the end of the day.

Note as well that these forums—like freelancing sites—also have job listings. So, you have the option to either advertise your skills and wait to be contacted *or* proactively make yourself known to clients that are looking for particular jobs.

Other Forums

In business terms, we might describe this strategy as a "go-to-market" strategy. We have simply *gone to* where all the webmasters and marketers that can benefit from our services might be.

But if you aren't a web developer, Internet marketer or writer, then that might not be your ideal market.

Fortunately, there are plenty more places that you can go to sell your skills. **Stack Overflow** (https://stackoverflow.com) is a well-known forum for developers that has a Developer Jobs section. You'll find something similar for pretty much any niche that you're interested in entering, whether that's photography, design, or business consulting.

But the sites don't even need an official "job listings" section. There's nothing to stop you advertising your skills on general programming forums, or in groups on sites like Google Plus (be sure to check the sites' policies first though). The same goes for Reddit. As a general rule though, you'll find that you get a lot more success if you spend some time developing a good reputation in those communities first. And of course, you can advertise "passively" by mentioning your skills in a signature block, for example, and then going around solving people's programming quandaries!

Gumtree is also another less-obvious place that you can list your services— pretty much anything you can think of in fact!

LinkedIn

LinkedIn (www.linkedin.com) is a fantastic tool for networking and making new connections. It can also be a great way to find work—and some of my most exciting opportunities have come from here in fact.

LinkedIn is not a freelancing site but rather a social network for professionals. Nevertheless, recruiters definitely use this as a place to scout for talent. Not only that, but it can also act as a great additional tool to combine with other approaches. For instance, if you don't want to list all of your work experience on a site like Warrior Forum (and as a general rule, you should ask permission before using previous clients' projects in this way—it's not very professional otherwise), then you can simply link to your LinkedIn page. You can even directly connect Upwork to a LinkedIn account, and the same is true for many other freelancing platforms.

LinkedIn essentially allows you to create a profile, list your skills and experience, and then add connections from your professional (and personal) networks. You'll also be able to join groups, send messages, and give and receive endorsements for people you have worked with.

Using LinkedIn works like a game of "degrees of separation," and the really exciting part is that you can contact your second- or third-degree connections using something called InMail. So, if you're trying to reach the CEO of a big company and it just so happens that someone you went to school with is the company's marketing manager's daughter, you now have a direct way to get in touch.

What that means is that you should cast your net far and wide. Whereas you might think twice about adding that old school friend on Facebook, on LinkedIn you should aim to add *everyone* that you ever come into contact with. You never know where a connection might lead.

Don't blow these powerful connections though! Wait until you have something truly worthwhile before directly messaging your biggest contacts. Or better yet, ask your mutual contacts to give you an introduction.

Tip Consider using LinkedIn Sales Navigator. Previously known as Rapportive, this tool allows you to see the LinkedIn profiles of people who contact you via e-mail. That way, you can more quickly grow your network.

Creating a Website

If you're interested in finding work as quickly as possible, then simply posting ads on forums and creating profiles on freelancing sites is a good way to go about it.

But in both these cases, you are "going to" the clients. In an ideal world, as you grow, you want to get to the point where the clients start coming to you. And one of the most important things you can do to reach that point is to create a website.

This will then act as a showcase and portfolio for your work. It will serve as a "landing page" to which you can send potential clients and as a way to build trust and authority. In a moment, we're going to talk about using advertising to drive potential clients to your business—and having a website is pretty much a requirement for those sorts of strategies.

But even without an advertising campaign or profile on another platform, a website can bring in visitors through SEO and then build enough authority for you to charge higher prices.

Content Marketing

Imagine for a moment that you're a business owner and you enjoy reading content related to your work in your downtime (it's lame, but we all do it). You've found a website by a great app developer, who talks about the app market, who shares brief tutorials, and who provides tips on things like user interface (UI) and smart code. You don't know much about the subject, but this blogger seems to really know her stuff and has a genuine interest in providing the best information out there.

Now you find yourself needing someone to program an app for your business. It just so happens that the blogger you've been reading for the last few months also provides that service. What are the chances you're even going to bother looking anywhere else? This is the idea behind "content marketing."

For this to work, you need to be able to make your work interesting to people who *aren't* already developers/web designers/writers. You need to appeal to your potential target demographic by showing the art in your craft. If you do that, you'll build a following, and that following will become a huge pool of potential clients for you. Not only that, but the more followers you have, the more *clout* you will have and the more you will be able to charge. Those followers become testimony—and that puts you on the in-demand list. Sure, this strategy takes time, but the potential benefits of writing a few blog posts about your work every week *massively* outweigh the cost.

A well-written blog post on "how to find a developer" can also bring direct traffic from interested buyers through Google—if you understand the basics of SEO—and thereby become an ad for your business. Once again, if you provide something truly useful and then subtly use this to promote your own services, then you can help more people discover you while at the same time building trust *and* targeting precisely the right kind of client. If you keep posting regularly, then any post could conceivably make it to the top of Google. Again, this is the power of content marketing!

There are also things you can do to encourage a blog post to rank highly, as described a bit later in the section "SEO Basics."

But the most important reason to create a website is so that you can develop yourself as a brand. This is how you will transition from taking odd jobs on freelancing sites to being an in-demand, online megastar who can set their own salary. A website lets you show off your skills and expertise, your portfolio, and your social media influence. And it gives clients a way to contact you directly, with nobody taking a cut or limiting the way that you choose to work.

How to Create a Website

So, with all that said, how do you go about creating a website? Most tech professionals already know how to do this, so I'm also not going to go into a lot of detail here—there are entire books dedicated to website creation. Feel free to skip this section if you already know the routine, but if you're looking for the basics or a quick refresher, here are the steps to create a website:

1. Find web hosting.
2. Install WordPress.
3. Create a brand.

Find Web Hosting

Finding web hosting means getting space on a web server where your website files will be stored. You'll also need a domain name (URL), which ideally will be your own name or brand. Whenever someone types that domain name into their browser address bar, your site will be shown. Hosting will likely set you back $5 to $20 per month depending on the bells and whistles you choose. Lots of sites offer both web hosting and a domain name as a single package, such as **Bluehost** (www.bluehost.com), **GoDaddy** (www.godaddy.com), and **HostGator** (www.hostgator.com). You will find that these sites vary a little in terms of their bandwidth, storage, downtime etc. For our purposes, these differences are largely negligible - seeing as you likely won't have huge amounts of traffic, or be required to upload huge files.

Install WordPress

WordPress is a content management system (CMS), a framework that can be used to very conveniently create new websites, change their design, install new features, and manage your pages and blog posts. WordPress is a completely free tool that powers around 25% of the entire Web. It is behind many of the most popular sites in the world, from BBC America, to TechCrunch, to Sony Music, to Bloomberg Professional, to the New Yorker … There's a huge community surrounding the platform, and it's also completely customizable and open source. In other words, there is no downside. It makes creating a website incredibly simple (we're talking several clicks simple) and ensures compatibility with the vast majority of ready-made tools and themes. Building a site from scratch will involve significantly more work and make any future updates much more complicated. Even if you are a professional web developer, it often makes sense to use WordPress as your foundation, as that way you'll spend less time tweaking code and will have out-of-the-box support for many useful plug-ins and tools. Not just that, but WordPress is a proven commodity when it comes to things like SEO. You know it *can* work for a successful big business. Don't let your ego get in the way and insist on building your site yourself unless you have an actual reason. Focus on providing value to your clients.

At the opposite end of the spectrum, site builder tools like **Squarespace** and WiX.com are no easier to use, but rope you into recurring payment plans.

To get started with WordPress, log into the hosting account you chose in step 1 and look for the option to install WordPress in the control panel. Often you can do this with a single click. If your web host doesn't offer this, then you can install the platform manually by downloading the files from the official site (www. wordpress.org) and then uploading them to your server and following the instructions. Once installed, you will log into your WP admin panel and then choose a theme, add plug-ins, and write content all via the menu on the left.

Create a Brand

If you want to be taken seriously (tip: you do), then you need to think hard about the design of your website and how this will speak to your "brand." A personal brand is different from the kind of brand associated with a larger business, but it is a no less important part of your strategy.

Depending on how you intend to present yourself, you may or may not want a logo. But at the very least, you'll probably want a stylized font. My advice here is to use a professional designer (unless you are one or have experience) as this really is a very important first impression and should be used across your social pages too, as well as on your letterhead and so forth. And *listen* to your designer—this is their job and they aren't as close to the project as you are. That actually makes them better suited to making design choices, as they can see your business the way your clients will.

Make sure that the designer provides you with a vector file, such as an .AI format. This will enable you to edit and scale the logo without losing any quality. Likewise, think about consistent coloring and design cues to use across your website, in any social media, and so on. All of this attention to detail will help potential clients to associate their experience with a single provider: you. And if your site looks polished and professional, it will help to instill trust in your service. Ask yourself this: Can my website realistically compete with the best in my niche? If not, then it needs more work.

After you complete the preceding three steps, it's then simply a matter of adding content, writing up a home page, and filling the site with your portfolio, testimonials, and more, all of which is easy to do with WordPress.

SEO Basics

The ideal scenario is that your website brings in paying clients directly and not *just* via freelancing platforms and social media. To accomplish this, your aim is to get people to discover you via Google searches—which means you need to consider search engine optimization, or SEO.

As mentioned earlier, SEO is all about understanding which keywords and phrases potential clients might use in search queries in order to find your services. There are keyword research tools out there to help you find these phrases, but you can also use some common sense. For instance, if you are an app developer, then "freelance app developer" might be something that people search for.

Consider, though, that the most popular terms with the highest search volume will also be the ones that are the most difficult to rank for—due to the large amounts of competition you will face from other sites and service providers. So, it might take a lot of work and luck to reach number one for "freelance app developer," but you could have more luck with "freelance Unity developer" or "freelance Unity Android developer." The good news? You don't have to choose just one! You can pick a few to target with your site's homepage, but then target individual keywords with each blog post.

To use the keywords, you will subtly include them in your text in a way that seems natural. The ideal "density" is around .5% to 2%. That means that for every 200 words, you might include the keyword one to four times. My advice is to be conservative and to mix up your keywords with synonyms and related terms. This is called latent semantic indexing (LSI) and it is the best strategy to conform to Google's latest algorithm (called Hummingbird at the time of writing). The key is to communicate to Google what your pages and posts are about, while still prioritizing the user experience and being natural and organic in your writing.

Content should be well written (short sentences, lots of headers) and ideally long-form (over 1,000 words). You should link out to other useful resources and you should include images and pull quotes. Try to include keywords in the opening and closing paragraphs where possible, in one H1 or H2 header, in the image alt tags (HTML tags that show text when an image fails to load) and file names, in the SEO title, in the file name/permalink (the URL of the specific page), and in your meta description (this is a HTML 'tag' that is seen by Google).

Another important consideration is to ensure that your website loads quickly and displays properly on mobile devices (meaning it needs a "responsive design"—most WordPress themes will take care of that for you).

That's your "on page" SEO in a nutshell, but you also need to build a backlinks profile, which means getting as many other sites and blogs to link to yours as possible (with the caveat that these must be *high quality* connections—well-written and trustworthy websites). Often, you'll do this by writing free content for other sites and requesting that you be able to include a link back to your page in return. This is called "guest posting." These links then help Google's spiders (programs that read websites) to find your content by following them. They also act as testimonials of sorts, which Google sees as votes of confidence regarding the quality of your information.

Sound confusing? I could go on for an entire book, but again the information would be outdated within months, so my advice is to do some research into the subject of SEO if this is something you want to invest in heavily. To help you along the way, there are some good WordPress plug-ins that will help you to see where the SEO of each page and post could be improved. I highly recommend **Yoast SEO** (https://yoast.com/wordpress/plugins/seo).

Of course, another option for those professionals with sufficient funds is to invest in an SEO company to handle all this for you.

Note that a good website also needs to be updated regularly with new content. This creates more work for you, so you need to decide whether this is a strategy you want to pursue or whether your time could be better spent elsewhere. If you are starting out, then maintaining a basic static page to sell your services is definitely a good idea. Once you start charging more, though, you might start considering investing time into building your brand and your influence.

YouTube

Another option if you want to build a brand for yourself and position yourself as an authority/thought leader in your industry is to create a YouTube channel. This can be used in a similar way to a blog. While it's not as effective as an online portfolio, it is another way that you can demonstrate your knowledge and experience, show off your personality, and build a big following. Creating a successful YouTube channel is in some ways easier than launching a successful blog, as you'll be going up against less competition. If you happen to be charismatic and engaging, then this is a great way to use those assets to your advantage.

For an example of how this might work, check out any "fitness YouTuber." These creators post regular videos sharing their training regimes and tips but will often allude to paid programs and books that they sell from a website. The idea is to build an audience and establish trust and then to direct their audience to a sales funnel that will ultimately result in sales.

You can do the precise thing with programming tutorials. There is actually a fairly large market for online programming tutorials, and you only need a piece of screen capture software to make these—**Flashback Express** (www.flashbackrecorder.com) is a great, free example. It works with videos on web design. With videos on digital marketing. With videos on coaching or law. Demonstrate you know your stuff, build a big audience, and the amount you can charge will go up—as will your discoverability.

Social Media

Social media similarly gives you another avenue to market yourself and to connect with a large audience. This is a way to manage a brand that involves a lesser time commitment as compared to running a blog.

For instance, you might create an Instagram account to post pictures of your web design work. Or you might use it to promote the "laptop lifestyle" (that's a popular hashtag you can have for free!) and show off photos of yourself working on sunny beaches or coding in your snazzy home office. You may then build your following here by posting regularly, liking other pictures in your niche, and using smart hashtags.

Tip   You can use up to 30 hashtags on Instagram and it's recommended that you do. As one video I watched put it: Why would you enter the lottery once if you could enter 30 times for free? Ideally, look for terms that have around 300,000 recent tags. These are popular but not overly competitive. Choose a few more at either end of the spectrum though.

Either way, social media can help you to build a following and you can then include a link to your home page, LinkedIn or other portal in your profile description, and the occasional photo description (the text below your image). Then, just browse through other users' profiles and post useful comments. Don't try and sell yourself (you'll eventually get reported for spam); just comment on other users' sharing their work and say something encouraging or offer a tip for free. If those users then click your name (and many will), that's a way for someone else to discover what you're offering.

This works best in visual industries of course, but it can be effective for any type of professional. The key is to "sell the dream" as it were. Look for the emotional hook in what you're doing and try to express that artistically through your posts. Even in a dry, tech-oriented business to business (B2B) scenario, you can still find things that will get viewers excited: whether that means useful tips, or photos that demonstrate the power of technology to connect businesses. Ask: what is it that gets your target audience excited?

Likewise, you can achieve similar things with a Facebook Page or a Twitter account. This also gives your potential clients more ways to contact you. Facebook even has call-to-action (CTA) buttons so that clients can order straight from your page.

Again: post regularly and provide value—don't just try and sell your business, or be so afraid to show any personality that you end up looking dull and boring. The WORST company social media accounts are the ones that do nothing but occasionally post about their latest special deal, or how good their main product or service is. Why would anyone follow that?

Let your mission statement and brand identity drive the way you talk online, and don't be afraid to act "un-business-like" if it means you stand out or get shares. This is where you can really express yourself as a brand, and brands that try to appeal to everyone will ultimately end up disappearing into obscurity. Knowing what your brand stands for and expressing that through social media will help you to gain real fans, not *just* customers.

Whatever you post, try to update regularly if possible. If you built a blog, then this is the perfect place to share your new blog posts to try and gain some traction for them.

One more thing: remember to speak with your followers. Facebook is primarily a communication tool, and it works best when you treat it as such. The same is true for Twitter and Instagram to a lesser extent. Respond to comments on your pictures, ask your fans what they want to hear about next, and let people see a little behind the scenes. Using live streaming is also very useful for this, as it lets your audience feel as though they're talking to you directly.

Running all this social media can be time consuming, but it should pay for itself in the long term and you can ramp it up as you build momentum. A quick tip is to use a tool like **IFTTT** (https://ifttt.com) which can automatically cross-post your updates for you—meaning your Instagram feed will help to populate your Facebook page.

Persuasive Writing for Selling Your Skills

If you're going to be posting ads on forums or listings, then your success will likely come down to your ability to write a good pitch and to stand out from the crowd. Likewise, if you have a website that you use to sell your services, then your sales skills will once again play an important role.

The question, then, is how you can go about describing the services that you provide in a way that will make you seem like a fantastic option for any potential client looking to hire. The answer is by using persuasive writing techniques.

Be Clear and Avoid Jargon

The first and most important tip—as mentioned previously in the context of freelancing profiles—is to make sure that you are absolutely clear about what it is that you are offering. And this means that you can't use any jargon or buzzwords.

The WORST business websites are the ones that say things like:

> *Offering high-level, digital enterprise solutions for companies with big ideas! Leveraging digitization, big data, and the cloud to help our clients meet their targets and goals.*

This might sound clever, but it tells the reader *nothing* about the service actually being offered. You have a couple of seconds in which to win over the audience (remember, most visitors will spend less than 30 seconds on a website or page) and most professionals aren't in the mood for riddles. If you can't explain what you do clearly, then there's a good chance you don't really know yourself!

So instead, open with something like:

> *Digital marketing consultation for companies looking to enhance their presence online.*

Or:

> *Top-tier Android app design and development.*

This makes it *absolutely clear* what you do.

A single succinct sentence is the ideal, and you can then use a couple more sentences to expand on this and share some of your alternative services.

Engaging and Holding Attention

Another thing to consider regarding those short attention spans is that you need to do everything you can to grab your audience's attention quickly.

If you were selling a tacky e-book, you would target your audience with rhetorical questions (these get us to reflect on what we're reading), with a narrative structure (they say that "storytelling is SEO for the human brain"), and with lots of short sentences ending with cliff hangers. You'd talk directly to your audience, using the first person.

> *Are you sick of that flabby stomach?*
> *It's harming your confidence, your relationships, and your energy levels. Right?*
> *I used to have a similar problem. Not anymore!*
> *Today, I'm all rippling abs and broad smiles. Life has never been better.*
> *And I owe it all to one weird trick! You'll never believe when I tell you.*

Fortunately, you are not selling a tacky e-book. And I don't condone these transparent methods. If you want to be taken seriously as a professional, then you need to present yourself as such. But that is not to say that you can't still take a few leaves from this book.

Try to be as direct as possible. Avoid large paragraphs. Use stories and examples where possible to create more emotional involvement. And make big, bold statements!

Address Concerns and Pain Points

From there, you then need to demonstrate what it is that sets you apart and why companies should hire you. You can add more detail regarding your experience and accomplishments at the bottom of your profile, so for now keep it simple by pointing out your years of experience and maybe mentioning one or two of your most high-profile jobs.

Explain that you are easy to work with and try to address any "pain points" or nagging questions your reader might have at this point.

You've told them that you have lots of experience. But isn't that what all developers/writers/consultants say?

You've told them that you offer fast turnaround times and a reliable, transparent service. But many of your clients will have been burned in the past and thus be wary of such promises.

Your job is to address each of these concerns and thereby prevent them from being deal-breakers for your readers. Remember: human beings are naturally risk-averse. Your job is to remove *any* potential risk from dealing with you.

You can do this in a number of ways:

- Acknowledge the problem and set yourself apart ("Don't risk your reputation on a less-qualified designer . . .").

- Offer a money-back guarantee or similar.

- Provide examples/qualifications that your competition can't.

- Use testimonials and social proof to back up your claims.

- Suggest that the client put in a very small order to begin with because you are "confident your work will speak for itself."

- Offer a free e-mail/Skype consultation (only if you charge enough to make this option worth your while).

- What do they have to lose?

Likewise, your buyer might be worried that the process is going to be time consuming and thus put it off to handle later. Try to make ordering as easy as possible and explain *precisely* the details you need in order to get started on the project. If you are selling from a web page, then you can even include a form embedded right there!

Know Your Value Proposition

Similarly, you also need to demonstrate how the service you provide can benefit your buyer. Sure, you offer app design that is of a higher quality than the competition. But why does that matter? And why should your clients bother with an app?

This is where it pays to get inside the mindset of the buyer and to understand their goals. Another useful business term here is "buyer persona." This is basically a fictional biography of your ideal target, filled out in as much detail as possible and brought to life in your imagination. How old is your typical buyer? What are their goals? Where do they spend their time online?

While you will have clients that deviate from this template, your buyer persona is your "prototypical" average buyer, and when writing sales pitches, this is who you are writing "for."

If it's a small business owner looking for a mobile app, then they probably want to expand their reach, avoid falling behind the competition and becoming dated, and improve the experience for their customers. This is your "value proposition." In other words, it is the way in which the service you provide is going to be valuable to them. The old adage goes that you "don't sell hats, you sell warm heads." Similarly, you don't sell apps, you sell happy customers and better profits.

And if you can point out how your service is in fact an investment that will pay for itself many times over, then you can overcome another barrier to sale: the cost.

Paint a picture of how much better your client's business and life will be once they've secured your services and get them to view it.

Teach Something

If you really believe in the service that you provide, and you believe it is important, then you should know how to impart this same belief to your reader. And by showing them *how* to use the service you offer and why they should, you will be in a very good position.

For instance, you might explain why an Android app is important for marketing by explaining the usefulness of being able to send notifications to the user. You might point out how it can be used to direct a customer to a store. Or you might stress the value of sticking to Google's Material Design guidelines.

You can then close by saying that even if the client doesn't use your services, they should ensure they hire a developer that understands these things. (But isn't it easier to just hire you?)

This is something you will also be doing through the use of your blog posts and content marketing.

Go in for the Kill

The thing to remember is that most purchases—even in business—are driven more by emotion than logic. This is why it's so important to generate a sale (or at least capture an e-mail) before the visitor leaves your page. If they go away and think about their decision, often they will opt to save money or forget all about you.

Instead, you want to work them into a fever pitch where they feel compelled to call or fill out that order form.

You can do this by painting a negative picture of what could happen if they *don't* use your services. Either they get left behind by the competition and damage their reputation or they use a lesser provider and end up wasting their money.

Another way to create this anxiety is to invoke urgency, scarcity, and rarity. That means encouraging the reader to act right away rather than going away and thinking about it. You can do this by offering a limited-time special offer, or pointing out that your calendar is very busy and you only have space for a couple more clients. Again, the aim is to get them to order *now*.

Putting This All Together

When I sell my SEO writing services, I'm targeting companies that might be used to using very low-quality content written by non-native speakers, working for agencies that are still using outdated SEO techniques (such as "keyword stuffing" to the point of getting the site penalized). The writing is very often unreadable, or at the very best it is bland and uninspiring.

My challenge is getting over the fact that the competition will often work for less than $1 per 100 words. And the key to success is to use all the techniques we've looked at here.

I begin my pitch by stating confidently what I do. I make that more niche—I am not just a writer but an SEO writer. I am not just an SEO writer but an SEO writer specializing in fitness, self-development, online business, programming, and technology[1].

Then I list some of my previous experience. I am a published author, I've written for large online brands (see my LinkedIn page), and I have worked as an editor for a print magazine with a circulation of 3 million.

Then I explain that in order for a website to generate a following and gain authority, it needs content that isn't just technically proficient but that says something NEW. It's not enough to hire a good writer. They need to hire a good writer that is passionate about the subject and that knows it inside out, so that they can say something new that is *of value* to the target audience. And they need to say it in a way that demonstrates an understanding of that community. That's why I *only* write on my chosen topics. And in a way that is entertaining, engaging, and conforming to the AP Stylebook. Cheap alternatives cannot offer this.

I ask them to think of the sites that they read daily. Do they hire writers with no passion for the subject? Do they publish articles with poor grammar and lots of repetitive keywords? No. They read sites that are filled with magazine-quality content, written by unique personalities that love their subjects. That's how you build a *brand* with a following—rather than a spammy site that will get penalized.

The sites that are filled with poor-quality content are the ones you click away from immediately. They're the sites that you make a mental note to *avoid in the future*.

If they are to succeed, they need to be able to compete with the very best sites in their niche. That is true of their website design and of the content that fills the website.

I offer that top-quality content. My work has *been featured* on the very kinds of top-quality sites they are competing with. And I do all this with rapid turnaround and at a *very* fair price.

Not to mention that my writing can help them generate more sales, improve their SEO, and build relationships with their followers. I understand their business goals and the technicalities of the industry.

Finally, I'll point out that my time is limited and I will be operating on a first-come, first-served basis.

---

[1]You can check out my LinkedIn page here: www.linkedin.com/in/adam-sinicki

You see how this might work? Now go and do the same thing for your own services![2]

Advertising

If you have a website or even a post on a forum where you are selling your services and you have written your sales pitch well, then it follows that you can create more work for yourself simply by ensuring that more people land on that page.

How effective your website/post/page (which I will refer to henceforth as your "sales page") is at generating sales will be referred to as your "conversion rate." This describes the rate at which visitors become paying clients.

So, if you have one new client for every 100 new visitors/views, then you might consider this to be a conversion rate of 1%, which is a very good conversion rate, but certainly not unheard of if the traffic is targeted (meaning that the people looking at your ad are the kinds of people who might want to buy from you!).

Now, let's work out the average amount each client might spend with you. You can figure this out by looking at past work or based on the hourly rate or per-gig rate that you are charging. If most projects take you five hours and you charge $100 per hour, then you are making $500 for every customer. Or $500 from every 200 visitors. Remove any overhead—which probably is minimal for a coder for hire, for example.

Note For now, we'll assume that each client will only buy from you once. But were they to order multiple projects, or to pay you a recurring fee to manage their website, then you might be able to multiply this by the number of orders per customer to work out your customer lifetime value, or CLV.

Now you have the amount of money that you earn for every 200 visitors, you know how much every 200 visitors are worth to you.

And that in turn means that you can start *paying* for your visitors. You might do this through pay-per-click (PPC) advertising. This basically means that you're paying each time someone clicks an ad, rather than paying for the ad itself. You can set a "maximum bid," which is the maximum amount you will

---

[2]Of course, these techniques will work best when targeting smaller organizations, start-ups, and entrepreneurs. For larger projects and clients, the decision will likely not be made so quickly and may even come down to a whole procurement department or at least a team meeting. Depending on the type of projects you are looking for, you should adjust your approach accordingly.

pay for a click (if there is no competing ad to be displayed in the same space, then the cost will be less). Likewise, you can set a daily budget so that your ads will stop showing after you've spent $X amount.

If you pay $2 per click, then that is $400 per 200 visitors. That means you're spending $400 (maximum) for each $500 job and making a $100 profit. But it might just be that you can find a niche angle and only pay 10 cents for each click.

The two most popular platforms for PPC advertising are Google AdWords, which shows ads on Google's SERPS for specific keywords, and Facebook Ads, which shows ads on Facebook's home feed based on the user's interests and preferences. For example, you could use AdWords to show your ad to anyone who searches for "affordable web developer" or "estate agent website developer." Or you could use Facebook to show your ads to the owners of small startups with interests like "business." (Or something more specific relevant to your niche.) Decide which platform will bring you the most targeted clicks and invest there.

Of course, this sort of strategy will significantly increase your overhead and you need to weigh that against the benefits. But for the right type of work (highly paid with long-term clients) and with the right website, it can be a useful way to generate some work. What's more is that using Google AdWords can be a good way to jump straight to the top of Google for your search terms and that way test which terms bring you the most customers before investing time into a targeted SEO campaign.

Other Forms of Advertising

Of course, there are many other forms of advertising. PPC gives you the advantage of being able to closely control all the variables and track your stats; but you could likewise pay to display a banner ad on a website, you could pay for a "solo ad"[3], or you could even pay for an ad in a magazine or your local paper. How about handing out fliers?

Approaching Directly

Many of the options we've discussed so far involve creating some kind of profile or ad and then waiting for clients to come pouring in.

But if you want to be more proactive, then you can also try approaching potential clients directly where you spot a need. In fact, much of your success is likely to come down to your ability to identify and act upon opportunities.

---

[3]A solo ad is a shout out to an existing mailing list.

And this can mean simply looking for companies that might be in need of your services and then approaching them.

How many times have you visited a company website and found yourself thinking that it looks outdated or poorly designed? How many times have you looked for a restaurant's app in the Google Play Store and found yourself left wanting?

I have a friend who worked as a roofer for a while and the way he ensured he always had enough work was simply to drive around his area looking out for external signs of wear and tear. He'd then knock on the doors of those homes and offer his services.

You can do the precise same thing as a tech entrepreneur, or any kind of online freelancer. Look for companies that are at about "your level" and try to find opportunities to work together.

And this doesn't have to be something you do online either! You can just as easily ask store owners in person if they have a website or app. Have they considered e-commerce?

The key to success when doing this is to be polite and positive (don't imply that they're doing something wrong) but to also demonstrate how your services could help them. Try to demonstrate that you're familiar with their business and even that you're a fan. If you're contacting a blogger, for example, perhaps open by commenting on a recent post that got you thinking (while not beating around the bush too long). There's nothing worse than receiving generic e-mails offering services that don't relate to you, from people who clearly haven't done any research. Don't be that person.

From there, use the techniques we've discussed: share your expertise, allay any fears they might have, and so forth. This can be a surprisingly effective way to procure new clients. If you really want to capture their imagination and demonstrate your commitment, then you could even try creating a mock-up of the project you're offering to work on for them, where applicable. This is how I landed one of my biggest clients as an app developer! It works because it lets them see the value you'd be offering and massages their ego—though of course it means there is a greater loss in terms of time spent if you don't get a lead from your hard work.

Networking

Another great way to find clients is to look to your personal network. Most of us know people who run their own businesses, or who are close enough to management that they could put in a good word for us. If the service you provide is business to customer (B2C) rather than B2B, then you can try approaching friends of friends. I say "friends of friends" because in the very next chapter I'm going to explain why you should never work for friends!

But in short, don't underestimate the value of your *existing* contacts and who you can reach through them. Likewise, it might be that through your personal network you have access to some great "route to markets." For instance, if you happen to know the editor of *Restaurant Owner Weekly*, then this would be a great place to advertise app or website development. You could always ask them if they'd do you a favor, or at least offer mate's rates. You might be surprised just how many opportunities your friends and contacts can already offer, if you think a little outside the box.

Tip This is another good opportunity to check out who you're already connected to on your LinkedIn page. Maybe you know another online freelancer who has clients they can pass on to you? If you don't ask, you won't know.

And of course, you should strive to keep expanding that sphere of influence by networking. One of the best ways to do that is by attending events and conferences and speaking to as many people as possible. Likewise, attending hackathons and working on open source projects can be great ways to gain more contacts *and* to get yourself noticed. You may even be headhunted!

For other types of work, you can likewise attend tradeshows, conferences, and other events. Put yourself out there!

Perhaps you got into coding, or whatever other creative endeavor, because you like working alone and you're a natural introvert. I hear you. But making the effort to put yourself out there, meet people, chat, and build relationships will have a huge impact on your career trajectory. Try to get good at networking and selling yourself—it will be a massive asset to you.

Chapter Summary

At this point, you should now have an understanding of how the gig economy works and how to find work through both conventional and less-obvious channels. You've got all the skills and knowledge you need to start generating clients, in other words.

But being successful as an online freelancer is about much more than just knowing how to find the clients. You also need to know how to *keep* them. That is where Chapter 4 comes in.

Choosing Your Gigs and Rates Wisely

Something you'll learn early on is that not all gigs are created equal. Now that you know how to find work, the next step is knowing what *kind* of work to find.

At the same time, you need to know how to arrange your working relationship with the client and what to charge (which will also impact the kinds of people that your ads attract).

Ideally, you want to attract high-paying projects that you can finish quickly, and you want work that can help you further your career. This chapter will explain how you do that.

What to Charge

I was on the plane back from Germany a while ago when I happened to overhear two other passengers' conversation, as you tend to when travelling alone. They were two middle-aged businessmen presumably on their way back from a business trip, discussing the logistics of getting a website designed for the company.

© Adam Sinicki 2019
A. Sinicki, *Thriving in the Gig Economy*, https://doi.org/10.1007/978-1-4842-4090-8_4

What I managed to gather was that they needed a very basic website that they could use as a showcase and portfolio for whatever B2B service it was they provided. They were talking about several proposals they'd had from potential web design companies and, from what I could gather, they were looking to spend around $2,000-$3,000. If you are a tech professional, then chances are that you're now thinking what I was thinking at the time: *I could do that in a couple of days.* (At the time I had a very full work-schedule, or maybe I would have spoken up!)

A similar experience, I recall, was being propositioned to build a website for a company. A friend worked at an insurance company and let me know that his company was looking for a very basic site that could act as a portfolio. Keeping in mind that I wouldn't be writing the content, designing the logo, or even securing their hosting and domain.

He assumed that I'd be interested (this happens when you work online—even if you're not a web designer), but because I had a problem saying no at the time, I said I'd think about it.

"Just to get a rough ballpark figure that I can take back to them," he asked, "how much roughly do you charge?"

As it was a friend, and I was not yet experienced in negotiation, I told him that I could do it for a few hundred dollars. And what he advised me was that if I went in with that pitch, no one would take me seriously. All the other web designers would be charging ten times that, and if I didn't follow suite, the assumption would be that I was an amateur.

You and I both know that building a website these days is as easy as installing WordPress, choosing a theme that looks modern, and setting up a few plug-ins. For a basic portfolio, that's *all* you need to do. It isn't a stretch to suggest that this could be done in a very short time indeed.

If the client wants a custom theme built, then of course things would get a little more complex—but then we're still just talking a few lines of PHP most likely to edit a premade template.

If they want an internal web portal for collaboration and exchanging files, then sure, that would be a much bigger, more complex undertaking, and I'd have to charge a lot more. But the point is that a lot of managers and buyers still don't know the difference. In this case, there is a huge gap in terms of knowledge and, depending on what your morals will allow you to get away with, this can be a *massive* advantage. Like when I sold to my five-year-old sister a rock on a string and told her that if she tied it to her ceiling, it would wobble to warn her of earthquakes. Except now Mom isn't present to force me to give the money back.

How Much Are You Worth?

While this might seem a little bit like a scam, the thing to remember is that it really shouldn't matter how long it takes you to make something or how hard it is to build. That is of no concern to your clients (never ask how the sausages are made).

What *is* their concern is what the end product can do for them. How much will that product earn them? In the case of a website—especially with a bit of SEO—it could earn them *millions* over a course of a few years (depending on their service or product). In that sense, it would be worth every cent they pay to have the website built.

And how is this really any different from what a doctor does, or what a consultant does? There are consultants in various fields that charge hundreds of dollars per hour just to give advice. Again, the company is paying for the profit and the information. And in the digital age, knowledge and information are *the* most valuable commodities.

Or how about those courses and retreats that cost *thousands* of dollars per person for a few days? Those aren't even one-to-one!

(By the way, these are valid avenues for a tech professional to make money from eventually—and we'll be looking at that later on in this book!)

You can also liken it to selling e-books. This is a side hustle I've experimented in a few times: creating a PDF file and then selling it from a "landing page," or to an established online audience. Typically, a book on getting six-pack abs or building an online business can cost you $30 all the way up to $150. That book costs *nothing* for the creator to produce. There are no overheads: no delivery, storage, or anything else. People are willing to pay because they think the information is worth that amount of money to them.

There is a skill deficit here. A knowledge deficit. And THAT is the value you are providing. While you think this job is easy, the reality is that it's only easy because you invested the time and effort to *learn* that skill.

You might have only spent a few days building a website, but you took *years* learning your craft and building up to this point. *That* is what you are charging for.

And remember from Chapter 2 what a potential client's other options are at this point:

- Hire someone/a team in-house, which will cost a large amount of money.
- Take on a local employee for a fixed-term contract, who will probably need training.

- Outsource to a large development firm, which will charge ten times as much and give them less direct interaction with the coder they are using!

Gold isn't inherently worth anything. As metals go, it is actually particularly *impractical* for pretty much any application. It is valuable because it is rare and hard to acquire. And so are you.

Imposter Syndrome

If you still feel uncomfortable about charging thousands of dollars for something that takes you a few days, then there might be something else psychological going on here. You may be experiencing "imposter syndrome." This is a common phenomenon that causes even the most talented and qualified individuals to feel as though they are just bluffing their way through—that they don't really know what they're doing.

This usually comes down to a very human tendency to underestimate ourselves—and *overestimate* everyone else. You think that your boss knows everything about the industry? They're probably making it up as they go a lot of the time too. And what's more is that they will have started out knowing even less.

Knowledge really is valuable. Knowing even just a *little* more than someone else is something that we can charge for. And all of us bring unique skills and knowledge to the table. But if you don't value yourself, then you can't realistically expect anyone else to either.

Okay, So What Do I Charge?

With all that said, the amount you're going to charge will be dictated very much by the market you're entering and what you can pursuade people to pay you.

The first thing to do is research what others in your niche are charging. This is a form of "benchmarking"—looking at other businesses that are comparable to yours and identifying what works for them. Take a look at how your competition is offering the work and use that as your base. From there, you're then going to look for ways to improve the setup.

Choose: Will you undercut the competition and charge less in order to present a more compelling offer? Or will you charge more and set yourself up as the premium option?

If you choose the former, then you need to acknowledge that you're going to be competing with some *very* aggressive pricing. In particular, you'll be competing with people from overseas (India in particular) who are able to charge less thanks to lower costs of living. You don't have that luxury.

This is why it can be useful to calculate exactly how much you need to live off of, then to realistically think about how much work you can complete and how many "dry spells" you can expect to face. This way, you can work out your absolute minimum that you can charge and still live off. I have a policy that I need to earn $150 every single day as my minimum. Ideally, I earn a lot more. But having a minimum works as a very useful waypoint for calculating my fees.

Now obviously the smart thing to do is to set a base rate that is slightly higher than your minimum, as that will give you wiggle room when it comes to negotiating, introducing special offers, and so on. It is very common for people who get in touch from an ad to expect that you're going to lower the price at least a little. Or of course, you might choose to greatly increase your prices in order to earn more and work *less*.

If you choose to go for a higher rate, then you need to justify your increased cost. What can you offer that the competition can't? Experience is probably the best bargaining chip in this case. But if you're going up against foreign freelancers, then your location might help too. Some clients will want to meet to be able to discuss the project in person and "easy communication" is also a big plus. Being local might be even better then. People are willing to pay a *lot* for convenience and a sense of security.

If you're going to charge more, then make sure you emphasize your justification for this in your sales copy/profile. Point out why you are the "premium option" for companies that care about getting the best-quality end product and the best service. Ideally, this will mean showing how they'll earn more and improve their business by spending that little bit more with you.

Charging more also means being able to show the high caliber of work you've done previously. Building up a big portfolio and getting your feet wet early helps a great deal in this regard—more on that in a moment.

There are other value adds you can include too, such as "free revisions" or "clear and comprehensive commenting." What is your unique selling point (USP)?

Of course, you can also charge more or less depending on the rarity of your particular set of skills, which will likely also correlate with a sparser supply of clients.

Multiple Prices

There's also nothing to stop you from experimenting with different prices. Go in high and if no one bites, lower the amount you charge. On Fiverr, it's common practice to alter the fees continually depending on the number of orders in the queue. As work starts to pile up, you increase your rates to deter future orders (and make sure that any overtime work is more than worth it).

When things slow down, you lower that price again to attract more people. This also works because someone with a large queue appears inherently more valuable than someone that isn't in such high demand.

If you are selling work from a website or via a mailing list, then there's nothing to stop you from running "special offers" for a short time. Likewise, you can post to sites ads that announce your special rates. This can help you to attract and hook new clients, bring back old ones, and fill those quieter patches.

Alternatively, consider charging more on one site than you do on another to experiment with different pricing strategies: but be very careful when doing this, because if you get discovered, you can end up putting noses out of joint.

The strategy I've used for a long time very successfully is to do a minimum amount of work for an agency every day (more on this shortly) and then to take on additional, higher-paid work on top of that. The agency work earns me my minimum $150 but it only takes me half a day. For that second half of the day I can work on higher-paying work and take more risks knowing that I've got my "basic salary" already in the bag.

Increasing Your Price with Existing Clients

Eventually, you'll likely find a few long-term clients. This happens in almost every line of work, whether you're an app developer, a writer, or an Internet marketer.

This is a good thing because it means you'll rarely have any dry spells. But it's also a bad thing because it means you're now tied to a certain price and working arrangement and you might experience friction if you try and change that. It's very easy to become comfortable working for a meager wage and thereby to miss out on fulfilling your potential. Eventually, this can become essentially identical to traditional employment!

Now is the perfect opportunity to advertise for very highly paid work. If nothing comes of it, then nothing is lost. If an opportunity does arise, you now have a choice to make. Will you take the risk of leaving a reliable client behind to do more work for a higher-paying one?

But you should also give your existing clients the chance to keep working with you by asking them to agree to your higher wage. So how do you approach this difficult conversation?

One option is to try and show how you are justifying that increase in price. This can be personal (new baby, new responsibilities) but it can also relate once again to the work you're completing. For instance, explain that you're now charging a bit more but in return you will provide extra revisions, or you will increase your turnaround times. If you're a programmer, you can add more detailed comments, or offer a "maintenance" service. If you're a writer, how about including links to resources and better formatting?

You can also use this same strategy if you want to change the service you provide in any other way. For instance, when I decided that I would no longer write on *any* subject matter and would only write on topics that were my specialty (fitness, self-improvement, business, tech, psychology), my original plan was just to announce this to my clients. My wife pointed out that this would go down much better if I could show how this would benefit *them* and spin it into a positive. The pitch then became that I would be able to offer higher quality writing *and* faster turn-around times (TAT to use the industry lingo!) by focusing exclusively on topics I knew well. Everyone wins. So always find something sweet to help make that bitter pill a little easier to swallow!

But there are more ways to increase your wages too ...

Explain Yourself

As mentioned, "personal reasons" can also work as an excuse. If you're not sure about how you can increase the apparent value of your service, then an alternative approach is to explain why *you* need the extra money. This is the approach that many people take when requesting a promotion in a traditional employer/employee relationship. "I have a kid on the way, so I need more money for childcare!" Then there are outside forces like inflation and the rising cost of supplies and materials.

Personally, I'm not a huge fan of this option, as it's not that far removed from begging for a raise and it puts the power in the hands of the client. In the gig economy, it is always important that *we* call the shots. We provide a service, and we choose how much it costs.

Still, if you have a good relationship with the client, and you want to explain yourself, then this can be a good option.

Shopping Around

If you have other offers, then you can always just be brazen and express to your existing clients that you have a new price and that you have other clients willing to pay it—but be prepared for them to cease giving you business. Being able to get your existing clients to "bid for you" is a great way to increase your salary, but just be careful not to rub anyone the wrong way by doing so and damage your working relationship with them.

The key to victory in *any* negotiation is almost always being willing to walk away. So, if you can secure higher-paying work elsewhere *before* expressing to your existing clients that your fee is going up, then this will put you in a much stronger position. Then make sure that you really *are* happy to leave.

The thing to remember here is that, ultimately, having a loyal client is more important than having one that will pay a larger amount only once. So, you need to "test out" these new clients before you decide to potentially burn your bridges with older ones.

Taking on more work than you can cope with is never going to be easy, but if you plan for it, then there are options: try working an extra hour, for instance, or outsourcing some of the simpler parts of your job/getting help in. Even if that means that you end up spending any increase in profits, it will ultimately prove beneficial if it means that you find a high-paying and loyal client that you can keep going forward!

You can also tell your current clients that you are taking a week of holiday and then actually do work for other clients during that time! You are simply taking a short time off from one client, but not the other.

Just don't be tempted to keep both old and new clients and try to earn double at the expense of your sanity. Not only is burning the candle at both ends a one-way ticket to severely impaired productivity, but it also means you lose the flexibility to increase your rates *further* in future.

Go Incremental

Finally, why not take a lesson from Dr. Stanley Milgram's famous psychological study of obedience? (Sorry: psychology graduate here!) This study aimed to find out if normal people could be persuaded into carrying out acts of atrocity. They were therefore asked to take part in a fake "experiment" during which they would play the role of an assessor, while another "participant" (who was in fact an actor) would be made to answer questions. For each wrong answer, the unsuspecting subject was instructed to deliver an electric shock (fake) to the "learner." And each time, the voltage would go up. The actor (who was on the other side of a wall and could only be heard by the participants) would cry out in pain each time, even complaining of a bad heart and begging for the experiment to be called to an end. Eventually, they would stop making any sound at all. (This was 1963—the obvious ethical issues involved in this study would prevent it from being carried out today!)

Toward the end of the study, the participants were willingly delivering shocks of 450 volts to their pleading "learners," despite the warning sign "Danger: Severe Shock" being plastered right over the button.

How were ordinary people convinced to deliver potentially *fatal* electric shocks to people they had never met, and who were presumed perfectly innocent? There are plenty of factors, but one of the most important was the incremental nature of the increasing voltage. While it would have been hard to convince someone to *start* at 450 volts, that same number apparently seemed a lot less of a big deal when participants had just delivered a 435-volt shock! 30 volts isn't that much more than the harmless 15, and 45 isn't that much more than 30…

Afraid of raising your prices? Then try increasing the amount by just 10 cents per hour. This is miniscule and will almost certainly not drive away any loyal clients. But, by the same token it will actually add up to 80 cents a day, $4 a week, and $16 per month (roughly). That is $192 per year—not nothing! And then you put it up again in a few months. And again.

This method also happens to work particularly well with the aforementioned option of explaining why you "need" the money. Increasing your prices by 10 cents might seem a little petty, but if you explain that you have higher overhead, or that your cost of living has increased, then it will seem perfectly reasonable. That 10 cents increase reflects the 10 cents increase in your electricity bill, for example.

As you have no doubt realized at this point, there is actually a whole lot of psychology involved in marketing and dealing with clients. When you enter the gig economy, you become a one-person business, and that means wearing multiple hats. In this case, that might include learning how to persuade your clients to let you get your way!

Note as well that these small increments in price are psychologically easier to swallow if you break down your "wage" into the smallest possible units. Asking for a raise of $192 per year might be harder in conventional employment than asking for a raise of 10 cents an hour.

Better yet, if you deliver your work based on the number of words or the number of lines of code, then you can charge something seemingly *miniscule* like .1 cent per extra line of code—and actually have it translate to an even bigger fee hike!

More Negotiation Techniques

If your clients don't agree to your new rates right away, then there are a few other strategies you can bring to negotiations.

Keep in mind that your negotiation will often be won or lost in many ways before you even begin asking for more money. The impression they have already formed of you, the timing (and their current mood/financial situation), and your own confidence/qualifications will all play a very big role in determining the outcome.

With that in mind, make sure to keep negotiations in mind from the word go. Do what you can to overcome that imposter syndrome, fill your résumé with impressive qualifications and experience, and do the best work you can. Another useful tip is to try and create as much of an in-person impression as possible. In typical negotiations, it is often "you" that the buyer will really be investing in, rather than your service. Obviously, creating an-person impression is harder when the relationship is maintained entirely through e-mails and

Slack, so to steer things in your direction, it can be a good idea to spend some time building more of a personal connection. That might mean through Skype, or in the case of newer clients, it could also mean by creating a presence on YouTube/social media.

Likewise, it's always a good idea to time your negotiations carefully. Are you coming off of a very successful project that you just completed? Or better yet, does your client rely on you for something even bigger that's just around the corner? At this point, you will be in a much stronger position.[1]

You could be even more manipulative by doing a favor for your client before announcing your increased prices. This taps into our innate desire for reciprocity—we hate being in debt and feel compelled to offer a gesture in return. Normally we feel so compelled that this gesture is of far greater value than the original "gift." It's a powerful trick.

This is why when I was on a family holiday in Turkey, all the stall owners would offer me a cup of tea and a free piece of jewelry for my younger siblings before trying to sell me something much larger!

Priming, Anchoring, and the Zone of Possible Agreement

Similarly, try setting the tone for the negotiation early on with a well-placed question. For instance: why not send an e-mail asking if your client is happy with the work you provide? They will likely say "yes," and at that point, you have essentially *primed* them to view your service as worthwhile.

You could even turn this into a formal process by presenting a feedback form. You could then include more questions that provide some insight into how your clients view your services and use this as a good "litmus test" to see if they're likely to be amenable to increasing rates. If not, then you can see areas for improvement to work on so that you *can* go in with a better chance of success.

Likewise, you can use this strategy if your offer is turned down. Simply ask: what could I do to increase my value to you? Then work hard to meet that requirement, leaving them with no further excuses.

Another spin on this is anchoring. *Anchoring* in negotiations refers to the process of encouraging your discussion to revolve more around one specific price point, pitch, or idea—this becomes the "anchor" or reference point. If a certain price gets brought up more than any other, it takes on a focus and very often you'll find that everyone settles on that by the end. Very often this will be the first price presented at the start of the negotiation—see the primacy and recency effect in psychology.

---

[1]To be honest though, most of my pay hikes have been entirely the result of generosity on the part of my clients. They simply told me that they felt I deserved the extra money. The best way to increase your rates? Find good clients and do great work!

So if the entire conversation revolves around why you *can't* be paid an additional $1 per hour, then you may well find you end up walking out with that extra $1. This is why you must never tell someone to "watch out for that tree!" As soon as you move their focus in that way, they can't help but drift toward it.

Of course, if you're going in with an opening bid, then it is very important that this be something realistic that isn't going to be offensive to the other party. You need to have a rough idea of the *zone of possible agreement* or ZOPA. This is the bargaining range defined by the maximum that the client is willing to pay and the minimum you are willing to accept. Your opening gambit should be somewhere in the middle here, but perhaps skewing a little high.[2]

Consider as well, though, the power of compromise. If you are pitching to increase your wages in exchange for more value and the client turns you down, make sure you have a counter-offer in your back pocket to respond with. This might mean slightly reducing the extra value that you're offering, but at a slightly lower cost to them as well. For example:

"My new coding service includes detailed comments, ongoing tech support, and three free revisions for an extra $5 per hour."

"I'm afraid our budget will not allow for that."

"I really feel that by adding this extra detail and flexibility, you will be able to get a much better end product that helps you accomplish your goals. How about an extra $2 for the free revisions?"

This relates to a concept called *contrast*, which we will get to in a moment.

One last tip is to take advantage of politeness and uncertainty in the language of your clients. People are naturally keen to be liked and they hate breaking social protocol. Therefore, if you ask a client if they can pay you a little more, they will often say something like:

"I'm not sure if our budget can stretch that far."

Or they'll try and blame someone else by saying

"I don't have the authority to make that decision and my manager is very strict on price increases."

---

[2]How do you find out the ZOPA? One option is to try surveying a similar business—perhaps an old client that is no longer using your services. Ask them out of interest what their budget was for the project and what they might have been willing to pay. You can then enter negotiations with *future* clients armed with this information. It's not a bulletproof method, but there's a chance it might be equivalent.

Your job here is to pounce on the probablys and maybes and to ask the client if they can check their project budget or consult with their manager. Offer to speak with the appropriate person. You could even suggest ways that they could bring their overhead down! If they don't explicitly say no, keep on pushing it. I call this the "polite weak point."

You're breaking social protocol and it's likely that they won't thank you for it—but sometimes being unpopular is a small price to pay. Just as being confident in the value you provide is a powerful tool for negotiation, so too is willingness to ignore social protocol. It's actually an ability that is worth practicing!

When to Charge

Now you know how much you can charge, and you know how to increase the amount you are asking for, the next question is *when* you ask for your money. As you will see, this is actually a more complicated question than you might initially have imagined!

Up Front vs. On Delivery

One important consideration when choosing when to charge, is whether you should charge up front or on delivery.

Charging up front means that the cash will be wired to you before you begin on the project. Charging on delivery means that you'll get paid when the project is sent to the client and they are happy with it. Of course, the former is better for you, but the latter is better for the client.

There's no hard-and-fast rule here. The best choice is going to depend on you, the nature of your work, and the client in question. While you might have a preferred modus operandi on this one, my advice is to be steered by the following factors:

- *The size of the job*: If the client has ordered a logo or has ordered a single 300-word article, then you can comfortably charge on delivery. You won't stand to lose too much if the client proves to be untrustworthy, and it will look a bit churlish if you quibble that you want your $40 right away. Conversely, though, if this is a first-time client who is ordering a *massive* app project that's going to take you months and months to work on, then you should definitely ask for at least some of that money up front and possibly at set points throughout the project.

- *The potential risk to you:* Sometimes if you do a job and the client turns around and says they don't want it, you may find that you're able to use it elsewhere or sell it to someone else. In that case, you might choose to chance it and ask for payment on delivery.

- *The client:* If this is a long-term client who has paid on time for years, then you shouldn't pester them for money up front every time. That said, there should also be a limit to how much money you're willing to "loan" them in this way. Unfortunately, you can't really trust anyone when it comes to business. These are not your friends. They are people looking to make some money. And they have their own commitments. On the other hand, of course, if you get a bad vibe from the client and you don't know them, then you should absolutely charge up front. Check out their reviews if they have any, or even consider asking others in your community.[3]

- *Whether there is a contract:* If there is a contract, you've read it through, and you're happy with the terms, then there's no real reason not to go ahead and invoice upon completion.

- *How valuable is the gig to your career:* Would you potentially do it for free if it came to it? If so, then you likely don't need to be paid up front.

Remember that this isn't an either-or kind of thing. There are plenty more options and agreements in terms of how you want to get paid. If you can't come to an agreement, then the old "half up front, half on receipt" works well.

And if you are getting paid daily for the amount of work completed (e.g., number of lines of code, number of words, number of minutes of edited footage) then this entire matter may be moot. Likewise, you can ask to be paid for your hours put in at the end of each day.

---

[3] I speak from experience here—I once had a steady client who had been using my services for *years*. In fact, they were my first client that allowed me to move out of home and try going full time as a "web person." Then one day they missed a payment (we had an agreement where they would pay monthly for a set amount of work at that point) and told me that they were having problems with their bank. I took them at face value and continued working for them the next month. After missing another payment, they told me that if I needed the money they would send it via PayPal. I said "yes, please" and they eventually came clean and told me that their own clients weren't paying, and they had to prioritize the salaries of their in-house staff. Fair enough, but they could have told me that months ago. As it happened, this breach of trust almost entirely destroyed my business. It was only by employing my "transhuman business model" (which you'll learn about later) that I managed to dig myself out of that hole!

And I learned my lesson. Today I am forgiving . . . up to a point.

Should You Give Free Samples?

Some leads will get in touch with you and ask for a free sample of your work. This might be a quick icon design, a short 200-word article, or a quick installation of a comments section on their blog. They'll tell you that if they like the work you do, they'll be ordering "large amounts" soon.

It seems like a reasonable request, so should you do it?

Simple answer: no.

Because when you really think about it, just how reasonable is it?

If you have a portfolio of your previous work, then they can see your examples there. Why do they need you to create something specifically for them in order to ascertain your caliber?

If they're uncertain, then why don't they just put in a very small order? If they were to buy that forum installation or small article, it would only cost them very little if they didn't like it. Why should it be you taking the risk?

The reality is that there's a very good chance this person has zero interest in an ongoing relationship with you. They just want a free logo and are looking for a schmuck willing to make it for them. I am highly suspicious of anyone who tells me they will be making "lots of big orders" in the future.

Apart from anything else, accepting this early on will set a bad precedent in your relationship. Right away, that places the power firmly in the hands of the client. They know you're desperate, so don't expect them to be willing to pay the best rates in the future, or to respect your free time when you request not to be called at 9 p.m.

This is actually true of nearly all relationships in life: the patterns and precedents that you set out during that early "get to know you stage" will very often define the nature of the relationship for many years going forward.

Per Job vs. Per Hour

When taking on any kind of project, there are lots of different types of contract that you might end up agreeing to. But one of the most fundamental questions that you'll probably find yourself presented with when working as a freelancer is whether you should charge for each completed task or for each hour that you work on a project.

Of course, there are pros and cons to each, and the decision will also come down to what the client is willing to pay to some degree. Ultimately, the objective either way is going to be to get paid as much per hour as possible—ask yourself whether the job will take you longer than the client expects (so you want to pay per hour) or whether it will take less time than the client will expect (so you want to pay per project).

Although there is no "right answer" here again, I will say that as a personal preference, I very much lean toward per job (even though I am forced to take on both types of work). The reason for this is that I work very fast (which you will too once you've read Chapter 5), which means that I can earn a lot per hour and still provide incredible value. This also gives me far more flexibility to decide how and when I want to dedicate time to a project.

More to the point, when you charge per project, there is no question of whether or not everyone is being fair and honest. If you charge per hour, the temptation to drag a project out is always going to be there. And if you don't, you might end up getting paid less than you should. If you work fast and to a high standard and reflect that in your per-hour price, then you will find it hard to compete with seemingly cheaper competition. And even when you go full speed, you might still find that some clients quibble about how much you charge and how long the project took you. That's where the time clock and screen-recording software comes in, which as we've already discussed will actually undo a lot of the benefits of being self-employed in the first place.

And what about that time you spend "half working"? What about the few tweaks you made that evening just because it was convenient? Or all those interruptions you suffered answering emails from clients at odd hours?

If you procrastinate at all, or if something comes up, then you can't as easily "make up the time" elsewhere.

Again, consider this on a case-by-case basis, but do keep those drawbacks in mind.

Other Options

Also consider that per job and per hour are just two options and there are *always* more options out there. Even better for us than charging per project is to charge in smaller increments, as discussed earlier. For a writer, that might mean charging *per word*. For a programmer, it might mean charging per line of code. For a video editor, it might mean charging per one minute of footage.

This system gives you even greater flexibility to decide how much you want to earn in a day, and it means you have the option to negotiate being paid in smaller increments rather than at the start or end of a project (which might also suit the client better). You can then use the many strategies I outline in Chapter 5 to increase the volume of work you can output and *thus* the amount you earn every day!

Packages

For both new and existing clients, offering different "packages" is another option and one that can completely change the game. This means changing the way that you actually pitch your services in order to get as much money as possible from clients *without* losing the clients that can't afford to pay that much.

Let's say that you currently have an SEO content writing service and you write for $2 per 100 words. You've decided that's not enough to pay the bills and you want to increase your rates—but you're afraid of losing your most loyal clients.

So, what do you do? You explain to them that they can *continue* to use your services at that rate *or* they can upgrade to a "premium" package. This might mean that you now provide three revisions, better formatting, and links to external sites that you've researched. Maybe for a little more, you could also provide multiple proofreads.

If you're a developer, then you could do something similar by offering a premium service that includes a faster turnaround time, thorough commenting throughout the code, and ongoing support.

Of course, you don't need to limit yourself to just *two* packages either. You can have different options to meet every kind of budget!

This is also *great* for attracting future clients as it means they'll be able to select the package they want and that suits their needs. If they choose the cheaper options, then their expectations will now be lower, and you can work faster. But *a lot* of clients will choose the more expensive options.

And actually, once you have multiple different packages with different prices, you can start using this to your advantage to get your clients to pay more than they otherwise would. Once again, this means taking advantage of human psychology and a concept known as *contrast*.

In other words, how does having a budget package impact the *apparent* price of the more expensive package?

Let's say that you have three different packages, each priced differently. Let's call them Basic, Premium, and Platinum++.

First, by making the difference in price between the Basic package and Premium package fairly large, you actually make the Premium option seem *more* premium. The assumption will be that this option offers a *lot* of value, and that in turn will encourage many clients to pay the extra amount. Who wants a shoddy job done on their coding?

And now, if you make Platinum++ cost just a *little* extra than Premium, you can nudge clients to go that slight bit higher than they would otherwise.

For instance, a company might have a budget of $1,000 to spend on a basic website—which happens to be the cost of your Premium package! But if they see that they can upgrade to the Platinum++ amount for just $100 more, then they very often will. For just that little bit more, why not get the *very best* that money can buy?

Likewise, if someone is making the *emotional* decision to have a website built (largely for ego perhaps), then they might decide that they can't justify forking out for the most expensive option. But they may therefore "compromise" by going one tier lower. That way, they can justify their splurge by telling themselves:"at least I went for the cheaper option." This way, you can anticipate and counter buyer's remorse. And by having more than one "cheaper" option, you might avoid their going for the *very* cheapest.

Trying out different pricing schemes and experimenting with packages can yield great results—so conduct some tests and see what brings in the most profit. This is again something you'll have a lot more flexibility to do as a result of using packages.

Bulk Orders and Long-Term Deals

Another option you can present to your clients is to save money by putting in a bulk order; the obvious benefit to you here being that you will now have guaranteed income for at least a significant period of time. The same goes for recurring or standing orders.

For example, you could offer to design website icons for $30 each, or to do 20 for $150. Alternatively, you could offer regular site updates and security maintenance for $10 per month. Again, think about what works best with the lifestyle that you want to achieve, and think about how you can get the best pay for the time that you're putting in.

It's Not Just About the Money

You've decided what you're going to charge and now you know how and where to find your clients. But of course, being willing to pay is not the only prerequisite for a good client. There are many other factors to consider when weighing up whether or not to take on clients, some of which are actually more important than the potential profit.

The Complex Morality of Freelance Work

When you start working as a freelance coder, writer, video editor, coach, or anything else, you might not expect to find yourself dealing with moral gray areas. And for the most part, you probably won't have to.

But every now and then, a job will come along and you won't be sure if you should take it or not. This might be because the work is very low quality—because it is "trashy." It might be because the product that you're selling is not worth the asking price. Worse, it might be that the subject matter is illegal or destructive.

For example: would you write an article about how to get started as a drug dealer? Would you build a website for a brothel?

Those are extreme examples and not particularly common, but you might well find yourself feeling uncomfortable writing the sales pitch for a multilevel marketing scam, for instance, or a product that promises weight loss but is likely to do more harm than good. I have been asked to write content that expresses political opinions that go against my own beliefs (which in some ways is a fun challenge). I've been asked to make websites with topics I felt uncomfortable with and create code that was overly derivative of others' work. You have to judge each project on a case-by-case basis.

One stance to take is that you are just a "hired gun" here: that it isn't your place to question why. You provide a service, and it's not up to you what other people choose to do with it. When you buy a product in a shop, the shopkeeper doesn't have to like what you plan on doing with it! And where do you draw the line? Do you need to test every product before you agree to build a website for the company?

Then again, though, you could also take the stance that you want to improve the amount of quality information on the Web and help people. Like I said at the beginning of this book, the Web is an *incredibly* powerful tool ... and you know what comes with great power (sorry: comic book fan here)! Apart from anything else, there's the matter of not wanting to be associated with low-quality garbage. Plus, you need to consider the trustworthiness of the clients that would ask for this kind of work.

Ultimately this is your call. But deciding how you want to approach these decisions and writing yourself some moral "guidelines" can help you to prepare for those less straightforward cases. I have lines that I won't cross and every now and then I need to reassess these when a job comes along that I haven't been ready for.

Taking on Jobs That Progress Your Career

While finding work that doesn't go against your moral compass is an important consideration for any creator, just as important is to find work that you find *fulfilling*. This isn't only so that your soul is fed, and you don't quickly start to hate yourself—it's also so that you'll be able to maintain focus and productivity *and* build on your own skills and portfolio.

I talked earlier about imposter syndrome and about how you need to be ready to accept a lot of money for potentially "easy" work. But you know what? It's honestly unlikely that you will be getting paid thousands of dollars for a few hours of work any time soon. Even though you have the same skills as people that do demand that kind of money.

Remember that web design gig my friend tried to get me to bid on with his insurance company employer? Where I was advised to increase my prices significantly? I ultimately decided to turn down that opportunity (because you shouldn't work for friends, as discussed a bit later). However, if I *had* gone ahead, the company likely wouldn't have wanted to invest that kind of money in me at the time anyway. (Plus it would mean indirectly working with a friend - which I'll get to in a moment.)

Why is that? Because I lacked the experience or the credentials. Even though I could probably deliver the exact same end product, most companies would be much more confident hiring a bigger outfit with a richer background and more experience.

But since that time, I have:

- Worked on two very successful apps (including a collaboration with a large YouTuber)

- Presented development tutorials on a large media outlet

- Authored a book on Android development

- Given talks on Android development and internet marketing for high-profile audiences

- Built my own online brand with a large following

At this point, I could arguably charge a lot more for the same services and probably compete with other "big players."

But I'm still not going to hold a candle to an ex-Google employee, or an app-boom millionaire.

You have to prove what you can do, and you have to pay your dues. It's less about what you can *actually* do and more about what you can *show* you can do. Who can vouch for you? How impressive will you sound on paper when the person hiring you explains to their manager why they chose you?

A lot of this comes down to your hustle, which unfortunately doesn't always come easily to the stereotypical, introverted developer. Moreover though, it comes down to building up a backlog of experience and impressive accomplishments—which of course also helps give you the *confidence* to charge the higher rates. And puts the swagger in your hustle (we'll call this swaggle).

And this is always worth keeping in the back of your mind when taking on jobs—not only when choosing your jobs but also when deciding what kind of pay you will accept. This is how you become the "superstar developer" or the "superstar editor." It's about building *authority*.

In fact, I would argue that it is often the savvier move to take the jobs that will raise your status over the jobs that pay the best. Your priority should be to build your own personal brand. Don't think of yourself as a grunt, but rather as an image that you can craft in order to put yourself high in demand. Imagine the kind of service provider you want to be, and then work to *get yourself* in that position.

This is also why I think that *everyone* should consider creating a website, a blog, or a video blog (vlog). At least a fully fleshed-out LinkedIn account! This helps you to build that brand, to gain notoriety in your niche/industry, and show the kind of work you do.

This is absolutely essential for those in the gig economy, to my mind. But you know what? I also think this is something a lot of other people could benefit from even in the world of traditional employment. Create a killer LinkedIn page, create work that you are really proud of, and look for opportunities that will help you to further your career. Be confident in what you have to offer and what you've proven. And then feel confident charging for that. It takes time to get to this point, but it feels fantastic when you arrive.

Jobs That Increase Your Skill Set

Another thing to keep in mind is that some work will also increase your skill set. I find this when writing coding tutorials, for instance: by choosing subjects that I don't already know inside out, I can use this as a way to effectively get paid to learn skills that will benefit me further down the line. Of course, this will also mean the projects take longer, so you need to weigh up the pros and cons each time.

All the work you take on, though, is going to have this benefit to an extent. The more jobs you do, the more you'll get used to dealing with different people, using different tools, managing your own productivity, and so forth.

Again, it's about paying your dues and building your way up to the top strategically and patiently.

Finding *Good* Clients

Here's something else that might surprise you: the higher-caliber clients that *want* that kind of career-progressing work also tend to be the ones that are great to work with. You might think that the more money you are being paid, the more fuss and hassle you would have to endure. The reality is very often the precise opposite—which is because *serious* businesses and professionals don't want to waste their time with petty complaints either. It's invariably the low-quality work that will result in unfair demands, last-minute changes, late payments, and other issues.

Of course, there are exceptions to this rule though, which is why you still need to be discerning when it comes to picking clients. Trust me: a "bad" client is almost *never* worth the amount of money that you are getting paid to provide their services.

The biggest sign that a client is going to be difficult to work with in the long term? A desire to have very long conversations prior to working with you—or to share overly complex instructions. I've had experiences where clients have requested that we have a Skype call before they order work, and in some cases these calls have gone on for an hour or more. Others have sent me videos where they explain in detail precisely what they're looking for—complete with editing and motion graphics! Sometimes these videos are 20 minutes long!

Ask yourself: what serious professional has the time necessary to do that? And more to the point, how much time is the client going to want from you going forward? The worst part is that nine times out of ten, the work you then get hired to complete will be relatively miniscule. I've had it where after hours of talking, I've been given a job that will only take an hour to complete. You're not being paid for these calls or to "play business," so try to cut the "communication overhead."[4]

Another bad type of client to look out for is the sort that believes they can get you to do all sorts of odd jobs for them. If you're a web designer, that doesn't mean it's your job to fix all their alt tags, or to rename all their image files and re-upload them. If you're a writer, it's not your job to collect contact details and put them into a spreadsheet. This is work for a VAS, or just work that the client should do themselves. Accepting this sort of work actually devalues you, and it is ultimately a waste of your time. Again, learn to say no in these cases.

Of course, you won't really know the caliber of a client until you actually begin working with them. But just don't be afraid to turn down opportunities to work with someone if you get a bad feeling ... Not every opportunity is a good opportunity!

---

[4]For more on this, check out *The 4-Hour Workweek* by Tim Ferriss (Crown Publishing Group, 2007) or *The Personal MBA* by Josh Kaufman (Portfolio Penguin, 2010). Both are great books that I recommend for anyone looking to make a living online.

One Last Tip: Never Work for Friends

You know who is almost *guaranteed* to be a bad client though? Pretty much any single one of your friends. While this may sound a little negative, it's unfortunately also true 99% of the time.

The problem is that when you work for friends, they will either expect you to work at a "friend's rate" or insist on paying the usual amount. Both these situations are a little awkward.

In the first case scenario, you will end up potentially resenting them for the work you're doing. Even if you don't, you'll inevitably make their work lower priority than your big *actual* clients who are paying twice as much (or should), which means you might not do your best work possible. Then when your friend complains that they're still waiting for you to deliver, you'll resent the fact that they're complaining *despite* your working for them at such a heavy discount! Either that or they'll be really happy with your work and you'll end up doing *more* for them at this low rate that isn't really enough to pay your bills.

On the other hand, if they pay the full amount, then they might find they resent you for that on some level (even if you protested the polite amount), or they might "over-correct" by making sure to be just as firm with you as they would be with any other service provider. Either that or they'll feel guilty and say things like "don't worry if it's a bit late." The bottom line either way is that no one is fully satisfied, but it's awkward if anyone says anything!

If you must work with friends, then make sure you have a strict agreement in place before you start. Consider offering a small discount that might be equivalent to what you would offer one of your best clients (maybe 5%) and explain why you can't afford to offer them a deeper discount. Better yet, consider using an intermediary as a go-between!

But it's just much easier to avoid this whole mess in the first place. And yes, I speak from experience.[5]

Variety Is the Spice of Gigging Life

The last thing I'll leave you with is this: in the ideal world, you should aim to get a broad range and variety of different types of clients. That means clients who offer steady, ongoing work, clients who offer occasional big projects, and clients who are one-offs. This mixture will allow you to keep a basic "salary"

---

[5]You know what else is annoying? When everyone you speak to assumes that you don't have work and offers you jobs as a kind of "favor"! Here is how the conversation will go: "What do you do for a living?"; "I'm a web designer"; "Oh, I might have a job for you"/"Oh, you're in luck, my company is looking for a new website." Actually, thanks mate, but I'm currently booked back to back with pretty high profile clients!

coming in (discussed in Chapter 7), while at the same time expanding your career and maintaining the freedom and flexibility to take on more interesting opportunities.

If you're *really* lucky, you might find some non-urgent long-term projects, or even clients that will take work whenever you provide it. Both these things are blessings because they give you work that you can fall back on when everything else is quiet. But of course, you need to keep looking around and know how to market yourself if you're going to attract those kinds of opportunities.

Chapter Summary

So, in this chapter you learned the importance of finding the right clients, the right projects, and the right pay. Hopefully, you have a better idea of how to identify high-quality clients and jobs, and how to charge for your work in a way that is fair to you while also remaining competitive.

The next step? Actually *delivering* on that work! And predictably, that's what we'll be delving into in Chapter 5.

Delivering Great Work

If there is one thing that has allowed me to be successful as an online service provider, it is this: I always deliver my work on time.

That might sound overly simple, but you would be surprised how many people working online *don't* do this. This is a sentiment that I hear echoed by clients all the time, and it's the reason I've become indispensable to several organizations I work with.

Having tried to hire writers and programmers myself, I know just how flaky many people are who work on the Web. It's all too easy to stop answering your e-mails when there's a job you are running behind on (or that turns out to be harder than you thought). When you don't have to face an angry client *in person*, it's much easier sending off a quick e-mail to tell them their work will arrive late.

And that's fine. It happens. But if you let it happen a few times, it will get to the point where those organizations feel they can't trust you and that they can't rely on you. That in turn means that they can't consider you for those big projects that would help to further your career, and it means that they're not going to recommend you to their own business partners.

On the other hand, if you're the kind of provider who delivers work on time, every time, then companies won't want to let you go. This is even truer if you're also the kind of person who overdelivers with attractive bells and whistles, or who sends work in early. This is such a rare commodity, that they'll go out

© Adam Sinicki 2019

A. Sinicki, *Thriving in the Gig Economy*, https://doi.org/10.1007/978-1-4842-4090-8_5

of their way to look for things for you to do, just so that they don't lose you! Better yet, some companies might come to rely on you to such an extent that their business couldn't operate without you. This then puts the balance of power firmly in your court (apologies for the mixed metaphors there), which in turn means you can start picking and choosing projects, influencing the direction of the business, and increasing your rates.

You want to become indispensable, and that means being reliable first and foremost.

Being reliable comes down to being able to work quickly and efficiently. And that's a pretty important skill for a whole host of other reasons too. Of course, the faster you can work (without sacrificing quality), the more you can earn and/or the earlier you can clock off.

In fact, if you can churn out huge amounts of work while remaining absolutely focused, you'll gain a *huge* advantage over the competition. This chapter will show you how.

Why Focus Matters

If you are working as a freelancer from home, then this has many advantages and disadvantages. Sometimes those advantages and disadvantages essential boil down to the same thing.

For instance, you probably love being able to set your own work pace and being in an environment of your choosing. Great advantage, right? Well, yeah, except it can also be a disadvantage. Of course, the challenge now is *actually working* when you're meant to be, and not allowing yourself to become distracted by television, game consoles, food, tea, coffee . . .

This is something that will come with practice. When I first started out freelance writing, I would write 4,000 words a day on the very best days. At my peak as a writer, though, I managed 10,000 words as a minimum and often much higher. This is purely a matter of practice and training the brain to focus intently for such extended periods.

In the typical working day, many of us will waste a whole lot of time answering e-mails and calls, dealing with awkward clients, making cups of tea and coffee, going to the bathroom. And then there are all those times that you allow yourself a quick minute to check Facebook and that then turns into 20 minutes. Or you catch yourself reading your favorite blog on your phone. Or playing "five minutes" of *Fortnite*. Or staring at your work and typing one line of code per every ten minutes.

Suddenly, an "eight-hour day" becomes three or four actual hours of work. This is true in the office especially thanks to all the unnecessary interruptions and the meetings mandated by management. There's also less incentive to make your working hours "pure work." In fact, this is sometimes discouraged by management (and certainly by insecure colleagues who don't want to look like slackers by comparison!).

But if you work for yourself and you can work for stints of *completely* uninterrupted focus, then you will be able to transform the way you operate—outstrip the competition and potentially send your earnings through the roof.

Shouldn't working from home mean that you afford yourself a little slack? Not work twice as hard?

Sure, but if that's what you want to do, then why not work solidly for three hours and then clock off at midday? Rather than half-working, half-procrastinating and wasting so much time? If you've been working in an office, then you might actually have to "untrain" yourself out of the usual relaxed approach.

Flow States

So how do we achieve this intense focus? The aim, as it is seen by many, is to achieve what is popularly referred to among psychologists as a "flow state." This concept—originally named by Mihaly Csikszentmihalyi—describes the experience of being so wholly focused on one task that all other awareness seems to fall away, even your sense of self. You lose your inner monologue and may even find yourself holding off on going to the bathroom for long stretches. You've almost certainly experienced this to some extent at some point in your life. And you probably eventually came up for air hours later and found yourself feeling disoriented—it might have even gone dark outside without your realizing! This is the same kind of focus we experience when watching a particularly engaging film or reading a great book (as you're no doubt finding right now . . .).

In this state, areas of the prefrontal cortex (used for self-criticism among other things) will shut down, leading to something known as "transient hypofrontality." Specifically, it is the dorsolateral prefrontal cortex that shuts off—contrary to popular belief, your entire frontal region doesn't stop working, or you'd be effectively lobotomized!

Flow states are amazing for productivity. Unfortunately though, the concept has been somewhat overhyped and overgeneralized, to the point where many marketers and writers treat them as a panacea for just about every possible problem or ailment. I am particularly put off by the notion that any self-reflection (or activation of the "default mode network," also known colloquially as "imagination network") is bad. Being "present" and being in "flow" is often considered as being this magical state that will make you happy, productive, and more creative. Mindfulness and presence are very much trending right now—while using your brain to daydream and explore ideas is often considered to be the root of all evil. Your "inner monologue" isn't just there to criticize you!

Different Productive States

In reality, we actually need both these contrasting states in order to function optimally. Flow states and other forms of intense focus are actually caused by a similar process to the fight-or-flight response (our physiological response to stressors) and can be considered "catabolic." In other words, the body is responding to a challenge by focusing all its resources to attend to the matter at hand. Your heart rate increases to supply more blood flow to the brain and muscles (reducing blood flow to many internal organs), your blood viscosity increases to ensure your blood will clot in the case of an injury, your senses are heighted, and your focus narrows.

The "challenge" could be a leopard that's about to eat you, *or* an impending deadline for an important coding project. Your biology doesn't know the difference—it is whatever you are extremely motivated by in that moment. Other things can also make us more catabolic and stressed, such as when the body detects low blood sugar or is subjected to extreme cold. This is why we get "hangry" and it's also why a cold shower is so invigorating and so loved by many productivity gurus.

What we focus on is determined by our "executive attention," a.k.a. "attentional control." This in turn is handled by the executive control network of brain areas, which includes numerous frontal regions such as the anterior cingulate cortex. We have a "dorsal attention" network, which is our consciously driven attention (I "choose" to focus on work), and we have a ventral attention network, which is triggered as a reflex and is largely unconscious (such as when you turn to look for the source of a sudden loud noise). To maintain focus you have to ensure that your psychology and physiology both agree that the task at hand is the thing that demands your full attention.

The key distinction between stress and flow is that you are still calm and that you are *enjoying* the important task. It is the difference between being psyched up and being psyched out. We also become entirely focused on the moment during a panic attack or other "negative" forms of stress—but the experience is rather different. That difference from a physiological point of view may have something to do with levels of neurochemicals neuropeptide Y and DHEA, and potentially "heartrate variance." This rabbit hole goes pretty deep (and you can read about it more over at my blog, www.thebioneer.com), but suffice to say that a flow state seems to keep more of our faculties intact as compared with simple stress. Flow seems to maintain at least some degree of self-awareness and creativity.

And this goes to show that self-reflection isn't always a negative force. This is why we might stutter when delivering a speech—because the response has effectively shut down our ability to plan ahead and think abstractly. Sure, it might have been your little voice that got you *into* this mess, but it's the resulting *lack* of introspection that is causing the problem.

So, our aim is to be motivated to complete our work and to be engaged by it, while at the same time *not* being so stressed by it that we feel nauseous and experience our minds going blank.

At the other end of the spectrum you have the opposite state—"rest and digest" (these two states can also be described as sympathetic and parasympathetic nervous system responses, respectively). This is when the body is comfortable and well fed; when no danger is present, and our biology can busy itself with processes like digestion, wound healing, and the formation of new neural connections. This state can be considered "anabolic," and it's when our mind is allowed to wander. It's when we find ourselves daydreaming or coming up with new ideas. It's why studies have shown a correlation between lying in a more supine position and creative problem solving. When we are relaxed, we have less "tunnel vision."

Likewise, it explains the long history of people coming up with great ideas when taking scenic walks (lush green environments also lower stress!) or while engaging in menial and repetitive work (Einstein's discovery of special relativity during such work at the patent office being the most famous example).

While flow causes less tunnel vision than high stress, it still can't hold a candle to the truly out-of-the-box thinking that occurs on a long walk, then. In other words, being "in your own head" is useful for creativity, while being highly engaged and focused on the task in-hand is useful for sheer output. Flow leans a little more toward the latter and can be *highly* useful. But we also need that down time and a little introspection to come up with our very best ideas.

Top Tips for Being Highly Productive

So, bearing all of this in mind, how do you ensure that you maintain a high output *and* creativity?

To increase focus specifically, the key is to make the work you're doing seem "important." This happens when we know that we'll be in trouble if we don't complete a deadline (remember in school how you used to write your entire essay the night before it was due?) but also when the task itself is inherently rewarding and engaging.

In other words: we focus on what we find pertinent and interesting. Remember how I said that being in flow is similar to the feeling you get when watching a well-made film? That's because a good story is engaging and dramatic. You're invested in the characters and your biology believes the outcome to be of great importance to them.

Importantly, this needs to be an *emotional* feeling. It's not enough to tell yourself you *should* do something—you need to *want* to do it. And you need to remove the stress and the doubt that will put you off from even trying to begin with. Motivation and the attention networks are governed by emotions rather than logic—which is why it's so hard to force yourself to do something that isn't at all engaging.

And you also need to try and separate your creative thinking and your intensive output. Embrace these two opposite ends of the spectrum and leverage them to do your best work.

Here are some tips that will help with that.

Just Start

When you know what the task you need to complete is but you're struggling to stop procrastinating, the key is to just *start* working. Whether that means writing, coding, editing, or whatever else. Don't let your uncertainty about the task or your ability put you off. Don't stare at a blank screen or page (this is incredibly intimidating); just start creating anything you can. Remember, you can always come back to it and improve it! The key is simply to *start* that flow. The first half hour might be rough, but once you've gotten over that hurdle, you'll enter the right mental state.

Intrinsic Motivation

This is the part where we make the task as engaging and rewarding as possible. To do this, try to remember *why* you're doing the thing you're doing. Although the data entry job you're doing right now is probably rather dull, remind yourself that it will lead to something amazing—the lifestyle, freedom, and success that you want. Picture yourself succeeding and try to feel the motivating emotions that come from that.

Better yet, try to make the task itself *more* interesting and "intrinsically motivating." An easy example is when writing: if you've been told to write something that is really dull, think about ways you can spruce it up or make it more engaging. Writing blog posts for a brick-laying company? Get creative and turn it into more of a narrative, or think about the aspects of brick laying that you *can* get interested in: project management perhaps, or the physical health benefits of manual labor. Or do some research and learn about the intricacies of brick laying. There's something interesting to learn about almost every topic if you look deep enough. This will hopefully also be more interesting for the reader as a result.

Another seemingly obvious tip that often gets overlooked is just to *actively do your very best*. If asked to build a boring piece of software, ask how you could make it better and make this your best work. That might mean creating a unique and compelling user interface, or it might mean writing the most elegant code you possibly can.

If you're interested in what you're doing, then you will find you also create better work. And there is art and craft in pretty much *every* type of work if you look for it.

Priming and Inspiration

In psychology, the term *priming* refers to the process of creating a certain mental state through a prior activity or exposure. For instance, you might prime someone to respond positively to questions by first putting them in a good mood. Alternatively, you might prime someone to answer a question relating to fruit by placing a bowl of fruit in the room with them.

The point is that by implicitly getting someone to use certain areas of their brain, you then "excite" those relevant neurons and make them more likely to fire in the future.

And the way I like to use this is by "priming" myself for a particular task. For example, before going to the gym I will regularly watch action scenes from my favorite movies or TV shows. And in just the same way, I can prime myself for coding by listening to music from *The Social Network*. Or I can put myself in the mood to be highly productive by watching the ad for *Limitless*. Simply: priming puts you in the right state to do great work, and that makes a massive difference.

Another great option is to look at inspiring examples of the work you're about to do. Commissioned to make a website? Check out some beautiful web designs first to get those creative juices flowing. Writing a sales pitch? Read some great examples. Now challenge yourself to create something that good or better!

Feedback Loops

Often it is hard to work on a lengthy project because there is no immediate feedback or sense of reward. On the other hand, coding actually tends to lend itself very well to intense focus because it involves lots of immediate feedback (specifically when you test the program, make a few changes, and then test again).

If your project doesn't have this kind of feedback loop ingrained, then you can introduce it by breaking your work down into smaller chunks or looking for other ways to monitor progress—such as a word count.

This is another reason why getting paid "per increment" works so well. Watch your pay go up with each line of code you complete!

Clearly Defined Goals

Similarly, it's very hard to churn out massive amounts of work when you lack direction. If you have 20 different jobs to complete and you're not sure which one should take precedence, you'll often end up doing neither—or switching awkwardly between tasks.

True flow states usually require at least 10 or 20 minutes of intentional focus before they kick in (hence why you should just *start work* as soon as possible), and switching between different tasks will interrupt this state. In other words, you need to pick a task and stick to it—then forget about all those other jobs!

A way to do this is to write a to-do list at the start of your day before diving into the thick of it. This gives you a much more concrete order to finish your work in and removes any element of guessing.

Removing Distraction

Remember earlier we met the dorsal and ventral attention networks and saw how they were driven by conscious and unconscious stimuli? The point is that if you're hungry, if there's loud noise, or if it's too hot, this will continuously drag your attention *away* from the task at hand.

Wearing noise-cancelling headphones with loud music and using a large monitor (such as an ultra-wide monitor, or an array of several screens) can help make it easier to achieve that kind of tunnel vision—effectively by forcing a kind of sensory deprivation so that all your senses are completely flooded with what you're currently doing.

And it's why making sure you're comfortable and all your most basic needs (hunger, thirst, warmth) are met before trying to focus on those "higher" cognitive tasks (you could even go so far as to relate this to Maslow's hierarchy of needs!).

The Right Environment

Another way to avoid having your attention pulled away from whatever you're doing is to change your environment to one that is more conducive to work. What I find works the absolute best by *far* is to head to a coffee shop. This is one of the most valuable tips I think I can give you when it comes to succeeding in the gig economy.

There's something about the buzz of a coffee shop that puts me in a creative state of mind. At the same time, the fact that I know I'm being "watched" means I feel as though I *can't* procrastinate. If someone were to look over my shoulder and see me playing computer games, they might well question why I don't have anything better to be doing on a Monday morning! That little bit of social pressure is very valuable.

Another option is the collaborative workspace, or co-working space. In response to increasing demand, these places are popping up in cities around the world, and provide access to an office-like environment for a monthly membership fee. This is cheaper than renting an office on your own (which of course is also an option) but provides many advantages such as networking opportunities, social interaction, and often the use of powerful tools and resources. If you were attracted to the gig economy by the promise of getting *away* from people, then this may prove counterintuitive. But for those that want a little social interaction, or who find coffee shops to be too full of distractions, this is another great option. Just do a Google search for co-working spaces in your area, and you will likely find a few to choose from. This can help you to avoid some of the background chatter that *is* a little distracting that you otherwise get in coffee shops.[1]

Then there's the fact that a co-working space, coffee shop, library, or other productive work space will provide you with much needed separation between work and relaxation. There is a very serious danger when you work out of your own home that you will lose the ability to mentally "switch off" once you finish work. Moreover, it can make it hard to mentally "switch on" when you need to *start* working! Being in a coffee shop or any other environment that isn't your home can help to alleviate this issue.

Then of course there is the coffee, which is a whole other story!

Failing that, make sure that you at least have an area of your home that you have designated specifically for work. This will help you to create that kind of separation.[2]

---

[1] It can be hard not to overhear certain exciting conversations, for instance—I've witnessed a fair few job interviews and even a couple of breakups in my time!

[2] There's another reason that some people claim coffee shops work so well for productivity. That is the fact that they provide the perfect kind of background hum. When you are working in a coffee shop, you'll notice that the people around you are chattering in a way that isn't quite discernible. You can hear "hubbub," but you can't make out the precise things people are saying.

This is the ideal type of noise because it eventually becomes "white noise." The brain eventually recognizes that there is no important information here and thus you become desensitized to the sound. This works in just the same way that you might tune out the sound of a ticking clock after a while, only you still have that slight relaxing background hum.

So popular is this sound, in fact, that you can actually find coffee shop chatter tracks online to listen to. One good one can be found at https://coffitivity.com. Other people like the sound of rain, in which case you can try www.rainymood.com.

Scheduled Breaks

There is a limit to how long you can (or should) sustain your attention. Eventually, you will find that you become tired, hungry, or just burned out. When this happens, your mind might begin to wander again, and you'll find that the quality and quantity of your output take a big hit.

To avoid this, it is advisable that you schedule breaks and "rewards" during your work. This might mean getting up to have a coffee, or it might mean allowing yourself to check e-mail at certain points throughout the day. Maybe it just means giving yourself a "budget" of 90 minutes throughout your eight-hour working day to spend as you wish. Just so long as you have allocated this time, it doesn't matter how you structure it.

Personally, I don't recommend setting this at a hard and fast time though. There will be times when you feel completely in flow and you know that if you keep going, you can finish your current project within the hour. Don't break that concentration—it is priceless.

Likewise, there will be times where, try as you might, you just can't bring yourself to get anything done. Don't sit there forcing yourself to work: instead give yourself a set ten-minute break to do something you *want* to do and then come back fresher.

There's another important reason to do this . . .

Separating Creativity and Flow

As mentioned earlier, we shouldn't think of flow as being a magical solution to all our problems. In programming, one of the worst things you can do is to spend hours banging your head against a wall trying to solve a single problem or issue. In a huge number of cases, the solution will present itself only when you take a *break* from the task at hand, or better yet, change your environment.

Almost every programmer reading this will have at some point found themselves struggling with a coding problem and wasted hours on it . . . only to then get up and go to the bathroom and have the answer come to them there!

This is because being in a new environment and allowing your mind to wander will help you to explore different possibilities and different neural connections. When we are highly focused (stressed), we have tunnel vision—creative thinking wouldn't have helped early man much when being chased by predators! When we relax, we're able to explore different neural networks and combine them in unique ways. After all, creativity is really just the marriage of existing, disconnected ideas.

You can see how relaxing makes your thoughts more abstract and creative when you sleep. This is your most anabolic, parasympathetic state—and it's also when your thoughts really start to become abstract.

If you try to "brute force" your way through a problem, your tunnel vision will blind you to alternative solutions and you'll end up wasting a great deal of time. This has been demonstrated in countless studies, such as the "candle problem."

THE CANDLE PROBLEM

The candle problem is a cognitive performance test that challenges participants to overcome their "functional fixedness." This is a "cognitive bias" that essentially limits our ability to think of objects as having a use other than their intended one. Here, participants are given a candle, a hammer, and a box of tacks and are asked to attach the candle to the wall so that it can burn there and light up the room. They invariably try to hammer the candle to the wall directly, which results in mess and failure.

The actual solution is to empty the box of tacks, hammer *that* to the wall, and then stand the candle in it. This requires the subject to overcome functional fixedness as they are now viewing the box of tacks not as a box for tacks, but rather as a *shelf*—or just a cardboard resource.

Researchers have measured the time it takes people to come to this realization and have found that applying incentive (reward) or time limits actually makes them *less* likely to come to the right solution. A more relaxed approach allows the necessary "out of the box" thinking.

In other words, then, it may be pertinent to separate your creative endeavors and your "grind." This way you can maximize your productive time by just thinking about how you're going to approach a problem later on. Driving or walking somewhere? Waiting in a line? Think about solutions to coding problems, cool ideas for your web designs, or structures for your blog posts. Then when you sit down to work, you'll have everything already mapped out and you can just *produce*.

Likewise, if you find yourself hitting a creative brick wall, take the time out and head into a different room. The act of being in a different room also activates different neural networks and therefore helps to further break you out of your "tunnel vision."[3]

---

[3]Incidentally, this is also where the "doorway effect" comes from—that tendency to enter a room to get something and immediately forget what you went in for!

Finally, it can also be a good idea to prepare all your research and do all your learning prior to the actual task. Again, this means you can then just sit down to work and *get on with it*. This is also a good idea if you plan on working in a coffee shop (or if you're a digital nomad). You never can rely on good Wi-Fi being available!

By doing all the thinking, all the research, and all the prep while you are more relaxed, you can absolutely maximize those few hours of intense output.

Optimum Performance

If you follow all the tips in the previous section, then you should find that, with practice, you can hone your ability to stay deeply focused for long periods of time, thereby enhancing your output, increasing your income, and simultaneously providing the most reliable service possible. All without a boss breathing down your neck.

The next piece of the puzzle is the "wetware"—your own physical condition. Do you sleep well? Do you eat well?

Are you generally fit and healthy?

In a traditional business model, you can increase your company's output in a number of ways: by increasing your staff, by investing in automation, via process fixes, and so on.

While some of this is possible to an extent as a freelancer, the most straightforward way to increase your revenue is just to increase the amount of work you're able to complete. I call this the "transhuman business model"— you are simply scaling up the amount of work you can complete by upgrading yourself.

Yes, if you're paid per completed project, then being able to work quickly and efficiently becomes imperative. That means not only upgrading your work habits but also making sure that you are the best and most focused version of yourself. Here are a few tools you can use to accomplish that.

Sleep

Sleep is absolutely essential to ensure your best performance. Too often, it is easy to see sleep as something that you can "trade in" for more work. You might be tempted to work into the early morning if you haven't completed your tasks for the day, for instance. But in almost all cases, you will get more high-quality work done by going to bed early and then having a more productive day *tomorrow*.

Getting better sleep will ensure you wake feeling refreshed, energized, and more productive. It will also help to improve memory (indeed it is now thought that neural connections go through an essential "pruning" process during sleep) and it is essential for your long-term health.

So how do you sleep better?

- Try to go to bed at a consistent time and wake up at a consistent time. Our biological rhythms love this kind of predictability.

- Consider shifting your bedtime and wakeup time by one hour either way and monitor when you are most productive. We all have a "chronotype," which dictates when we are at our most productive. It may be that you operate better earlier or later! Find what works best for you, then stick with it.

- Get sunlight during the day, especially during the morning. Try using a "daylight lamp" to simulate waking to a natural sunrise.

- Avoid looking at bright monitors for one hour before bed. This artificial light stimulates the release of cortisol, which acts as a counterpoint to melatonin (the sleep hormone). Another reason not to work into the night!

- Better yet, avoid anything stimulating. Taking at least half an hour to read a book before going to sleep can make a huge difference.

- If you haven't finished your work and you absolutely have to get it done, then it is better to wake up earlier tomorrow morning and work then, than it is to work later tonight. As long as you get it in before the client's next working day starts, there should be no problems.

- Take a warm bath or shower before bed to try relaxing your muscles.

- Sleep in a cooler environment by opening the window slightly.

- Improve your sleeping environment: get blackout curtains, invest in a more comfortable mattress, try to eliminate sources of light (LEDs from alarm clocks), and so forth.

- Avoid caffeine after 4 p.m.

Exercise

Why would exercise be important for productivity and work? Think of it as being similar to the "general physical preparedness" used by athletes. Athletes that are trained in specificity (to be top performers in *one* specific sport such as sprinting or powerlifting) still need a basic level of fitness in order to perform optimally. This involves basic cardio, mobility, and health. In other words, a powerlifter still benefits from jogging.

The same thing goes for your productivity. Apart from the fact that exercise has been shown on countless occasions to increase creativity, focus, memory, and more, it's also true that having more energy will help you to perform at a higher level for longer. If you can run ten miles without keeling over, you're going to find that you don't become as mentally or physically tired after typing 10,000 words or coding for five hours straight.

Meditate

On his podcast, Tim Ferriss (author of *The 4-Hour Workweek*) has been interviewing countless "high-performing individuals," including famous athletes, tech entrepreneurs, musicians, and many others, to identify their habits, routines, and "secrets." He repeatedly points out that the thing that most of them have in common is the habit of regular meditation.

Meditation is nothing mysterious or esoteric. It is simply the practice of focusing the brain for an extended period, thereby gaining more control over what you focus on the rest of the time. The only thing that really varies is how you go about doing that: depending on the form of meditation, you might clear your mind, reflect dispassionately on the contents of your own thoughts, watch a flickering flame, engage your peripheral vision, deeply consider a prayer, focus on your breath or body, or repeat a mantra over and over. These are the methods used in mindfulness meditation, transcendental meditation, religious meditation, Hakalau meditation, and more. You can even practice "mindful ironing"! And whichever you choose, meditation has been shown to have countless benefits, from improving focus, to helping to improve mood, lower stress, enhance sleep, and even increase the amount of gray matter in the frontal cortex and "whole brain connectivity" (a strong predictor of IQ).

The bottom line is that meditating for just ten minutes a day can be a huge benefit. There are plenty of guided mindfulness meditations that you can find online for free.

Nootropics

I'll leave you to do your own research on this one (might I suggest my own blog, www.thebioneer.com?), but suffice to say that nootropics are supplements, nutrients, or drugs that can help to enhance brain function in some capacity.

Now of course, this is a potentially controversial subject. Nootropics such as modafinil, while powerful, don't necessarily "improve" brain function in an objective manner and may in fact come with unwanted side effects such as addiction (this hasn't actually been shown in the case of modafinil, but there is a lack of long-term studies). Modafinil is available by prescription only in the United States, which means you can obtain it legally only by consulting a qualified healthcare provider and establishing that you require it for an FDA-approved use. Like most drugs, modafinil is available online from unregulated sources—never a good idea, not only because such a purchase is illegal but also because you don't know what you are getting.

Conversely though, there are countless other nutrients that we can take safely to increase focus, memory, mood, and more. These include good-old caffeine (and I'm sure most coders reading this already live on coffee), as well as omega-3 fatty acid, inositol, vitamin D, MCT oil, L-theanine, creatine, and many others. These are all things that are found in our diet but which many of us aren't getting enough of. And they can drastically improve everything from brain plasticity (learning) to focus and mood. The bottom line? Eating a healthy, nutritious diet improves brain performance, unsurprisingly. If there are things you're currently failing to get from your diet though (and that's very likely), a little supplementation may help to give you an edge.

Passion for What You Do

One last thing to mention—though it is perhaps in many ways the most important point of all—is that you will find it MUCH easier to work quickly and efficiently if you have a genuine passion for what you do. If you're *excited* to begin work each day, then you're going to find that nothing can stop you and that you *willingly* put in more hours than you have to. You know what they say: if you love what you do, then you will never work a day in your life!

So, when choosing what kind of work you want to provide, make *sure* that it is something you love doing. If you only like programming in the context of games development, make sure that this is *precisely* what you are offering. If you want to be an action film director, then offer to edit action films. Make sure that what you're doing makes you really come alive, and your quality *and* quantity will benefit. This is superior to taking on boring work and trying to find ways to convince yourself it's actually quite interesting!

Other Strategies

There are countless other strategies that you can use to try and improve your physical and mental performance and thereby to increase your output and profits.

Some people find that intermittent fasting helps them to greatly increase their focus and energy levels, for instance (myself included). Others benefit from cold showers or the Wim Hof breathing method. Power naps are helpful for others. Try changing your routines and focusing on your health to see how this measurably improves your performance. Once you find what works for you, stick with it!

Making the Work Easier

Another way to work more efficiently is to streamline your workload by making your job as easy as possible, so that you can complete the work faster. This is something that should be right up your street as a developer: after all, programming is really about finding complex ways to be lazy.

Cookie-Cutter Projects

Ideally, look for "cookie-cutter" projects: jobs that you can repeat multiple times. This is the natural evolution of creating packages and "productizing" your service.

For instance, instead of being an Android app developer, you could become a developer who makes a specific *kind of app*.

How about advertising your service as this: "Two-Page App with Information and Contact Form." You can then set a specific price for this that is more reflective of the value your clients will get from it, rather than the time and effort you're putting in. For you, it's a simple matter of taking your two-page app framework and then inserting the content and graphics that your clients provide! Likewise, you could offer to convert an iOS app into an Android app. Or you could offer to build an infinite-scrolling website.

When you control more of the variables, you will get fewer "difficult" projects, and you'll be able to streamline the way you provide the service over time. You'll be able to deliver complete projects much more quickly because the framework is already there.

This type of offer is *ideal* for Fiverr, by the way!

Eventually, you might even evolve your service into a type of product. If you add social functions to websites, then you can eventually start implementing essentially the same code—the same product—into different websites with just a few customizations. I did this with my app Multiscreen Multitasking when working with phone manufacturers in India. I designed versions of the same app for different OEMs (original equipment manufacturers) and let them add their own branding. I was thereby providing the service of "adding multi-app functionality" via variations on the same product.

This way you can charge much more for work that takes you far less time to complete. The result is you deliver work faster and can clock off earlier/take on more clients.

Waste Not

Of course, as a programmer, reusing segments of code should be your bread and butter. If you use an object-oriented programming language, then you can regularly reuse chunks of code (classes) in different projects. The same goes for methods or libraries across both object-oriented and functional languages.

If you're a video editor, then you will find that you have motion graphics and presets you can use. As a web designer, you'll be able to reuse royalty-free assets that you've purchased, or chunks of HTML/CSS/PHP you've written.

When writing, I often end up deleting paragraphs from projects. But I *never* let them go to waste. I paste them into a large document and then I reuse them whenever I'm working on a relevant piece of content in future.

Be strategic when you create *anything* and don't let it go to waste.

Taking on Easier Jobs

If you stick with a more general "service provider" approach, then you can still choose which jobs to take on the basis of how difficult they are likely to be. If you are getting paid per job rather than per hour, then you should naturally gravitate toward work that you can complete quickly and easily, in order to increase your turnover.

That doesn't just mean taking on shorter jobs; it also means taking on jobs that don't require you to learn a whole new concept or skill—perhaps a new API for coders—that you have no experience with.

The exception to this is taking on work that will progress your career, which we talked about in Chapter 4.

More Ways to Work Better

Sometimes working faster and better doesn't come down to your own capabilities, *or* the kind of work you're doing. Sometimes it comes down to the way that you're approaching your projects. Which means that a few small changes can often make a huge difference ...

Outsourcing

It's also worth noting that you don't have to do *all* of the work yourself in many cases. Depending on the nature of the work you're doing, you might find that you're able to outsource elements to other individuals or companies. A particularly good example is to use a virtual assistance service (VAS), which, as introduced in Chapter 2, is an organization that handles any kind of odd job or small task. Essentially, anything that can be done remotely online (i.e., that does not require your physical presence) and that doesn't involve "specialist" skills can be handled by a VAS. These companies are often based in India and other countries where living costs are lower, meaning that you can sometimes pay as little as a few dollars per hour. Of course, you do get what you pay for, and those looking for more impressive services might be better served by a more premium option based closer to home (this will also reduce potential language barrier issues).

So, for instance, if you have been asked to create a website with a large directory page that links out to useful resources, then you could hire the VAS to assemble all the links and site names for you. You then just have to make them look pretty with a bit of CSS. And hopefully the time you saved will pay for the VAS while still keeping you in profit.

You can even hire a VAS to remove the dreaded communication overhead. Why not have a representative to find the work for you and deal with clients? Then all you have to do is to handle questions they can't answer and *do the work*. The result is that you spend more time working and less time chatting, thereby earning more than you otherwise would. Just make sure that you choose a good service that will represent you well, and make sure that the client feels as though you value them and are giving them your attention. This runs the risk of being impersonal.

Or, why not use another service or individual to help find higher paying work? If you want to charge more but don't want to risk losing your current clients for a newcomer who won't stick around in the long term, then you can take on more high-paying work *on top* of what you're already doing, and then use a service to manage the extra that you can't handle on your own. This doesn't have to be a VAS, either. You can also hire other individuals or companies to handle aspects of your work that are unnecessarily time-consuming. In fact, I have often gotten my wife or a friend to step in when my work has been a bit too demanding!

Of course, though, you will need to weigh up the benefits of using third parties against the cost. Are you earning more as a result of using them? Or are you at least able to provide a better service and potentially enjoy your own work more? Likewise, consider that involving third parties can also introduce more variables and more things to go wrong. You will inevitably spend some time chasing *them* down, which can be equally time-consuming unless you find a truly exceptional service.

In Chapter 9, we'll be looking at the ultimate evolution of this concept: service arbitrage.

Automation

You may find that automation is an even better option than outsourcing. In other words, is there a piece of software that can handle some of your workflow for you?

Or if you can't automate a job, could you find a tool to help you produce better work, faster? Technology is a force multiplier: it should allow you to put in the same amount of energy but get *greater* output. A hammer is a perfect example of this, because the same amount of force that is needed to drive a nail into a piece of a wood with a hammer would *never* be enough if you were just using your fists.

Likewise, perhaps you can find a library or plug-in to help you code faster? Maybe you can find a piece of wireframing software that will improve the quality of your web designs?

And the best part about being a tech entrepreneur is that if a productivity-enhancing tool doesn't exist, then *you can just build it*! When I was mainly getting paid per word for my writing, I actually increased my income by writing a piece of software I called "Word Boom." This allowed me to use common shorthand, but it would then swap those words for longer expressions—thereby increasing my word count. So, I would write "don't," which would earn me my rate for one word, but Word Boom would automatically convert that to "do not," which would earn me *two words*. Likewise, it might change "but" to "on the other hand," thereby increasing my profit for that one word by 300%. Of course this is a bit of a simplification, and this was back in the day when clients wanted content for content's sake - it's not a practice I particularly advise in itself today! Point is, if you're creative, you can find ways to lessen your workload and create your own force multipliers.

Take a look at your current workflow, find the repetitive tasks that consume time on a regular basis, and then think about how a piece of software could save you time.

The Risks

Note that using software to handle your work, or outsourcing it, can also sometimes introduce new problems. Our aim here is to be more productive and thus provide a *better* service: not to look for shortcuts at the expense of quality.

An example of automation gone bad is the "article spinner." For those not familiar with SEO, one of the most important factors to consider is originality. That is to say that Google doesn't consider content to be valuable unless it is unique; so, if you were to copy a blog post from another website and publish it as your own, you wouldn't get to the top of the search engine results. In fact, you may even be penalized! This means that as an SEO writer creating blog posts, you can't sell the same writing to two clients.

Unless you use a content spinner, that is. This is a program that basically takes your content and then "reorganizes" it to create multiple unique posts that will pass Copyscape (the industry-standard tool for checking that content is original). In some cases, spinners require content to be written in a certain way to begin with: perhaps with different versions of the same sentence written inside triangular brackets.

Either way, though, the result is content that is almost *always* nonsensical and certainly not very inspired or interesting. Worse is that some unscrupulous service providers will actually use content they didn't write originally and run it through a content spinner—which is still a breach of copyright, not to mention entirely unethical.

Using cheap strategies like this might work in the short term, but in the long term they will almost always be limited. Clients will quickly catch on, and soon the negative reviews will start piling up.

Likewise, using a third party is only a good idea for the unskilled portions of your work. Once you start to outsource the mission-critical aspects of your work, your clients may notice a dip in quality, or at least an inconsistent tone. You'll lose the unique "flavor" that your service provides. And people will leave. Either that or they'll realize they can get the exact same service elsewhere and cut out the middleman!

So, yes, use tools and third parties to work faster and better. But never do so at the expense of quality. And always make sure to *check* anything that you didn't create yourself by hand.

Process Fixes

If you aren't a programmer, you can still benefit from *thinking like one.*

A "process fix" is a change that addresses the way specific work flows are designed to make them more efficient. For instance, if you run a blog for a company, then you might find yourself taking the following steps each time that you write a new post:

- Writing the post in Word

- Proofreading the post

- Uploading the post to WordPress/the blog

- Adding pictures, alt tags, and so on

- Clicking the Publish button

If you were to apply a critical eye to this process though, you might notice that it involves going over the content *twice*: once to proofread the text, and once more to add in the images. Likewise, you might find that pasting the text into WordPress is introducing formatting errors and mistakes that slip through the net.

So instead, you could proofread the post at the same time as inserting the images—*after* the content has been pasted into WordPress. The new process would look like so:

- Writing the post in Word

- Uploading the post to WordPress/the blog

- Adding pictures, alt tags, and so on and proofreading

- Clicking the Publish button

You've effectively removed an entire step (or at least combined two), while at the same time moving the proofread closer to the point where you'll click Publish. The result: less time spent on each post, and fewer mistakes.

And if that saves you 10 minutes per blog post and you usually submit five blog posts per working day, you might find that you're now able to submit *six* blog posts in that extra 50 minutes. That's a 20% increase in profits *every day* if you get paid per completed blog post.[4]

---

[4]Note by the way that little tricks like this can increase your salary by a greater degree than you would *ever* be likely to encounter in traditional employment! The same goes for negotiating a seemingly tiny increase in your rates per word or per line of code.

There are many more examples of how this might work in different lines of work. As a video editor, perhaps taking the time to name your files (so you can find them more easily in Premiere) could help you to save a significant amount of time. As a programmer, maybe creating a reference of variables, classes, and methods to keep handy could save you a lot of searching around.

Even making the decision not to completely turn off your computer in the evening can make a huge impact if it means you aren't waiting five minutes for it to boot up every day.

All I'm really suggesting here is that you sometimes take the time to be critical of the ways in which you are working and to address your work flow. Again, this comes down to being able to step "out" of your business for a moment and to work *on* it instead of *in* it.

Hardware

Finally, investing in better hardware can make a big difference to your ability to work quickly and well. This is an investment that is highly important and very much worth making. Don't try to save money in the short term by cheaping out on your hardware, because at the end of the day it's going to slow you down and actually cost you.

Starting with the basics, you need a computer that can handle the work you will be doing and that boots up quickly. You don't necessarily need huge amounts of horsepower unless you're working with 3D models and you need it. Just so long as it launches quickly, and it isn't prone to crashing and losing all your hard work. Likewise, you should make sure that the typing experience is comfortable and quick (important for both writers and coders). Many people appreciate using mechanical keyboards, but your mileage may vary. You should also give yourself enough screen real estate to see what you're doing. Having a widescreen monitor or a multi-monitor array is something that many people find beneficial. If you need to work on the go, then getting a laptop that you can plug into a monitor when you get home is one option. Another is to look for a laptop with a large, high-resolution display.

You don't need the best overall computer, but look to invest in the best computer for your specific type of work. It may be that there are certain features and benefits offered by specific types of machine that you can't find elsewhere. For instance, graphic designers might benefit from the stylus that comes with the Surface Pro, and the ability to detach the keyboard and use it as a canvas. Alternatively, you might decide to prioritize battery life.

And it's not just about your "main" computer, either. Having backup machines, smaller devices for working on the move, or machines that serve specific purposes can also be very useful. Likewise, it's also important to think about the rest of your setup.

Obviously, you will need a comfortable desk and place to sit. Make sure your desk is large enough that you can spread out and arrange documents there without it looking like a bomb site. A messy desk can create the wrong kind of stress, cause you to waste time searching for documents, and so forth. A comfortable chair will further help to ensure you're comfy and so less distracted (not to mention looking after long-term health).

Great headphones can make a big difference to your focus, as we've already discussed. Likewise, you should think about the quality of your mobile phone, which will serve as your primary communication device and will often be the primary tool you use to respond to e-mails and queries on the fly. For smaller computers and phones, a power brick can be a huge boon.

You don't *need* the latest and greatest tech in order to get started making a living in the gig economy, but it really will help you to work faster and better. Simply by making the experience of working more enjoyable, a better computer will boost your output and your focus, thereby increasing your output. And then there's the fact that you might have to meet with clients, colleagues, or business partners and they're not going to be impressed if the "tech genius" has a laptop that's held together with tape.

So, when you can, invest in your tech setup. We'll talk about how you can afford to do that a bit more in a future chapter.

Chapter Summary

In this chapter, the aim was to demonstrate how you can increase your own efficiency, productivity, and even creativity. When you're entirely self-employed and paid per output, this can be the difference between just getting by and truly thriving. Whether you choose to use this productivity to do *more work* or whether you just want to clock off an hour early, you'll find that working on the "wetware" will pay off in dividends.

The only problem? Other people. With the best will in the world, you're going to need to interact with clients, service providers, and customers from time to time. The next chapter will help you to do that part better too.

Communication and Collaboration

In Chapter 5, you learned how to work in a highly focused, highly productive manner for significant blocks of time. This is an incredible skill to have in the digital age.

The only problem is that no man or woman is an island. Being part of the gig economy means that you need to wear many hats. It's not enough to be a programmer, editor, or writer: you also have to be a marketer, a complaints department, and an administrator. You are part of a community now.

And seeing as many people who choose a life of working online are introverts by nature, this won't always come easily, especially when it means that focused flow ends up being interrupted by clients asking questions, wanting revisions, or asking for invoices.

Don't think of this as an irritation. Your communication is actually *part* of the service you provide. And it will make a huge difference to the experience of your clients and therefore their likelihood of recommending your services/ using them again.

Read on then, and we'll look at how you can minimize the time wasted with useless communication, as well as how to use modern collaboration tools to become a great team player.

© Adam Sinicki 2019
A. Sinicki, *Thriving in the Gig Economy*, https://doi.org/10.1007/978-1-4842-4090-8_6

Staying Communicative

One of the most important things you need to do as a freelancer is to maintain communication. And to maintain it *well*.

This means: Updating your clients as to the state of their work. Being transparent when asked questions. Being *responsive* to their communications. And communicating in a way that is professional but friendly—and that leaves a good taste in the mouth of the client. Tasty communication, then.

In other words, you ought to get familiar with spending time in your inbox. And you need to think about this as being part of your job, without letting it eat into your productivity.

When to Send E-mails

A good question to address early on is how many e-mails you should be sending and how often.

Depending on the service that you provide, you might be able to set some clear rules in this regard. For instance, you might provide an SEO service that includes detailed weekly reports. This allows the client to see what you've been doing, and it makes life easier for you, because there is no question that you aren't being communicative enough when you send an e-mail once a week.

If you are working on a long-term project for a client and you haven't promised any kind of regular progress report, then sending e-mails at occasional milestones (halfway through, for example) can be a good way to provide a little encouragement and to inspire some confidence that the work is actually on track and being done to a satisfactory standard.

Providing examples of work can also be a good way to ensure that you don't go too far in one direction before having to hit reverse. Again, you might detail this in the description of your service; for instance, by saying that your logo design service will include "three options" right at the start that the client can pick from.

You can also give the client access to the project as you're working on it. For instance, you might place the work into a shared Dropbox folder or Google Document (which we'll talk about more in a moment). This does invite potential complications though, especially if the client has the tendency to be a bit too involved! Use with caution.

In many cases, though, after an initial confirmation that you are beginning work, there is no real reason to provide constant lengthy e-mails in many cases. Rather, just let the client know that you are available for communication between specific hours and that they can ask any questions they might have. Then try to make sure you answer within 24 hours wherever possible (discounting weekends and holidays).

Order Forms

Other types of service may require that you work more closely with the client to begin with, which may in turn require a series of back-and-forth e-mails during the initial planning stages. Systemizing this process is a very good idea as it will help to smooth the process. That might mean that you provide your client with a form they can fill out in order to answer questions and provide the information you need to get to work. If you don't have a form or structure like this, you can end up sending a lot more e-mails and losing a lot in translation.

Even for simpler work, this can often be a great strategy. And it's also common with many B2C services, such as coaching, fitness training, and similar. You can use this to filter clients and make sure you only work with the right types of people. So, consider adding order forms to your site or providing them to new clients, even if you're just doing regular writing or coding work.

I provide online physical training programs, among other things, and using an order form has helped me to massively streamline the process—minimizing unnecessary back-and-forth e-mails, while making sure I have all the information I need right from the start.

Likewise, you can use other methods to get information and create a firm "direction" for your projects. In app, logo, and web design, it is a common practice for the client to provide examples of work they like so that you can get an idea of the direction they want to head in and can build a mood board. The same thing could work for aspects of a coding project, such as the interface.

Reducing Communication Overhead

I've mentioned the term "communication overhead" in this book a few times but haven't gone into it in great detail yet. Basically, communication overhead is the amount of time that you're going to spend answering e-mails and questions, taking Skype calls, and so forth. While we've seen that these are often crucially important parts of your job, they also *aren't paid*. That means that you are taking time out of your working day to do something for free, which reduces the amount you can earn. This really is an overhead, just like any service or tool you might be using! Unfortunately, it's not tax deductible either.

There are a few ways you can minimize this.

Batching

One of the most popular ways to avoid letting your day become a series of e-mails is to use something called "batching." This simply means that you answer e-mails in batches. Don't respond to e-mails as soon as they come in, but instead answer them at set points during the day. Maybe during those natural "breaks" in your flow states that we talked about in Chapter 5. To help with this shift, it's a good idea to turn off your notifications so that you aren't being pulled away from your main task every time a new e-mail comes in.

But it also requires something of a cognitive shift. You need to convince yourself that ignoring an e-mail for a couple of hours isn't going to result in the collapse of your business. Likewise, you need to be able to bear that tiny bit of social awkwardness that comes from ignoring *anyone*. Remember: it is ultimately going to result in better work *for the client* if you don't answer all of their questions immediately![1]

And the point is that you could be doing *anything* right now. For all the client knows, you're involved in a crucial face-to-face meeting. It's perfectly reasonable for them to wait a couple of hours to receive a response to a question. Or even an entire day.

This is why you might choose to say that you're available for contact via e-mail at certain times of day (maybe you could dedicate the first half hour of your day to responding to your e-mails, while you make that cup of coffee). Another trick recommended by Tim Ferriss in *The 4-Hour Workweek* is to use an out-of-office autoresponder to explain that you're busy but will respond within the next 24 hours. You can even provide an emergency contact just in case it really *is* urgent.

What you'll also find is that responding to e-mails too quickly can actually send the wrong message and *encourage* more inane communication. This shifts the power of balance in their favor. If you make a habit of taking a few hours to respond, you'll find the amount of communication actually drops. And as long as you answer the questions fully when you get around to them, and as long as you deliver fantastic quality work, your clients will still be happy.

Explaining

There will always be those clients that want to chat though, and sometimes they just won't take the hint that you are busy.

---

[1]By the way, this *also* includes ignoring friends and family on WhatsApp and Facebook. Don't ignore e-mails from clients during your working hours, only to then be a slave to your personal messages! Save it for your next coffee break. Turn off notifications.

In this case, it can be a good idea to simply explain to them that you work best when you are not distracted. Politely request that if they have multiple questions, they should put them into a *single* e-mail rather than shooting off lots of them. Likewise, if they keep wanting to make Skype calls, or insist on sending video recordings, you can politely ask that they communicate by e-mail instead.

And if they really won't listen, then you can try introducing the order form system to take control of the communication. If that doesn't work, then you have the next option . . .

Charging

If you find that your clients are taking advantage of your good nature by expecting you to send them essay-long e-mails on a regular basis, you can bring out the big guns: start charging for your time.

Remember, you provide a service and it's up to you how you want to structure your pricing. If you find you're spending too much time sending e-mails, then that can *include* a charge for communication—just like lawyers will charge for minutes spent on a phone call.

You may find that you feel rude charging someone to answer a question, but there are ways of introducing this system that will avoid friction.

One is to use the strategy we discussed earlier in another context: make sure you emphasize the upside. In this case, by charging for e-mails, you're able to spend *more time* doing great-quality work for the client. And they don't have to feel bad about getting in touch! What a win for them, eh?

You don't need to charge for *all* communication either. You can offer the first two, five, ten, or more e-mails for free. It's entirely up to you. Or you can offer free communication via e-mail, but then charge if and when someone requests a Skype call. Just explain that you don't have a lot of time for Skype and so unfortunately do have to charge per minute (this also encourages brevity). Conversely though, they are free to put their questions into an e-mail. You win either way.

Another tip is to make this crystal clear when you advertise your services. This also works well using the package system: you can include "five free e-mails" in the basic package, for instance, but then have "unlimited communication" in the premium option.

What to Do If You Fall Behind

Following the tips in Chapter 5, you should be able to increase your productivity and output to the point where it's highly uncommon that you fall behind. But with the best will in the world, there will always be occasions when things don't go quite to plan, and you're forced to send work in late.

So, what do you do?

The first thing to do is to make sure that you inform your clients and anyone else concerned as soon as possible. The temptation here is often to try and ignore the problem and hope it goes away until right at the last moment. In fact though, this only makes you seem *more* unreliable.

If you wake up one morning with work due that day and you don't think you'll be able to manage it, inform the client that it will be late as soon as possible. Better yet, try to give advance notice a few days ahead if you suspect you won't reach deadline in time. But don't be too apologetic (over-apologizing makes you appear *more* at fault and makes your reasoning sound more like an excuse) but do explain your reasons.

Another mistake to make is feeling pressured to make new promises that you can't keep. In other words, don't say:

> I'm really sorry that this is late. I'll get it to you this afternoon and will deduct 10% from the cost.

You're just setting yourself up to fail now, and you're likely to put yourself in a downward spiral. Likewise, it's a mistake to say anything along the lines of:

> I only managed this much today, but I promise I'll provide more tomorrow.

For the same reasons.

Actions speak louder than words. This is *definitely* true from your clients' perspective. And failing to do what you say over and over again will really hurt your rep. Aim to "under promise and over deliver."

Just state the facts and then try to work hard and avoid letting it happen again. Maybe take this moment to debrief and assess *why* you fell behind and how you are going to prevent it from happening next time.

NEVER simply ignore a client until they go away. It's tempting because no one likes being the bearer of bad news. But if you want to be taken seriously, you need to conduct yourself like a serious business person. Word does spread. In fact, breaking bad news occasionally is good practice: it will teach you to become a little more hardnosed. Be courageous and honest with your clients and they will respect you for it.

Prioritizing

When you face a day of multiple work deadlines and you know you won't be able to finish all of them on time, you may find you have to choose *which* client you're going to let down.

To make this decision, the obvious choice will be to prioritize your "best" clients. That means prioritizing the clients that pay the most, that will be best for your career, and that have proven the most reliable. The new client who doesn't pay much and has been a bit difficult is the obvious choice to delay.

But before you go ahead and do that, do keep in mind that another important factor is just how time-sensitive the work is. If a client wants content for a website that hasn't been built yet, then there is no real reason for them to need it urgently. Therefore, you will likely find they're much less upset if they receive their work 24 hours later.

On the other hand though, if you're developing an app that needs to coincide with a product launch, then you really need to make sure that's done on time.

Setting the Right Deadlines

One of the best things you can do to avoid falling behind is to set yourself more realistic deadlines to begin with. Obviously, you will sometimes find that the client has a deadline and that you don't get much say in the matter, but in a lot of other cases, the work will have no hard-and-fast due date.

The temptation that many of us will have is to claim that we can complete work in record time. We all want to please!

But what's actually more sensible is to be more conservative with your estimates. This way, you are more likely to under promise and over deliver. I mentioned this once already, so what does it mean?

This is a strategy used in a wide range of different business models. You encounter it, for instance, when you buy something on Amazon and find that the purchase comes with a free stylus for your mobile phone. That's "over delivering"—it's going above and beyond what was promised so that you come away feeling valued. Being pleasantly surprised by a product or service makes us much more likely to reflect positively on our experience and therefore to leave a positive review, or recommend that thing to a friend or relative.

This is also why delivery estimates should be conservative when you are selling a physical product. If you receive your product in three days and the delivery estimate was five days, then you'll come away pleased. If the same product arrives in three days but the delivery estimate was one to two days, then you'll feel let down.

And the same goes for providing a service. Sure, you might be tempted to offer a faster turn-around time (TAT) to make your service look more appealing than your competitor's, but rave reviews will ultimately serve you much better.

And on top of all this, leaving yourself a little "wiggle room" in terms of your deadlines is also a good way to account for those unexpected things that can otherwise set you back. Give yourself an extra day and you'll be able to handle that broken boiler, or corrupted file, without having to announce that the work is coming in late.

A good rule of thumb is to think about how long the work is going to take, and then estimate that you can do it one day slower than that.[2]

Dealing with Complaints and Revisions

Delivering work late is not going to be your only issue. Another problem is delivering work that is subpar, or that is seen to be subpar.

In other words, there will be times when you work tirelessly to meet the deadline, only for a client to say that they want to make a change to the work. And there will be times when you deliver the work and find out that you've made a big mistake.

And there will be times when you've delivered a fantastic end product and the client still has nothing but negative things to say about it.

So, what do you do in each situation?

Revisions

As far as revisions go—making cosmetic or subjective changes to a piece of software, content, or product—it is best to have a strict policy. Some clients forget that while this website or app might be their dream project, you probably don't have quite the same emotional connection with it. When they excitedly e-mail you with a list of ideas they suddenly want implemented, they may genuinely mean well and just want the best final product. But if you entertain their enthusiasm, it's going to cost you.

Likewise, if you've submitted a logo design and the client says they like it but would love to see what it looks like in a different color scheme, this kind of back-and-forth can again really add up.

---

[2]Of course, one argument against this is that you may feel more motivated to work quickly if you have promised to meet more stringent deadlines. The risk is that by giving yourself a relaxed deadline, you might end up taking it easy and thus earning less. The solution is to have a deadline that you share with your clients and a *personal* set of deadlines based on the volume of work you have and your goals for earning.

That's fine if you're charging by the hour, or per feature. But if you were charging for a finished product, then you should outline at the start of the project that you will provide X number of free revisions and no more. Factor this into your asking price (and again, consider using a tiered package system). Alternatively, explain that you love the idea, but it will take you just a little extra time and therefore that will need to be reflected in the cost. It's also important to point out that the delivery date will also likely be affected.

Mistakes

If you make a mistake, you should simply be willing to own up to it and fix it.

Maybe you've sent in a piece of software with a glaring bug that you failed to catch. Maybe you created a website and failed to take into account a key instruction because you read the e-mail too quickly. Maybe your content wasn't written on one of your best days and is full of errors.

In this case, you may need to make a small adjustment, *or* you might need to redo the entire project free of charge. This stings of course, but there's also no getting around it. If you take any other stance than this, you will risk upsetting your client, inviting bad reviews, and severely damaging your reputation.

When delivering the corrected version of the work, you might also choose to include a discount or some kind of free bonus by way of apology. This isn't always necessary, but if the work has missed its deadline as a result (another reason to set conservative delivery dates), or if it has damaged the reputation of the client, then this might help you to maintain a good working relationship.

Lastly, it's a good idea to include some explanation as to why the error happened (if it helps to prevent you from looking like a complete moron), but you again shouldn't try to "over-explain" yourself. Simply assure the client it won't happen again and make it right.[3]

Dealing with Difficult Clients

Then there are the clients that are going to expect unlimited free revisions of perfectly good work.

---

[3]If you're still finding this too painful, here's a little mental trick my mom taught me that can help you to do the right thing. Just remember: sometimes you lose money, sometimes you gain money. We've all lost currency, or had unexpected expenses because our cars have broken down. But likewise, we've all been given money unexpectedly by our kindly grandparents, had bonuses we weren't expecting (yes, this does occasionally happen in this line of work too!), or been undercharged at restaurants. The point is, it all balances out and, on average, you don't really gain or lose anything. This is just the same. A windfall will come and make it right at some point!

There are clients that will be rude and claim that your work is absolute junk. And there are clients that will engage in hostile action—such as demanding a reduction in price to reflect the fact that work was handed in ten minutes late.

Unfortunately, there are some people out there with seriously bad attitudes—and the anonymous nature of the Web makes it much easier for them to embrace that nature. Some clients feel very entitled and think that because they are paying you, they have a right to treat you like dirt. Some enjoy a bit too much the small modicum of "power" that hiring someone online gives them.

You cannot allow this to stand. Not only is it unprofessional, but it will almost always get worse rather than better. If you fold to the demands of such a client, they will continue to take advantage of you and ultimately, they will benefit from the relationship far more than you will.

This is again why it is a very good idea to outline the terms of your services early on. If you make it clear that your price includes "one free revision," then you can point the client to this when they demand more.

At the same time though, you also need to be ready to occasionally stand up for yourself and call out your clients' bad behavior.

What's important is not to become too emotional when doing this. Be dispassionate and logical, and try not to sink to their level. If their demands won't take you too long, then complete the task for an easy life but *then* cut ties. If what they're asking for is completely unreasonable, then either offer a partial refund or simply state that you have completed your end of the bargain and you won't be able to provide further revisions.

And then cut off ties.

Simply explain that while you've enjoyed working with them, you currently have other time commitments and regret that you won't be able to take on future work. If they rant and rave, you then have permission to ignore their further communication. Such clients are almost always all bark and no bite and chances are they're just looking for a fight. You don't have energy to waste on creative insults, and that's only giving them what they want anyway. So, rise above it and move on.

Note as well that some clients will be unreasonable in their initial request—trying to aggressively force you to lower your prices, for instance, or asking you to do things that are outside your job description. You might find yourself being asked to do grunt work (finding images for a website, or making a list of similar sites in their niche). This makes life even easier because you haven't committed to anything yet. Just say no.

It's corny, but if you don't value your skills as a professional, your clients won't either.

The Art of Good Communication

Good communication is absolutely key to thriving in the gig economy. We've already seen the importance of being able to write a good sales pitch. And if English isn't your first language, or you struggle with dyslexia, then using a VAS to handle your correspondence is a real option.

But ultimately, being able to write eloquent and detailed e-mails that make a good impression *and* convey all the information you need to is always the preference. This way, you can maintain a positive relationship, appear professional, and avoid breakdowns in communication that lead to errors.

How to Write Great E-mails

Writing good e-mails comes down to a few things. First, it means knowing how to communicate and write in general.

And the best way to remember how to write is to remember this:

Good writing is good communication.

You are simply aiming to convey information to the reader. The more information you can convey the more quickly, the more effective and efficient you have been in that task.

That means that you should be avoiding jargon, flowery language, and filler. Aim to get your point across concisely so that the reader has invested less time and gotten more out of it. Reread what you've written, and if you can remove words without losing anything, do so.

That doesn't mean your writing should be entirely concise and made up of short sentences and simple language though. Using your fuller vocabulary and a little more poetic license can help you to convey subtle emotion or detail. In other words, a bigger vocabulary allows you to say even more with less.

Your choice of language and the inclusion of jokes or colloquialisms, for instance, can help to set the "tone" of your voice, which in turn will communicate something about you and your perception of the relationship you are entering into. So good writing doesn't always mean extreme brevity—it just means "communication, not decoration." It means efficiency in your choice of words.

The Right Tone

And what should that tone be?

I find that in the gig economy, the general tone of e-mails is a lot more casual and informal than it is in the wider world of business. My wife is often dismayed at my use of smiley faces and jokes in e-mails! But this is simply the tone that I have picked up from the clients.

And that is probably the key. You should begin all communications as formally and professionally as possible (without being "stiff" or false with it) but then allow the client to set the tone going forward. If they're including smileys and asking personal questions, then you should feel free to do the same back.

Remember: many of your clients are similarly self-employed, or digital entrepreneurs. And like you, they may have been attracted to this lifestyle because they were fed up with the stuffy approach of big business and traditional employment.

They might even have chosen to do business with someone like you because they *want* to be able to speak directly to an individual with a personality— rather than the unknowable polished front of a large organization.

Rules of Engagement

That said about adapting your tone, during initial contact, there are some basic rules of professional communication to keep in mind:

- Use a formal sign-off. "Best wishes" is a safe and widely appropriate option. "Best" is also a versatile choice.
  - As you become more familiar with the client, you can also use "Thanks" or "Cheers." This makes most sense when you are actually showing gratitude, however, and can be seen as disingenuous or even *sarcastic* if you get it wrong. And I might only be getting away with "Cheers" because I'm British.
  - "Sincerely" is best saved for covering letters, or e-mails that began with "Dear."
- If you don't know the name of the person you are speaking to, use "To whom it may concern" or "Dear Sir or Madam." NEVER assume gender.
  - If you do know their name but this is the first time you're contacting them, it's almost always fine to use first names in the gig economy. This may not be true for larger organizations though.
  - Using "Mr." or "Ms." is generally best used when selling an expensive and serious service in a B2C capacity (e.g., legal advice).
- Use your own full name in the sign-off the first time—it is polite, and it ensures they know precisely who you are.

- Avoid attention-grabbing subject lines. Using "Re: *Subject of E-mail*" is generally a good structure. The same thing works without the Re: (which stands for "regarding" in case you weren't aware).

If you're unsure of just how formal you should be, then looking at the correspondent's own e-mails can help elucidate. Otherwise, check their blog or other material to see how they generally conduct themselves.

Using an e-mail signature block can be a useful way to ensure that your clients always remember who you are, and to give them a quick and easy way to get to your website.

Finally, note that as the e-mail chain gets longer and longer, you don't always actually *need* a sign-off, or to start every message with "Hey" or "Dear."

Making Friends Out of Clients

Remember in Chapter 5 we discussed the dangers of working for/with friends? Well, what happens if you flip this on its head and the client *becomes* the friend? How familiar should you be with your clients? How much should you know about them, and they about you?

This will once again be something that you need to consider on a case-by-case basis and often it will mean letting the client take the lead. How many questions do they ask? Do they elaborate when asking how you are?

As a general rule though, I would recommend keeping clients at a distance unless you're working long term in a collaborative manner with an individual or team. For more-straightforward client/service-provider relationships, it is often easier to avoid confusing the relationship or inviting unnecessary chatter (which also brings more communication overhead). I've had clients asking me for relationship advice in the past! While this can be a useful way to put the balance of power in your hands a little more (if they trust you to give advice on this, it suggests they respect your opinion generally), it's also a potentially dangerous move if you accidentally offend them or if they become overly familiar and start asking for favors.

Be courteous. Ask how they are. Wish them "Happy holidays." But otherwise leave it at that.

Social Engineering and Giving "Advice"

I did just hint at something perhaps a little tantalizing in the previous section. While I'm not condoning manipulating your clients, there are some subtle stunts you can pull and there are some other ways you can shift the balance of power in your favor. Specifically, I would say that there is a lot to be gained by giving advice.

For example, accepting work but "suggesting" they approach the project in a different way can often help to put you in slightly more of an advisory role *and* help you to do more work that you will benefit from. For instance, I was recently asked to write some articles for a company that built some security software. They requested titles like:

How [SOFTWARE] Can Improve Your Security
Ten Features of [SOFTWARE] You Won't Find Anywhere Else

I pointed out to them that the idea of content marketing is to create content people want to read. And no one wants to read a blog that consists of a company patting itself on the back and trying to sell its product. The same topics would work much better with titles that suggest actual value for the reader:

Top Tricks You're Missing to Improve Your Security
What to Look for When Choosing Security Software

That's content people would want to read.

This suggestion would (hopefully) result in an end product that would be more effective in achieving the goals of the client. That in turn would result in a happier client and a richer client. The richer client would in turn be more likely to hire me again. And I would have a more impressive success story to add to my portfolio.

What is good for your client is good for you. So, don't just sit on your opinions ...share them!

But there's also an ulterior motive here.

This demonstrates that you aren't just a service provider but understand the bigger picture, and it might in the future result in your having a bit more say over how things are done and the type of work you end up completing.

The client might next time *ask* you what you think they need. That then means you can suggest they order the services you *want* to sell.

At the same time, this increases your respect and you might find that the client ends up asking for your advice and seeing you as more of an equal partner. They might feel as though they now *need* you to operate! Which in turn means they're not too likely to stop working with you. Now you can help to steer the business a little more in the right direction for you.

I have worked with an agency that sold my coding skills in the past that actually asked me how they should grow their business. I pointed out that they had a problem with flaky programmers because they didn't pay enough to attract the heavy hitters. I recommended they should pay their coders *more* and they should make a big deal of the caliber of programmer they hire in order to attract bigger customers. They could even see themselves more as a talent agency, rather than a white label service provider.

They took my advice and, lo and behold, I got a raise and I got my skills promoted on the Web.

This is a dangerous game, but it's one that can really pay off.

Going Through Agencies

Speaking of agencies ...

If you want to make your life considerably easier, then one easy strategy is to use an agency or agent.

An agency is basically a company that is going to help you look for work and will then sell your services on your behalf. This is a "development company" or a "web design company" that works like a contractor: hiring freelancers to complete work on behalf of its clients.

That helps you to avoid dry spells, and also means that work can be spread between a team of service providers to better manage volume. But that's not the real benefit. The *real* benefit is rather that the agency will act as a buffer between you and the client. The agency will most likely want to keep communication to a minimum and so they'll simply pass on the clear-and-concise instructions to you.

And that means you'll be able to start each day with a list of tasks that you can simply work through. It means you'll never have to answer pointless questions, and it means you will get paid even when a client requests a revision or a refund (as long as you haven't made any glaring errors). That is no longer your problem.

Of course, agencies are also going to take a cut of your profits (a commission) in exchange for this. And sometimes it will be high.

This also means you're putting the power in the hands of the client—the agency *is* the client here. They get to choose what service you are providing and how it is going to be advertised and marketed. And negotiating a change in rates will be harder because they will still want to make a profit (so they're either reducing their cut or discussing the change in rates with their clients).

And perhaps most egregious of all: using an agency normally means that you're going to be uncredited a lot of the time. The agency doesn't necessarily want to advertise that it uses freelancers and may even try to maintain the illusion that it handles everything in-house in a big office. That means they can't tell the clients that you completed the work, which means your name doesn't go on it, and which means you may struggle to add it to your portfolio. (Although I did just explain one very specific and risky way around this limitation!)

This is why I personally choose to use agencies to provide just some of my work. I use agencies to earn a minimum amount via a steady supply of work, but I then use the rest of my time to hunt for more flexible and highly paid work. It's easy, stable work, with minimum hassle. And while it isn't terribly rewarding, it allows me to "bootstrap" my other ideas (self-funding my personal R&D—more on this in Chapter 9).

Collaboration Tools

Working online in the gig economy will often mean working with teams and individuals based in completely different parts of the world. More and more businesses these days actually operate without a base of operations at all and are instead completely distributed. I've worked with such groups myself.

This has advantages and disadvantages that go beyond the scope of this book. But suffice to say that there are plenty of great tools out there designed to make remote collaboration that little bit easier. And if you're being hired by an experienced business, then chances are that they're going to require you to fit into their workflow and adopt their tools.

I don't want to dedicate too much space here to collaboration tools, once again because the technology changes so rapidly that there is no guarantee the tools used today would still be around tomorrow!

But that said, there are several industry standards that have proven to be mainstays over the last several years and learning to use these can serve as a useful example of the kind of workflow you'll often enter into. So here are some that are worth getting to grips with.

Asana

Asana (`https://asana.com`) is a project management tool that allows teams to organize a wide range of different tasks simultaneously. Among other things, Asana will allow users to assign team members to specific tasks, to set and update the status of a job, to upload attachments, to schedule deadlines, and to discuss work.

So, let's say that you are working for a large organization and you've been asked to complete a small website. You'll then be sent an invitation to join the organization on Asana, and from there, you'll be able to look at the projects that the organization is working on and who is assigned to each one. You'll receive e-mails regarding your task that will inform you when someone comments on it, when it is nearly due, when someone uploads an image, and so forth.

If the team is using the tool well, then you'll be able to find a description of the work you need to do on this page, along with any links and resources that you might need—meaning you can check back here each time you need reminding what your next job is. If you have been assigned *multiple* jobs, then you should be able to see all of them in one place and thereby better manage your own time.

You can also use tool this independently if you like the system, adding your own tasks and projects here so that you have everything in one place.

Asana is just one project management tool used by teams. Another popular one is Basecamp (`www.basecamp.com`), and Trello (`https://trello.com`) is also up there. They all have their strengths and weaknesses, but the basic concept is very similar.

Slack

Slack (`https://slack.com`) can best be described as "WhatsApp for businesses." This is a communication tool that is useful not only for keeping up to date with the movements of your team, but also for asking quick questions, organizing meetings, updating the entire team, and creating a sense of camaraderie.

When you join Slack, you'll be invited to join a specific team (which will likely have the same name as the company or brand you're working with). From there, you'll be able to see a list of chats down the left-hand side, which can be individual one-to-one chats or group chats. You can create as many of these groups and permutations as you like. So, for example, were you a writer for a blog, then you might be able to discuss the brand as a whole in the General chat, chew the cud with teammates in the Off-Topic Lounge, or discuss work in the Writers section. There might also be a News Writers section, a private conversation you have ongoing with your editor, a conversation you have ongoing with two other writers who you're working with on a project, and a colleague who is having a baby that you thoughtfully decided to check in on.

You can use Slack through your browser or on Android and iOS, and you'll receive notifications when there's a new message in a one-to-one or small group chat, *or* when someone posts a message and tags you. They can also tag whole channels.

Slack can be useful, as it allows a colleague to ask a quick question at 7 p.m. When they need an immediate answer. Of course, it can also be a headache for those of us that like to switch off from work past 5 p.m.—so it's up to you (and your clients) if you are going to leave notifications on or off.

This ultimately allows the kind of chatter that you might naturally expect to encounter in an actual office and that in turn allows you to feel as though you're part of a team. It also enables the kinds of smaller questions that might be essential to the efficient operation of a larger organization.

BUT from your perspective this also poses a real threat. Remember communication overhead? Flow states? Batching your correspondence? Slack throws all of this out of the window and demands you to be constantly ready to answer questions, or worse—engage in small talk.

But some businesses really do need Slack in order to operate properly. So just make sure that the work you're doing is *worth* this intrusion into your workflow, and make sure the clients know when you will and won't be available to respond (you can snooze notifications).

Google Drive

Google Drive (https://drive.google.com) is one tool that you're most likely familiar with, seeing as it's something that a lot of us have used in office settings *and* in our personal lives. Essentially, Google Drive is a cloud storage system that lets you upload files and share them with others.

Google Drive is a very useful tool in a variety of scenarios—if you need to send a large video, for instance, or if you need to give access to a folder filled with different files.

But what makes Google Drive truly impressive is the included Office functionality. You also get

- Google Docs
- Google Sheets
- Google Slides

These tools let you create documents, spreadsheets, and presentations; just as you might normally do in Microsoft Office. You can do all this entirely through your browser, and then easily share the documents with other users. You can even invite others to edit your documents (use track changes to suggest edits without altering the original document), and in Sheets you can actually see other people using their cursor to select cells in real time! Of course, this does introduce the possibility for complication if more than one person attempts to edit the same document at once. But otherwise, it plays particularly nicely with other collaboration tools like Asana.

Google Calendar

Google Calendar (`www.google.com/calendar`) isn't so much a collaboration tool but can be very useful in our line of work. Not only is this a very useful option for managing your own to-do list, but it also comes with some powerful community features. For example, you can share your calendar with other users, which will let them see your availability—great if you are trying to arrange a consultation with a client. Better yet, you can also create events and invite other Google users, thereby ensuring the same meeting is in everyone's calendar and ruling out the possibility of mix-ups.

DocuSign

DocuSign (`www.docusign.com`) is a tool that lets you create, view, and sign contracts on the Web. This is used by many organizations to help overcome the issue of distance and it will let you sign with a stylus, or simply by typing your name. It also lets you store the documents you've signed so that you can check the terms you agreed to at a later date.

DocuSign is not free if you are going to be writing the contracts. If you're going to be drawing up a lot of your own contracts, then you might think that the DocuSign membership is worth it to make sure you make a professional impression on clients. Otherwise, simply sending a PDF and asking them to sign it, scan it, and send it back will work just as well. More often, though, you'll be on the receiving end of these documents when working with new clients, in which case you can use DocuSign for free.

Tettra

Tettra (`https://app.tettra.co`) is essentially a Wiki for small businesses—or a "knowledge management system." If you work for a larger organization, then it may use a tool like this in order to create company polices, FAQs, editorials, and more. This can help to avoid time being wasted on easy questions, and as an added bonus it also integrates with Slack.

Dropbox

Dropbox (`www.dropbox.com`) is an alternative to Google Drive that you can use for backing up your own files and sharing them with others. This tool is a little slower and gives you considerably less space on a free account. It also doesn't come with the office suite that you get with that option.

However, it does allow you to sync your folders on Windows, which means you can simply save documents and files there on one machine and carry on working on them on another.

OneDrive (https://onedrive.live.com) is the equivalent from Microsoft that works in a similar manner but has closer integration with Windows.

SharePoint

SharePoint (www.sharepoint.com) is yet another online collaboration tool, this time from Microsoft. It is a fair bit different from the likes of Asana, though, in that it integrates closely with Microsoft Office and is primarily useful for managing and editing documents. In fact, it's the tool that the publisher of this book (Apress) uses to work with its authors (such as me!).

It's a clunky tool and not particularly intuitive or quick. That said though, it's also very powerful for what it does and in many cases it really is the best tool for the job.

Bonusly

Bonusly (https://bonus.ly) is an interestingly concept that, like Slack, can help to create more of a sense of camaraderie for a team that is distributed online. The idea is that the management provides all team members with a certain amount of money—perhaps $50 per month—and those users can then choose who they want to give the amount to throughout the following weeks until the total is refreshed. If you have a group of programmers working on a project, then, you might find that members get given bonuses to reward them for fixing bugs, for putting in extra hours to meet deadlines, or to wish them happy birthday. The money can then be redeemed either through PayPal as cash or as gift cards to a host of participating online brands, big-box stores, and even restaurants. The tool also integrates nicely with Slack, so that you can see through there when it's someone's birthday, or when someone is getting a lot of moola.

Bonusly is a great idea in some ways but it can have downsides too if you are all about knuckling down. On the one hand, it certainly encourages you to work harder, and being acknowledged for your contribution to a piece of work is a great feeling. It really can help to create some camaraderie and it's a nice gesture on your clients' part. On the other hand, constantly having to remember birthdays and work anniversaries is a pain and another distraction from work. And there is always the danger it can become something of a popularity contest. You may wonder: wouldn't it be better if you just got *paid* more? Or could keep your $50?

Still, there's no easy way of opting out of this without looking like Scrooge, so you might just have to get used to it. And when it works, it's a very nice idea.

GitHub

GitHub (https://github.com) is a collaboration tool that is specifically aimed at programmers and developers and that can be used to create large projects.

This is a web-based Git repository service; Git is an open source version-control system from Linus Torvalds (of Linux fame) that lets you make changes to a project without overwriting the original. In that sense, this is "track changes for programmers." You'll have a master branch and you'll be able to create additional branches to experiment in that won't affect that core code.

This means that by using GitHub, you're able to upload entire projects to the Web for team members to view and comment on. More importantly though, they can also create their own branches, which might add new features, make changes to key elements, or just fix a bug. The changes you make are called *commits*, and these come with commit messages that explain what was done and why.

One other great thing about commits is that they also act as snapshots that let you roll back changes should a mistake be made. The creator of the branch can then make a pull request, which gives the creator the opportunity to accept the changes or discuss issues. If they are happy with the alterations, they can "deploy" and "merge" those changes with the master.

Branching like this is an integral and inherent feature of Git, and GitHub simply provides an intuitive UI and makes the program available for multiple collaborators.

Another feature of GitHub is that it allows for the creation of *forks*. These are copies or clones of repositories, which let you make changes to someone else's project without necessarily having anything to do with the original. This is a great way to learn: by finding simple projects, forking them, and then building off of those starting points—and it's very much in the spirit of open source. You do still also have the option this way to make a pull request to the owner if you think they might appreciate your alterations!

Chances are that if you have a need for GitHub, then you already know what it is. And if you don't, then you probably won't!

That said, this is potentially a tool that freelance developers will spend a lot of time with, so I included it here. It is worth noting, though, that GitHub has recently been purchased by Microsoft, resulting in many GitHub users jumping ship in protest. Alternatives include the likes of Bitbucket (https://bitbucket.org), GitLab (https://about.gitlab.com), and SourceForge (https://sourceforge.net). Personally, I still recommend familiarizing yourself with GitHub first and foremost if you want to make yourself as attractive as possible to coding clients.

Skype

Skype (www.skype.com) is a tool that most readers are probably familiar with once again, seeing as it is popular outside of business as well. Thus, you likely don't need me to tell you that it is a video conferencing app that allows you to chat with prospective clients (as much as we might try to avoid doing this, it is unavoidable at times). Google Hangouts (https://hangouts.google.com) is another popular option.

Zoom

Finally, Zoom (www.zoom.us) is a slightly more feature-rich version of Skype. With Zoom you have conferences with multiple people (this is also possible on Skype and Hangouts, but it's made a little easier and more streamlined with Zoom) and, more importantly, you can record your meetings for posterity.

This is by no means a comprehensive list of online tools for freelancers, but getting to grips with all these programs will certainly stand you in good stead for a lot of upcoming work.

You Don't Always Need Remote Tools—Setting Your Own Flow

You might find that certain clients expect you to be familiar with one or more of the types of tools introduced in the previous section and to fit into the client's workflow. Depending on the size and the value of the client, you may decide that adapting is in your best interests.

I've had to use every single one of the tools listed and a whole bunch of others too. Often this involved being dropped in the deep end—but being able to say that you're experienced with Asana is almost as much of a CV bragging right as being proficient in Microsoft Office or WordPress, so that's one advantage at least.

But keep in mind that in some cases, "workflow tools" can actually end up being more time consuming than anything else. This is certainly the case if your clients are only ordering small items like logo designs, articles, or apps from you, but insist on an elaborate protocol for discussing and submitting the work . . . it would be just as easy (or easier) to e-mail them!

And actually, much like screen-monitoring software, some of these tools can end up preventing you from working the way that you want to—robbing you of the flexibility that maybe attracted you to working online in the first place! I have at least one client that expects me to be available on Slack between set hours, attend group Zoom meetings at certain times of day, and upload video content to YouTube on a regular basis. This seriously undermines my freedom and flexibility. How can I work in a noisy coffee shop when I need to be ready to make Skype calls?

So, what do I do? I do the best job possible the way that works for me. That means meeting on Skype where possible, but also being willing to say that I'm not available. If the client decides that our working styles don't gel, then they're free to let me go. If they're happy to compromise as long as the work gets done, then we can work with each other.

There is certainly no requirement to use fancy workflow tools, and in fact you might find in some cases that it is preferable to keep it simple. If you are unsure, then don't be afraid to suggest to the client that you just send your work via e-mail instead.

Challenges of Remote Collaboration

If you're not a people person, then the idea of being able to work thousands of miles away from your colleagues and clients might be inherently appealing. That is, until you realize that you still do have to work with them. And that the best time to get in touch with them is 7 p.m. Your time.

Time zones are just one of the many struggles of remote collaboration. One of the solutions is to use World Time Buddy (www.worldtimebuddy.com), which is a convenient website and app for checking the time in any given location (there are many others too, of course).

Keep in mind as well that time zones can change sometimes. Here in the UK where I'm based, there is a difference between British Summer Time (BST) and Greenwich Meantime (GMT). That's because the clocks move forward an hour during the summer, putting us out of sync. This has led to more than a few missed meetings! So, double-check, and use Google Calendar for extra confidence. It's also worth ensuring that you and your client are both on the same page with regards to date formats. Depending on where you are located, 01/06/2019 can mean two very different dates!

It's not just knowing the time that's the problem though—it's also respecting it. It's very common to find clients based overseas messaging you during unearthly hours and expecting you to answer because it's during their working day. If they need the work completed quickly and there's a problem with it, they're probably going to think nothing of messaging you at 10:30 a.m. Their time—even if that's 8 p.m. Your time!

This is where you need to be strict and create some boundaries. In order to do your best work during the day, you need your downtime during the evening. Turn off notifications, set up out-of-office autoresponders, and/or let your clients know that they can contact you using your personal e-mail only if it is a *genuine* emergency. Let them know your timezone, so that they understand when you are likely to be unavailable. Again, if they can't work this way, then they're free to find someone based locally. There are plenty of fish in the sea.

There are some advantages to the time difference, though, too. Sometimes if I don't finish my work before a certain deadline, I can send it in the next morning and it's still technically on time! The fact that your clients often won't remember what time it is for you also means you can occasionally get away with being unresponsive or slow—just tell them you got up late or something!

Another challenge of remote collaboration is the issue of cultural differences. These aren't usually as pronounced as you might expect, but something I did realize early on is that in the UK, we are *very* polite. I mean to the point of psychosis. Meanwhile, business is conducted in a much more curt and aggressive manner in other parts of the world, and *that* took a bit of getting used to. My clients weren't being rude: they were simply conducting themselves the way they were used to. I bit my tongue a few times, and this led to some *very* worthwhile relationships in the long run.

Be slow to anger and don't expect everyone to behave the way you do!

Finally, there are the obvious logistical challenges of remote working. We've seen some tools that can help with things like working on large projects and exchanging files, but you will find that even these tools aren't enough to account for every setback and issue. Files will get lost. Wires will get crossed. It's all part of the fun of being an online freelancer . . . Enjoy!

Chapter Summary

In this chapter, you discovered how to communicate effectively with clients via e-mail and through a range of collaboration tools. This should in turn help you to avoid mistakes and complications, while also improving your ability to manage relationships with clients. Effective communication actually is one of the most fundamental aspects of working online, so give it the attention it deserves!

Once you've grasped these concepts, you now have all the tools you need to run your business. You know what to sell, where to sell it, and how to deal with the people who want to buy it. All that's left to do is cross your *t*'s and dot your *i*'s. That's where the "busywork of business" comes in, meaning tax, accounting, and legalities. It's not fun, but we've put it off as long as possible. It's time to do the paperwork!

The Busywork of Business

Over the last few chapters, we've discussed some of the slightly more abstract and theoretical aspects of providing a freelance service. We've seen how making small changes to your turn-around times, your wording, or your health can have big impacts on your ability to produce high-quality work and turn a profit.

But now it's time to get practical again. It's time to discuss the nitty-gritty details of running a business. That means taxes, legalities, contracts, budgeting, and more (oh my!). These aspects are not particularly fun, but they are, unfortunately, unavoidable. And it's definitely worth spending a little time getting into good habits now if you want to avoid some far worse headaches down the line!

Billing

Okay, so we've looked at many of the collaboration tools that are used as industry standard by many organizations. But how do you go about sending and receiving money? This once again depends on the client and the situation, but there are a few "industry standards" that you will likely fall back on in the vast majority of situations.

© Adam Sinicki 2019

A. Sinicki, *Thriving in the Gig Economy*, https://doi.org/10.1007/978-1-4842-4090-8_7

PayPal

Perhaps the most common way to send and receive money online is through PayPal (www.paypal.com). PayPal basically acts like a middleman so that you don't have to hand over your bank details to clients, and it also helps transactions go much more quickly and much more smoothly.

To use PayPal, you need to set up an online account using an e-mail address. Once that's done, anyone can send money to you via PayPal and all they need is that associated e-mail. Better yet, you can even send money to someone who doesn't yet have a PayPal account. Just send it via PayPal to their e-mail, and then when they associate the e-mail with an account, they'll be ready to receive it.

To withdraw or add funds though, you'll also need to associate add a bank account or credit card. To do this, you'll provide your account information and PayPal will pay you two micropayments (tiny amounts of money). You then confirm the value of those microtransactions by checking with your bank statement and reporting back to PayPal, and from there you will be ready to start adding and withdrawing funds from your new account.

You don't actually need to withdraw cash every time though. These days you can buy a lot of things with PayPal online, and you can even get a PayPal Debit Card for making real-world purchases! But if you're working online for your full-time job, then you will probably want to withdraw your funds to a bank account *eventually*. Most mortgage providers won't let you buy your house with PayPal, after all.

Likewise, PayPal will allow you to create invoices for your clients. This streamlines the process of requesting money, ensuring that they know precisely what they're being charged for and giving them the option to make the payment very quickly and simply.

For many of my clients, a typical workflow will be

1. Receive e-mail containing order.

2. Acknowledge the order and commence working.

3. Deliver work.

4. Send PayPal invoice.

5. Get paid within 24 to 48 hours.

This system makes getting started online incredibly simple and it means that if you have a PayPal account, you can potentially start earning money tonight and have it in your account immediately. Which is awesome.

More Features of PayPal

PayPal also comes with a host of other features that make life easier for you as an entrepreneur. For instance, it keeps a record of all the money that comes in and out of your account, which makes accounting relatively simple at the end of the financial year (more on this in a moment). It also lets you keep track of your invoices and bills, and remind clients who have yet to pay.

PayPal also integrates with a lot of other tools that you're going to find yourself using as a freelancer. For example, it works with Bonusly, Fiverr, and a number of freelancing sites, meaning you don't need to enter your bank details there.

For those interested in e-commerce and selling digital products, PayPal also lets you create Buy buttons that can be embedded in web pages, sales pages, or even e-mails. You can even charge for your services this way, especially if you ask for payment up front and sell them as packages.

Fees

Unfortunately, PayPal is not perfect, however. That's because it does charge fairly high fees, which clients will often expect you to pay for. When you advertise your services as costing "$40 per hour," your clients aren't going to read this as "$40 per hour + PayPal fees." This isn't a problem though; you simply need to factor the fees into the amount you charge.

The fees are subject to change and can vary depending on a number of factors such as sales volume and the way you invoice. Generally though, they range from around 1.9% to 3.4%. Not negligible, but small enough that most people can factor them in without it crippling their operations.

Other Options

PayPal is probably the most widely used of these online payment services. There are plenty of others though, with TransferWise (https://transferwise.com) being one of the more notable alternatives. If you are put off by PayPal's fees, then you may wish to do some research regarding these tools and see if one is better suited to your workflow. Just be aware that you might run into a little more resistance if the client doesn't already have an account/isn't already familiar with it (whereas you can practically guarantee they'll be PayPal pros).

There are many other options when it comes to billing that don't involve one of these sites at all. One is to simply ask for a bank transfer. This will normally be cheaper than getting paid via PayPal in terms of the fees. If the client is based in the same country, then it will probably be free. But if the payment is international, you may pay a flat processing fee plus a percentage on top of the overall amount being sent. The percentage will be lower, but the processing fee means that this won't necessarily be advisable for smaller orders. Checks are also an option, though you might require a foreign check if you are providing services overseas, and that can again incur costs.

Note that a downside of accepting international checks and bank transfers is that they will often take longer to process. If you're dealing with a new client and you haven't quite established that level of trust yet, then taking a small hit in order to get your money *sooner* via an online portal might be a smarter option. I once dealt with a client who repeatedly told me that the money was taking a long time to transfer, or that the transactions were being cancelled by their bank. In truth, it transpired that they simply didn't have the money to pay me and they were using this as a convenient excuse. I lost a lot of money as a result.

This is why the payment method will often evolve as your relationship with the client does. You might start out by doing the odd job for them and getting paid via PayPal and then "graduate" to a monthly long-term agreement where you're paid quarterly via bank transfer.

With all that said, if your clients are based in the same country as you, then sending money via bank transfer or check (even cash in hand!) becomes the simplest option as long as you trust them with your account details. This way, you'll pay very little in terms of fees and should be able to receive your payment almost immediately. At this point the only limitation is the need to log into your online banking to check that the payment has processed!

Bitcoin

Oh, and there is of course one more option: getting paid in Bitcoin. Bitcoin is a cryptocurrency that isn't tied to a natural resource like gold or silver. Bitcoin is instead controlled by a public "ledger" called the blockchain and is protected via encryption. Bitcoin can be transferred internationally without fees, and has historically risen in value immensely, making it a potentially attractive investment opportunity. Bitcoin and other cryptocurrencies can also be spent and invested by bots and scripts, creating the possibility of "algo-businesses" that entirely run themselves.

At this time though, Bitcoin is largely only accepted online (save for a few media-savvy pubs and other venues). It also requires a little bit of setting up in order to start trading. And if the client you're approaching doesn't know what Bitcoin is, they're unlikely to want to spend time learning about it in order to pay you that way.

However, if you're familiar with Bitcoin and your client is too, then it's certainly an interesting option. And one that is likely to become increasingly viable in the coming years.

Invoicing

It's also a common practice to provide your clients with an invoice. This helps them with their own tax reporting (discussed later in the chapter) as your services will be written off as an expense/overhead. At the same time, it also inspires trust by demonstrating complete transparency. They will appreciate getting a complete breakdown of all the services provided and how much each cost, for their own records, to show to their superiors, and in case they have any questions or issues with the work you provided.

How you go about writing your invoice is largely up to you, but you should aim to make it as professional as possible without spending hours on it. Remember: time is money.

This is another benefit of using a tool like PayPal, seeing as it has the option to send invoices built in. You simply fill out the services/goods provided, their quantity, and their cost per unit and then you click Send. The recipient can easily pay that invoice and also keep a record of it.

Otherwise, you will likely need to make something yourself using a PDF. Microsoft Word now allows you to convert documents to PDF simply by saving them in that format. So, you can create a table including each job/project and the cost, with a total payable down the bottom.

Other key details to include in an invoice are

- Your name
- Your company name
- Your address
- Your e-mail
- Your phone number
- The date
- The invoice number (if you deal with the client regularly)
- Your PayPal address OR bank details
- A logo (if you like)

An example might look something like Figure 7-1.

Invoice for Work Completed

Adam Sinicki
(NQR Productions)
1000 Imaginary Way
Imagination Land
IM11 777

Tel: +00 Wouldn't-You-Like-to-Know

Invoice to: Client World Ltd

Date: July 31st 2018

Breakdown

Title	Time	Amount USD	Amount GDP
Equipment Repayment		-50	
Tuesday 10th		100	
Wednesday 11th		100	
Thursday 12th		100	
Friday 13th		100	
Tuesday 17th		100	
Wednesday 18th		100	
Thursday 19th		100	
Friday 20th		100	
Tuesday 24th		100	
Wednesday 25th		100	
Thursday 26th		100	
Friday 27st		100	
Tuesday 31st		100	

$1250USD = £949.99GBP

Details

Name: Adam Sinicki
Invoice Number: 33
Amount: £949.99
PayPal: MyEmail@EmailAddress.com

Figure 7-1. Sample invoice

This is an actual invoice I sent to a client recently (with a couple of changes) charging for a few hours of work on each of those days. Of course, if you wanted to charge per completed line of code, or per finished project, then your invoice would reflect that.

Even if you are providing a B2C service selling personal training services (meaning they aren't likely to need it for their tax reports), an invoice like this will still be appreciated by your clients.

Currency

When billing, it is a common practice to charge in US dollars—regardless of what country you're in. This is the "currency of the Web," and while you can charge in your local currency, it will only lead to confusion.

Of course, what this also means is that your income is going to change a *lot* depending on the exchange rate. When the value of the British pound falls against the dollar, this can result in a hefty pay rise for me at times. It's a little strange for me, but I benefit when the economy struggles! On the other hand though, if things move the other way, then this can hurt my income.

This also means that you can potentially benefit *a lot* financially by moving to a different country. If you are being paid in dollars and you move to a region where the dollar is worth more, you can withdraw your cash and potentially live like a king. More on this in Chapter 8.

This is also a factor you need to consider when choosing your payment method. Depending on the service you choose, you will be offered a different exchange rate. PayPal's exchange rate, for instance, actually hides additional costs—the rate it offers is the "wholesale cost of foreign currency . . . plus a currency conversion fee." This is a mark in favor of TransferWise, which actually charges the mid-market rate in its conversion, plus a relatively small and simple flat fee.

Anything currency is acceptable, as long as it is agreed by both you and the client, and as long as you factor these potential extra costs into your budgeting and financial modeling. You may even find that you end up charging in dollars, but then converting that amount into your local currency when you bill the client. That way you can benefit from the exchange rate where it is in your favor without paying a conversion fee. If you find such a client, then stick with them!

Agreements, Contracts, and Monthly Payments

Another factor that is going to impact the way you get paid is the way in which you arrange your agreement with your client.

Earlier in this book, I recommended going after gigs that will pay immediately at the end of the day. I also mentioned that I prefer getting paid "per quantifiable unit." That's one option, but then there's the option of agreeing to a contract where you will work a certain amount per month/week/day. This might then result in a recurring monthly payment, as long as all the work gets done. As mentioned, you'll find that this type of agreement often "evolves" from a more casual working relationship and that this lends itself better to bank transfers. If there's a $15 flat fee for sending payments, that's going to be a much smaller issue when the total payment amount is $2.5K versus $50.

This type of work has other benefits too, as it means that you have at least some kind of stable and predictable income. It's a great feeling knowing that even when the clients aren't biting, you have at least some income guaranteed. And it can really help with budgeting. If you mix this with other types of agreement, then it can help to further diversify your client roster and create a more resilient business.

But of course, it also robs you of some of your flexibility and freedom, as it means at least a certain portion of your time is going to be already assigned at the start of the month. It also puts the power in the hands of the client once more—they're tying you down and setting the terms, and you're then agreeing to them. This is subtly different from *you* offering to provide website maintenance for a recurring monthly fee or for a one-off bulk purchase.

These types of agreement can be verbal, or they can be based on an actual contract. Contracts should in theory protect both you *and* the client from changing the terms without warning or agreement from the other party. But do keep in mind that such contracts can also be restrictive and include terms that don't benefit you if they've been written up by the client. Just make sure that you read them *thoroughly*. Pay special attention to the wording. Here are some questions to keep in mind:

- Precisely what is it that you are agreeing to? Usually this will be X amount of work per given period.

- What agreement is in place for when you fail to meet those targets?

- How is payment agreed?

- What happens if the client fails to pay?

- How soon will they pay once they have received your work, or on what day will they pay?

- How long is this contract valid for?

- If this is a recurring monthly agreement, then how will either one of you bring it to a close?

- If you are agreeing to complete a certain long-term project (another common use for a contract), then what is defined as "complete"?

- Who retains the rights to the finished work? How will they/you be allowed to use it?

Look out for other things that the client might try to sneak in there too. Some may try to prevent you from working with competing parties, which could end up limiting your ability to find other clients.

I often find it is the client that is most likely to write up the contract, at which point you are that little bit closer to being traditionally employed. You'll likely find this contract is developed with the help of software like the aforementioned DocuSign. If not, you might be sent a PDF that you can sign with a digital stylus, or that you can print out, scan, and return. If you're unsure, then ask someone with legal knowledge for their advice.

While I don't like handing over power to clients like this, it is very often a necessary evil in order to secure the best work.

Other Types of Contract

You won't only be signing contracts relating to the work you're providing. You might also be asked to sign contracts relating to nondisclosure agreements (NDAs). This means you promise not to discuss the nature of the work; this may be necessary if you are working for a client that is planning a big project and doesn't want the details to be leaked to the press or the competition.

Normally an NDA is something you can sign safely, though there are *some* examples of companies using them incorrectly (to prevent whistle blowing for instance). Again, it's worth a thorough read before you sign.

Another common form you might get from foreign clients is to confirm that you are based in whichever location you're based in (this is sometimes necessary for their tax purposes). For instance, if you provide work for a client based in India, then they may need to document that you are not based in India via a Tax Residency Certificate (TRC) Declaration or similar. You might be required to get the form yourself, or you might be sent one to fill out. The same rules apply: make sure you read the document carefully before signing. Foreign clients might also request that you send a scan of your passport or other documentation proving citizenship. This can feel a little invasive, but if you trust the client, it shouldn't be a problem.

Be cynical and very careful, but don't let that sour what could otherwise be a fruitful relationship with a big client.

Writing Contracts

Should you decide to write the contract yourself, then stay calm and don't panic! While anything "legal" can seem daunting, the fact of the matter is that this is actually quite a simple process. Your objective is to write out the agreement that you want your client to accept, in such a way that it is crystal clear what you are both agreeing to, with no room for alternative interpretations.

Try to keep your contract as short as possible. Respect the client's time by not asking them to read through 20 pages of fine print for the sake of a two-hour job. If you need a little help, then ask a pro or consider looking for templates online; there are plenty available!

Most contracts will include the following:

Overview

This is a little like the "upside-down pyramid" approach to writing a news story. The first objective is to succinctly describe who the contract is between (including company names and addresses), to summarize the project/agreement, and then to outline the cost. This is your abstract, or your statement of intent, and you can expand on this later in the document.

Responsibilities

You should also outline what each party is agreeing to. That might mean "sticking to deadline" or "paying on time." You should also include what you *aren't* taking responsibility for. For instance, you might agree to build a website but not to upload it to the server or secure a domain name. Expressly state that your client will be responsible for that side of things.

Scope

Similarly, the scope will include all deliverables. Precisely what is the client going to receive and, by extension, what are you agreeing to provide? Make this as explicit as possible. Likewise, be sure to leave room for changes and alterations, however: Will the client have the opportunity to request revisions? How many times? How will such changes be requested?

Ownership

Intellectual property is an important consideration. Does the client own the exclusive rights to the project? Or do you maintain the right to sell this same work on to other clients in the future? Can you use part of the work you've provided to the client? Do they need to credit you for your contribution?

Payment Plan

If you are asking for an up-front deposit, followed by a final payment on receipt, then this would be where you outline that. The same goes for smaller, more regular payments and other payment variations.

Warranties

Do you offer any guarantee with your work? What if there are errors in your code? How long will you offer troubleshooting? Is there a money-back guarantee?

Termination

What will happen if the project doesn't go to plan? How and when can either party pull out of the agreement, and what penalties are incurred for doing so?

Signatures

Of course, you should also include a space for the signatures of both parties. These should also be dated.

Not all contracts require signatures though. In their absence, this will not be binding and will work more as a written informal agreement that serves simply to keep everyone on the same page.

Either way, writing out contracts yourself is generally preferable as it means you get to define the terms of your relationship and keep the balance of power shifted in your favor. Then again, you're still agreeing to do something in a very specific way, and based on terms you have agreed with the client, which is always going to be *somewhat* restrictively. Personally, I prefer to work contract-free wherever possible as it gives me more flexibility.

Keep in mind as well that the protection a contract provides you is only valid if the contract is legally sound *and* if you are actually willing to take action should the client be in breach! Certain clients will ignore their own contracts and very often it's not worth your time pursuing them. So, while this does offer a little assurance, know that you're not completely safe!

Tax

Okay, now the bit that you've been dreading. Get used to that feeling, because you'll be dreading it every year!

If you are self-employed, then that of course means you're going to have to handle your own tax returns; either on your own or with help from an accountant. Either way, this can be stressful, for obvious reasons: you're spending a large amount of money, you can get into trouble if you get it wrong, and it can get quite complex.

Of course, the specifics of how tax is reported and collected is going to vary depending on your location. For that reason, I don't want to go into granular detail explaining how to fill out each form or what can and can't be claimed. What I *am* going to do is explain the basics of how tax works for the self-employed and provide some tips that I hope you can use to make life easier *and* help you to better account for the impact tax is likely to have on your margins.

How Tax Returns Work

First, for the completely uninitiated, let's go over how tax returns actually work and what it means to "take reductions" or "claim back" on your tax. Do you pay less tax? Can you get things for free?

In short, you are going to be taxed on your net *profit*. It doesn't matter how much money comes into your business; what really matters is how much money you get to keep at the end of the day. So, if someone pays you $1,000 to build a website, but you hire a designer to help for $200, then you're only going to be taxed on the remaining $800. (Except you need to multiply this process and calculate your total profit for all the jobs you completed that year.)

While you're only going to be charged for profit, you do need to *know* your other numbers—such as how much money came into your business (called your revenue).

So, to fill out your tax return, you will be using the following information:

- Your revenue (total amount paid to you)

- Your expenses (total amount spent on equipment, services, supplies, etc.)

- Your profit (revenue minus expenses)

You'll report this at the end of the tax year (April 15 in the United States and April 5 here in the UK) for the year preceding. In the UK we report to the HMRC (https://www.gov.uk/government/organisations/hm-revenue-customs), and in the United States you'll be making your payments to the IRS (https://www.irs.gov/) using Schedule C of Form 1040. Don't expect these websites to resemble anything made in the post-Geocities era.

Depending on your region, you will be asked to pay an amount of tax based on this profit. In the UK, you can earn up to £11,500 without any tax. Anything over that up to £45,000 will be charged at the "basic rate" of 20%, anything over £45,000 up to £150,000 will be charged at a higher rate of 40%, and anything beyond that is charged at 45%.

So, let's say that you had a revenue of £70,000 (well done!), but you spent £10,000 on computer equipment, software suites, website membership, and advertising (very convenient round numbers here). You'll report both these numbers and you'll be left with £60,000 as your profit for the year. You will pay no tax on the first £11,500—so that will leave you with £48,500 taxable income.

You'll be paying 20% on £33,500 (so that's £6,700) and you'll be paying 40% on the remaining £15,000—which will be £6,000. So, you'll pay a total of £12,700 income tax for the year.

If your total profit was £60,000, then you are now taking home £47,300 after tax.

In the United States the system is very similar, though the precise numbers are different. There are seven different brackets: 10%, 15%, 25%, 28%, 33%, 35%, and 39.6%. These numbers actually vary a little for single professionals versus those with "head of household" status. Ultimately though, you'll still be left with a similar amount of income "after tax."

Except you likely won't get to see all of it, as you'll also likely need to pay things like National Insurance contributions in the UK, SECA Self-Employment Tax in the United States (which includes Medicare and Social Security contributions), student loan repayments in the UK (which also normally increase inline with your total earnings), and so forth. In the United States, you may also be required to make payments to your state tax agency, meaning that the total amount of tax you pay can vary from one state to another.

While you can calculate all of this yourself prior to filing your tax return, it does actually get a little difficult to account for all these different factors and it is one of the major headaches of being self-employed. There are calculators online that can help, or you can make do with a rough estimate. The good news is that when it comes to reporting, you should only need to input your revenue and overheads, and the relevant website will do the rest. If you choose to file your tax return manually by hand (or if that's your only choice), then things might be a little more complex.

Again, I don't want to get into the nitty-gritty here as it's all subject to change anyway. The best advice then is to check the government web pages and then to follow the guidelines you find there. You can also try speaking with an accountant or financial advisor if you need a little extra guidance, or perhaps a well-informed friend.

For now, what you need to know is that:

- You get taxed on profit, not revenue, though you need to know your revenue too.

- Tax increases incrementally as you pass certain income thresholds.

- Even the highest earners will pay lower tax rates up to those thresholds—only the excess income is charged at the higher rate.

- There are other things to pay when you file your return such as national insurance contributions etc. depending on your location.

How you then pay will also vary from region to region. In the UK, you can pay by card, direct debit, or check. You can do this online, by post, or over the phone. Generally, you will pay your tax in two installments: halfway through the tax year, and then again at the end. The first payment is calculated based on your earnings in the preceding year (the assumption being that you will have earned the same amount), while the second payment is known as the "balancing payment" once your tax return has been submitted. This is when you will pay the difference based on how much you actually earned. For this reason, you won't pay any tax at all until you've worked for at least one whole year. Again, things are different depending on where you live, and in the United States you will pay FICA and estimated taxes quarterly.

Depending on your location and preference, it is also possible to pay tax at alternative intervals. For instance, you can choose to use PAYE (Pay As You Earn) in the UK and pay monthly tax contributions as though you were employed. That said, the changing nature of your income means that you will still need to pay a balancing amount. It is also often possible to pay deposits into your online accounts, so that you can space your payments out throughout the year in a manner determined by you.

Keep in mind that it is usually better to keep money in your own accounts as long as possible. This way, you can still make interest on that money, and you will have easier access to it should you have an unexpected expense.

For those in the United States, you can find all the information you need at the IRS Small-Business Tax Centers page (www.irs.gov/businesses/small-businesses-self-employed/tax-centers). The Small Business Administration (SBA) is also a very useful resource: this is a US federal organization created to help small businesses learn what they need to pay. You can find that here: www.sba.gov. SCORE (www.score.org) is also a useful resource as a not-for-profit, free business-mentoring and education network.

For UK-based businesses, Gov.uk has a useful guide to setting up as a sole proprietor here: www.gov.uk/set-up-sole-trader.

For everyone else, a quick Google search should help you to find similar resources relevant to your location.

Claiming Expenses

There is a little bit of misunderstanding and misconception surrounding the concept of "writing off/claiming expenses." Many people seem to think that being self-employed means you can get all sorts of things for free by "deducting them." This is definitely not what's going on!

What deducting expenses really means is that you are going to file something that you have purchased as an overhead/expense. In other words, it will be subtracted from your overall revenue and not included as profit.

So, if you buy something like a laptop that you are going to use for work, you can "write this off," meaning that it won't be counted as income. If I earned $35,000 and I bought a $2,000 laptop, then I can claim for the laptop and my profit will now be $33,000 rather than $35,000.

So, I don't get the laptop free, but I don't need to pay tax on it. And seeing as I would have had to pay 20% tax on said laptop, that means I *could* make the mental argument with myself that it is in fact costing me $1,600 rather than $2,000. While there was no money deducted from the laptop itself, I'm still paying $400 less tax than I would otherwise. So, this becomes a much more calculated expense for me. (Just switch the currency and the rate and the same will be true for wherever you are based.)

The nice thing you may have already have noticed is that we *are* in fact now paying "less tax" than our traditionally employed contemporaries. That's because there's a good chance you would have had to buy a laptop *anyway*. Being self-employed means you can get a nicer one, or pay less overall. Most employed people have a personal laptop/computer they use for browsing Facebook, chatting with friends, watching movies, playing games, and writing documents. As someone who is self-employed, you can make your work laptop double as your home laptop and claim it on tax.

The same goes for a lot of other things, including your mobile phone contract, portions of your electricity bill, your Internet service provider's bill, even your rent! In most areas it is permissible to deduct some of your rent from your taxable income, as long as you calculate what percentage of your home is devoted to work activities.

Again, you likely don't have a bigger house than you would have had otherwise, and therefore you are paying less tax than your friends. And it's all perfectly by the book.[1]

---

[1] If you recall that you aren't paying for a commute or parking either, it starts to become apparent that you can have much more disposable income on a much lower salary by being self-employed!

But this is also where things start to get a bit complicated and a bit muddy—what is an expense and what isn't? Should you claim everything you possibly can?

Dangers of Claiming Too Much

It's important that you read carefully what you can and can't claim as an expense. Depending on your region, this is going to vary drastically. For instance, in the UK it was once possible to claim back any money that you spent on "entertaining clients." That meant that you could take a potential client out to dinner and not pay tax on the cost of that meal for you *or* for them.

But then a lot of people began to take advantage of this (by paying for meals for their family and pretending they were potential clients) and so a few bad eggs ruined it for the rest of us. Today, "entertaining clients" is no longer a valid expense in the UK.

In reality, you can usually get away with blue murder as long as you aren't taking the mick, seeing as no one is going to check your expenses. In fact, in the UK at least, you don't actually have to show your expenses at all! You can simply upload a single number for your overheads and be done with it.

BUT there is the possibility of being audited, in which case you will suddenly have to explain where all that money went. The burden of proof is now on you to demonstrate what each expense was.

That means you are going to need receipts. And if anything is dubious (such as money spent on coffee in Starbucks), then you're going to need to demonstrate why it was a necessary expense and not a *personal* expense.

In the UK, you need to keep tax records for at least five years. This can be pretty painful as it means you're going to need a good filing system capable of storing five years' worth of receipts. Fortunately, in the United States it's a bit less stringent and you only need to maintain your records for three years.

As you can imagine, getting audited is an incredibly stressful and invasive experience and can result in your needing to make large amounts of back payments. It's much better not to push matters and not to draw undue attention to yourself! Then of course there is that whole *moral* angle. After all, you use the same services as everyone else and you're already getting some perks from being self-employed. It only seems right then that you should pay your fair share.

Even if none of this is of concern to you, there are still reasons it isn't particularly wise to claim everything. For one, when you claim a lot of expenses, that means that your official income is lower. Your tax return is the only demonstrable proof of your income, and so this can then make it hard to claim a loan.

So if I were to earn $70,000 one year—a very healthy sum—but then went overboard and invented $50,000 of expenses, my tax return would say that I only earned $20,000! I might think I'm very clever, until I go to the bank to try and get a home loan. They'd see that my income was only $20,000 and thus they wouldn't offer me the amount I needed to buy my dream home.

Our aim then is certainly *not* to push this as far as it will go. In fact, I personally prefer to keep my reported expenses very modest. That way, if I should miscalculate, I know I can still explain my workings. Not only that, but as a sole proprietor who works in tech, my overheads are legitimately very low. Rather than stressing about every receipt for the sake of a few quid (Brit-talk, sorry), I would rather pay a little more tax and avoid the stress. To be honest, the amount of time it would take me to count every train journey to attend a conference could be better spent just *earning more money*. I see this the precise same way as communication overhead.

Plus, it does go to a good cause. For the most part.

(Translation: If you work for the HMRC, please don't audit me . . . I'm good, honest!)

Some Common Expenses

Chances are that if you are a tech entrepreneur, or a B2C service provider working online, your expenses won't be all that high. So, what *could* you claim?

Here are some common categories that might constitute "expenses."

Equipment

The number one expense that many of us will have in the gig economy is our equipment. That's likely to mean a laptop (which is always fair game), but it could also mean things like webcams if you provide Skype coaching. Or it could mean things like graphics tablets if you are a designer, or a smartphone if you use it for your business.

Software

If you use Adobe Creative Cloud, or perhaps an IDE for coding that charges you a one-time fee/monthly subscription, then this can of course also be written off as an expense. Other examples might include virus protection, or Microsoft Office.

Marketing

If you are going to advertise your business via a pay-per-click (PPC) campaign, or even a magazine ad, then the money you spend here would be considered an overhead.

Premises

As I briefly mentioned, it is possible to claim a small portion of household bills back as a sole proprietor. That might mean a percentage of your electricity bill, your phone bills, your Internet service bill, even your heating bill and rent. This will be based on a calculation that takes into consideration the amount of space that is dedicated to work, and the amount of time you spend working there.

Of course, if you do happen to rent an office, or if you spend money to work in a co-working space, then that is fair game for a deduction too.

Supplies

Ink cartridges, paper, paperclips, packaging ... keep your receipts!

Mileage

If you drive to meet clients, or get the train to attend a tradeshow, then this can be claimed back too.

Loans and Bank Charges

If you have taken out a business loan, or a PayPal loan, then you can claim back the interest paid. And if this loan was spent 100% on your business expenses, then of course you can claim back the entire amount very easily too!

Likewise, you also don't need to pay tax on the fees that PayPal charges, or any other bank fees.

Services

You can claim back any services that you use in order to provide your own work. For instance, if you are a coder but you use a designer to create graphics, then you *either* charge the client for that expense *or* you can include it in your price but then claim back the overhead.

VAT

VAT is value-added tax and is something you will need to consider if your turnover exceeds a certain amount. Here in the UK, that's set at £85,000 per year. The US has something very similar called 'Sales Tax'.

VAT is a "consumption" tax that is added to products and services at every "point of sale" where value has been added.

In other words, if money has exchanged hands, then you can bet the seller is going to be required to charge VAT and then remit that to the government. Normally, this VAT charge will be passed on to the buyer.

So, if your business model involves buying wholesale goods, then selling them on to client, you'll need to pay VAT to the wholesaler because they have provided value, and you'll also need to charge VAT to your own customers because you've *added value* by making the goods available and delivering them. In the UK, VAT is set at 20%.

In the United States, Sales Tax is charged at the state level rather than federal level. This means it varies between states, anywhere from 1% to 16%. Tax is *not* usually added when products are exported to other countries, however.

As a consumer, you will likely have experienced VAT as a nice surprise when you reached the checkout. Companies often don't like declaring the VAT charge up front as that isn't the amount "they" are charging as such, and they don't feel that they should have to scare away their customers with what looks like a 20% higher cost. It's up to you how you want to play that.

If your turnover exceeds the VAT threshold in your location, then you will need to register for VAT and then charge your customers for the goods and services that qualify for VAT. BUT you will also get the nice bonus of being able to reclaim VAT that you pay on goods and services yourself.

Types of Business: Sole Proprietor vs. Business Entity

If you are self-employed, then you are technically a business owner. Congratulations! Even if you just cut your neighbor's hair, that still counts.

But there are many different types of business owner that you can be. In that example, you would be what is known as a "sole trader" or "sole proprietor," which means you are a single entity who provides a service or product and doesn't *usually* employ any staff (though this is not a requirement). If you are a tech entrepreneur planning to build websites, provide coding, or write articles, then chances are it will make the most sense for you to register as a sole proprietor.

Registering as a sole proprietor is much easier and more straightforward than setting up other types of business. Registering as a sole proprietor in most cases means nothing more than registering yourself to start paying tax i.e. registering as self-employed. There is no additional separate process required. Here, you *are* the business in a legal sense. It is not a separate entity. That in turn does mean that you inherently take on a little more risk. There is no such thing as your "business going bankrupt" . . . that just means *you* are going bankrupt! But it also explains why it is so much easier to set up from an administrative standpoint, whereas becoming a limited liability company is a significantly more confusing task.

Becoming Limited/Incorporated

Here in the UK, the most common next "step up" from being a sole proprietor is to set up a limited business - the close US equivalent of which is the limited liability company. A limited liability company will have the suffix LLC (or LTD for a limited business), and that essentially refers to the "limited liability" that the individual has for the company's debt. The owners will pay income tax, while the company itself will pay corporation tax. The responsibility for the company's debt is normally limited to the amount that the owners have personally invested.

In the United States, it is also common to see the Inc. suffix, which refers to an "incorporated" business. An incorporated company will act as an entirely separate legal entity. That means that money owed by the business will *not* be owed by the individual. Your finances will also be separate, and rather than keeping all of your income, you will need to set yourself a salary.

There are several benefits of being a limited or incorporated business. For one, you will be taking on less financial risk. Any loans will be repayable by the business rather than by you personally, and if your company should file for bankruptcy, it won't affect you in the same way. While sole proprietors normally *can* take on employees as long as they file the right forms and pay the right bills and taxes, it is easier to do this as an LTD or Inc. Apart from anything else, this will protect you legally from lawsuits that employees sometimes like to launch at their employers!

Likewise, it is easier for an incorporated businesses to take on certain types of client. Some clients might feel adverse to taking on sole proprietors for instance, as they run the risk of becoming viewed as employees (which then means more expense and legal work for the "employer"). If you work full time for a single company, you might legally be forced to register as employed rather than self-employed. This is something to keep in mind yourself: you can't "freelance" for just one client!

Finally, the clear divide between you and your business will make tax reporting a little easier in some cases—as it will be very clear what was a business expense and what was a personal expense.

There are more fees associated with setting up either of these types of business, however, as well as significantly greater administrative challenges. That's why many people will choose to keep things simple - at least to begin with - by remaining as a sole proprietor.

A limited liability company (LLC) is usually effectively a partnership: a business that can have multiple owners (called "members"). An LLC is less complex than a corporation but still needs to offer stock and it still pushes you further on the spectrum toward "administrative nightmare."

The next "step up" from being an LTD or LLC is to become a fully fledged corporation. At this point though, you're getting away from what we would traditionally call gigging!

Independent Contractor

Another option for freelancers is to become "independent contractors" (defined by the IRS here: www.irs.gov/businesses/small-businesses-self-employed/independent-contractor-defined). This means that you are working on a per-contract basis, and if you consider the "evolution" of working relationships with clients, this is basically what is found at the extreme end—where you are more committed to a single company but are not "employed" by them technically.

Independent contractors are still considered self-employed but may pay their tax differently and may or may not receive benefits from their employers such as sick leave, maternity leave, and so forth. Contractors *can* work for more than one company at a time, or might change organization on a month-to-month basis. The problem is that very often an employee will work solely for a single company over the course of several years and still be misclassified as an independent contractor. In other cases, the term independent contractor is effectively interchangeable with freelancer and has little actual impact on the way you work.

According to the IRS, "misclassification" of workers is rife, and this is actually one of the bigger dangers of the gig economy as a whole. Companies often feel it is in their best interests to misclassify their long-term employees as contractors, as that means they are not required to pay their Medicare and Social Security contributions. It also means that they *can* avoid having to offer holiday pay, health insurance, company pensions, dental coverage, and other benefits (though some will still offer this). It also means that an employer can let the contractor go at the end of their contract without explanation.

This is where companies like Uber, FedEx, Grubhub, and similar have faced criticism and legal challenges. And it very often leaves the contractor in an unfavorable position, as they find themselves with all the drawbacks of being employed (no flexibility, requirement to work set hours) and none of the benefits (sick pay, job security).

The gig economy is potentially incredibly beneficial to those of us that are willing to take responsibility for our own income, time, and budget. The danger is that it also makes it possible for companies to take advantage of their employees, especially those that are nervous to go "all in" and are tempted by the seemingly favorable compromise offered by a long-term contract.

The key, as I have said already multiple times throughout this book, is to make sure that the balance of power is firmly in your court. And this will depend on everything from the way you communicate to the way you structure your business.

Company Name

If you're a sole proprietor, then your business name may be your actual name, but you can still choose to trade under a different title called your "trading name" should you wish. You can then include this on things like invoices and letters. This also gives you the opportunity to create a logo that can help from a branding perspective.

There are only a few limits on the names you can use. You are not generally permitted to use "sensitive" words in your company name, for instance (Virgin was likely skirting this rule!); likewise, you can't use existing trademarks or other registered business names. Finally, you can't have "Ltd" or "LLC" in your company name unless that is an accurate description of your business structure! If you want to stick something professional sounding at the end of your name, then consider "Productions" or "Studios."

If you want to make sure that no one else can use your trading name/logo, then you will need to secure a trademark, usually via the US Patent and Trademark Office (www.uspto.gov) or your country's equivalent (it's the Intellectual Property Office in the UK: IPO.gov.uk). The first step is to make sure no one else has already trademarked the name (a good thing to check even if you don't intend on paying for the rights). After that, you can expect to pay somewhere in the region of a few hundred dollars in order to secure the exclusive rights for ten years.

Tips for Easy Accounting

Keeping track of all your revenue and your expenses might seem like a huge challenge, but if you go about it logically, it really needn't be that bad. Here are some tips that can help a great deal.

Use PayPal

Maybe you balked at the PayPal fees and decided it wasn't for you. That's fine. But if you *do* use PayPal or a similar service, then this can make your life a lot easier. You can quickly generate a spreadsheet of all your income over a set period, and if this includes the lion's share of what you got paid, then that will make life very easy.

Better yet, why not make your business purchases using PayPal too? I conduct the vast majority of all my buying through PayPal, and that means I can calculate my income and expenses for an entire year in a few hours max. In fact, if I make a business purchase through my PayPal account, then only my net profit need ever be withdrawn into my bank balance.

Use Invoices/Keep a Spreadsheet

If you opt to go another route, then this is where writing those invoices will benefit you as much as the clients. Keep a folder on your computer (ideally backed up to the cloud) and put all your invoices in here. Now when it comes to calculating your tax, you can just open them all up, look at the amounts, and calculate their sum total.

You can do the exact same thing for your expenses: just put any invoices you get sent into a single folder, along with any e-mail receipts.

Better yet, keep track of these as you go by updating a spreadsheet—or use one of many accounting apps that will help you to do this more easily. If you're a coder, why not make your own?

Go Paperless

There was a time that you had to keep a physical copy of every single monthly statement your bank sent you. That's a lot of pointless paperwork and a big filing cabinet!

These days, online banking gives us the option to go paperless. That will make your life significantly easier, not to mention being far kinder to the planet. Likewise, you should also be able to get your energy company, landlord/ mortgage company, and so forth to all send you bills via e-mail.

Banks are still going to send you pointless written correspondence (I'm offered a credit card about one a month) and this is incredibly frustrating. But hey, it is what it is until lawmakers sort them out.

You can go paperless yourself by scanning/photographing documents and receipts, and then shredding the originals. You'll even find programs with optical character recognition (OCR) that attempt to sort these for you automatically, and there are plenty of useful apps for this (such as Expensify: www.expensify.com). A shredder is a good investment for any business owner or freelancer, as it will also help you to keep your personal data safe.

Company Account

Another useful tip is to set up a company account. This means opening up a separate bank account into which all income will be paid and from which all expenses will be taken. This not only helps to avoid confusion between personal and business costs, but it also means that your bank statement will pretty much provide all the information you could need for your tax returns or even an auditor.

While your business might not be a separate legal entity if you are a sole proprietor, most banks will still let you set up a business account if you like. But to be honest, it doesn't even need to be a business account! As long as you have a separate bank account that is dedicated to work-related transactions, then you're good to go.

Preparing for Pay Day

Another very important bit of planning you'll need to do if you're self-employed is to prepare for those tax payments.

The best rule is simply to take a third of whatever you earn and to stick it into a separate savings account. Once you've paid your tax, you can put anything left over into a savings account. This way, you'll be able to keep things nice and simple, while also earning interest on your turnover throughout the year (another nice little bonus for the self-employed!).

Finding out precisely how much you earn by filing your return as soon as possible (at the end of the tax year) is generally a good idea. This way, you can prepare for the exact figure you need to save for and avoid any unpleasant surprises. If you can calculate the income for the previous year before your first quarterly payment is due, then you can also spread the amount due more equally across the year, rather than making up the difference with huge balancing payments.[2]

And if you *should* get caught short? Then you have options: you could take out a loan (such as a PayPal loan, which we will discuss in Chapter 10), you could ask for an advance from a client, or you could just work a few Saturdays. That's where the flexibility of working in the gig economy can come in handy again.

Just don't bury your head in the sand and hope that this is all going to go away. Checking your accounts on at least a semi-regular basis is a very good idea and can prevent potentially devastating surprises and mistakes. Like so many things, it's not stressful or complicated *as long* as you are proactive!

---

[2]That said, calculating your earnings late can occasionally play into your favor if you've had a much more profitable year than the one prior, as it means the first tax payments will be calculated based on the lower amount and you can hang onto your cash a little longer.

Should You Use an Accountant?

I did warn you going in that this wasn't going to be a fun chapter, and after all of the excitement and promise of the first half of this book, you might have found this to be a rather sour-tasting reality sandwich.

But while it sounds pretty daunting and you might currently be covered in a thin layer of cold sweat, the truth is that it isn't half as bad as it sounds. I've included a lot of broad detail here in the interests of being comprehensive, but I've given you an idea of what you need to look into further to determine what does and doesn't apply to you.

And you know what? Seventy-five percent of what we've covered may well fall into that latter category. Chances are that if you're entering the gig economy as a freelancer, then you are simply providing a service as a sole proprietor, with very minimal overheads.

And if you're willing to pay some small fees to use PayPal, or if you set up a business account with your bank, then accounting is pretty easy too. At the end of the tax year, all you need to do, then, is to get your total revenue, subtract your expenses (which is probably a few pieces of software, a proportion of your bills, and a laptop), and then pay the amount that is automatically generated online. It's really that easy.

In other words: no, you don't *necessarily* need an accountant (you could also consider looking into tax preparation software).

An accountant *can* save you a big headache by handling all your reporting and taxes for you. And in theory they should "pay for themselves" by saving you more money on expenses than they charge (they might set you back several hundred dollars depending on the individual service). The other good news is that you may be able to write off those expenses too!

One of the biggest benefits of going through an accountant is that it gives you some authority and some sense of security. Should you ever be audited, then you can just direct the auditor to your accountant. If you ever need to take out a loan, then having a tax return signed by an accountant can help you to gain the trust of the lenders, and so forth.

And sometimes an accountant will be necessary. For a sole proprietor in the UK, filing a tax return is pretty simple. But if you're setting up a limited liability company that needs to pay sales tax in the United States, then you might be looking at a whole lot more paperwork. In that case, an accountant might absolutely be necessary—and certainly a big weight off your shoulders.

But then again, you might find the process of using an accountant is stressful in itself. If you don't have a lot of expenses, then it might not ultimately prove to be worth your while. This is likely to come down to your personal preferences:

there is no right or wrong answer here.[3] My advice is to have a stab at filing a return yourself, and then to involve an accountant if necessary. Note that you should register your business as soon as possible when you start selling your services—even if you aren't earning enough to be charged tax. This will also give you a good opportunity to see the websites and forms you'll be using when you do file your returns.

A quick Google search for "Register a Business" or "Register as a Sole Proprietor" should get you started. Or you can use the resources such as the Small Business Administration website that I provided earlier. Look for the official government page. Ignore third parties that offer to get you up and running for a hefty fee. Those guys you definitely do *not* need.

The Financial Trials of Self-Employment

Whatever type of business you choose, you will find there are one or two things that become a little more difficult for the self-employed financially and legally. We've looked at a lot of positives so far, and so it's only fair that we take a look at the downsides as they relate to your accounting, financing, and more.

Pensions

One downside of being self-employed is that you won't be getting a pension plan from your employer. Instead, you're going to need to sort this out yourself with a private pension. There are good options out there, just don't forget about it until it's too late!

Sick Pay

Another challenge you'll face as someone who is self-employed is the lack of sick pay and health insurance. If you are ill and you can't work, then you don't get paid! And paying for your own health insurance in the US can get very expensive.

This can obviously add insult to injury, and it means that you might be in trouble if you have a long-term chronic illness.

There are a few ways around this. One is to set up some form of passive income to cover these additional expenses and unpredictable situations, which we will look at in the next chapter. Another is to factor a realistic number of "sick days" into your budget (which we'll also look at in the next chapter).

---

[3]For the curious: I do my own accounting!

If you have an ongoing medical condition, research what benefits are available in your area if any. You may find that you are eligible for certain government assistance depending on your circumstances.

Another good idea is to look into disability insurance that will pay out should you find yourself unable to work for an extended period of time. Shop around for health insurance and factor it into the price that you charge. Remember that this is what your employers would be doing were you to work a regular job. Only they also factor in costs such as the cost of renting an office, and covering maternity leave. You can charge less for your services than a big employer and still keep enough left over for health insurance. It just stings when you see so much of your hard earned cash disappearing before you've even had a chance to spend any of it!

Leave/Vacation

Yep, you guessed it: there is also no annual leave or holiday pay. If you want to take a week of holiday, then that's coming out of your salary, bub! Likewise, depending on where you're located in the world, you might also find there is no paternity/maternity pay offered by the state.

Remember: we're saving money in many other ways by paying less tax (by being able to write off expenses) and by removing the need for a commute. This is simply something to keep in mind when budgeting.

Loans/Lease/Finance

One last problem you may run into as a member of the gig economy is that no one quite knows what to do with you. That is to say, that as someone who is self-employed, you might struggle when dealing with more "traditional" financial institutions. Getting a loan can be tricky, as can getting rented accommodation. The problem is that these organizations want proof that you're always going to be able to pay the bills/loan repayments. When you're self-employed, there are no such assurances (at least from their perspective).

The best thing you can do? Keep your affairs in good order. Make sure that you aren't trying to claim back too much, avoid taking on unnecessary debt (consider a PayPal loan, discussed in Chapter 10), definitely make sure to keep your credit history in good repair, and try to demonstrate that your income is *increasing* year-on-year rather than going the other way. While you can't provide pay slips, you *can* provide your tax returns, letters from accountants, and potentially letters from your long-term clients who can provide assurance that they will be using your services for a while.

As more and more people enter the gig economy, this will become less of a challenge. But for now, be prepared to fight a little with those that you need to borrow from!

Chapter Summary

This has been a painful chapter, no doubt. But you should feel proud of yourself: we've gone over all of the most potentially officious aspects of being self-employed that are necessary to create a business that is run the way it should be. Once you've handled the basics, then you can officially say that you are self-employed/a business owner. Exciting stuff!

What's more is that this is all going to lead to even more exciting opportunities and possibilities. While budgeting and looking at expenses might seem pretty dry, you're going to learn in the next chapter that this really isn't the case. In fact, you're going to learn how through understanding the numbers, you can potentially create the lifestyle you've always wanted.

Lifestyle Design

If you are a sole proprietor, then effectively you *are* your business.

In that way, your business and your personal life are effectively inseparable. And while this can sometimes be a bad thing, we're also going to see why this can be an incredibly *good* thing. Because once you remove the arbitrary separation between "work" and "life," you start to realize that you have *much* greater freedom to live the precise lifestyle you choose. This is one of the true benefits of entering the gig economy.

This is the central idea behind "lifestyle design"—a concept popularized by Tim Ferriss in *The 4-Hour Workweek*, but that has been doing the rounds online for a while now. By understanding lifestyle design and how it relates to the gig economy, you can create a whole new kind of work-life balance.

What Is Lifestyle Design?

To understand lifestyle design, you simply have to flip a common sequence on its head. Because for those in traditional employment, the sequence goes like this:

Find job → Design lifestyle to fit around job

In other words, our lifestyle is dictated by our work. We need job security, so we look for the job first. That will then dictate precisely where we live, our disposable income, the kinds of luxuries we can afford . . . even the number of hours we have spare in the evenings.

Using lifestyle design, though, means flipping this, like so:

© Adam Sinicki 2019
A. Sinicki, *Thriving in the Gig Economy*, https://doi.org/10.1007/978-1-4842-4090-8_8

Choose the lifestyle you want → Design the job to fit around that

This is the "lifestyle business," a transformative way of thinking about work. Suddenly, your entire life isn't orbiting around your career: instead your career is playing second fiddle to your life.

This doesn't necessarily require you to be self-employed either. Rather, lifestyle design simply means setting up your business or career in such a way as to provide a foundation from which to build the life you want *outside* of work.

Let's say for instance that you decide you want to have more time to spend with family, that this is the number one priority for you (and a good priority it is too!). In that case, you might decide that you don't necessarily want to take on a high-paying job as the CEO of a huge corporation. While that might conform to traditional notions of success and achievement, it also means taking on a huge amount of stress, and spending more and more time in the office.

Maybe you originally just wanted to provide for your family. But what you hadn't realized is that in spending so much time away from them (and being emotionally unavailable the rest of the time), you're actually *hurting* them.

What's more is that you inevitably get accustomed to a certain quality of life and end up increasing your living expenses, thereby leaving yourself with the same slim amount of disposable income at the end of it all. The stress and debt is still there, in fact it is amplified.

So instead, maybe you do a "career 180" and decide you're going to be a garbage collector. Seems like a bad move, right? Until you realize that they're actually paid well enough for what they do, and that you could drop your commute into the city, thereby reducing your overheads significantly. More to the point, the hours are often very good. You might do a morning shift starting at 12 a.m. that allows you to get home by 1 p.m.

Now you're spending significantly more time with your family! You've achieved the thing you wanted to achieve, all the quicker. And when you get home, you get to "switch off from work."

But let's say that you don't want to give up on your current career trajectory. How about taking another option: working four days a week instead of five? You can almost always wrangle this with a boss if you know how to sweet talk them into it (and if not, then you could make a horizontal move and find an organization that *will* let you work this way). Go back to some of the negotiation techniques suggested in Chapter 4 if you want advice on how to broach this.

Again, you now have more time with your family, and more time to do the things you love. This is an *option*.

But what if you don't want that pay cut either? Well in that case, you could always choose to let students stay in your spare room. You could teach piano lessons in the evening or run a side hustle. Or you could look at your expenses and see if you can't *save* nearly one day's worth of pay per week.

In other words, there are many more factors and variables that impact on your income and lifestyle than most of us readily consider. Playing around with these can let you create the life you really want.

The Trap

Too many of us will find ourselves stuck in jobs that are well paid and perhaps even cognitively rewarding … but just aren't what we want (and many more of us will find ourselves in this pickle with jobs we *don't* enjoy).

The problem is that this is all we've been taught: that success means wearing a suit and getting to shout at people, regardless of what that does for our blood pressure. That taking risks is irresponsible when you have a family to provide for—and that anything other than traditional employment *is* a massive risk. We're so "risk averse" that we ignore the risks that we're facing *right now*.

We believe there is some kind of honor in working long hours and grafting hard. Staying at the office until 10 p.m. means you are conscientious or a team player. Working harder makes you a better person. Even if that work isn't particularly valuable. Even if that work means attending pointless meetings about how to market staplers, where nothing ultimately gets decided.

Working *in itself* is not something to be proud of. Doing meaningful work *is*. And so is looking after your family. But we mustn't conflate those things.

What's more is that we feel as though we're working toward some kind of green pasture. We think that when we become highly successful, we'll then be able to quit our job and retire to spend all that time with our families. We think that when we're successful our stress will drop away. We look forward to the day we retire.

But why are you waiting until you're old and gray to start enjoying life? What if you die tomorrow?

So many people have told me that they regret missing out on their children's younger years because they weren't home in time to tuck them in. The things I regret are not going on certain holidays, not taking certain opportunities because I was 'too busy'.

And what if—most tragically of all—you already actually had all the income and the success you needed to start enjoying life today but just didn't realise it? Your family won't benefit as much from an extra $2,000 per year as you think: they'd probably rather spend more time with you! Especially if you could just as easily get that same $2K by driving less and cutting some bills.

Don't aim to retire happy. Aim to love your work and your lifestyle so much that you don't feel the *need* to retire at all. Be happy now!

(Get a private pension just in case though.)

Were I a cynic, I might suggest that "the system" benefits from perpetuating fear and false expectations that drive us toward conventional employment. I might suggest that the promise of a golden retirement isn't that far removed from a similar promise that was once hung prominently for all to see:

> *Arbeit macht frei.*

Wow, that got heavy quick.

But I'm not that cynical, honest. I included this because I think it's an apt analogy and an example of how the promise of distant 'freedom' can cause us to endure even the most inhumane circumstances (not that most of us endure anything that is even comparable to that). In reality, I don't think there's any evil conspiracy going on here. I simply believe it's a hangover from a time when these tools didn't exist. We haven't yet adapted to our new way of life and the possibilities it brings.

And the system is so bloated and tired that it's going to take decades for it to catch up. If it doesn't collapse on itself first.

But you don't need to wait. You can create a job that you can love *right now*. That means pursuing goals and ambitions, yes, but not acting out of fear or trying to fulfill someone else's ideal of success.

What REALLY makes you feel alive? For me, among other things, it's working out. And so, I always make sure that I can fit in my workout first thing in the morning and start work at 10 a.m. rather than 9 a.m. I get to write and vlog about working out, and I get to test fitness trackers. I'm working on building a fitness app. Much of this work is stuff I can't *wait* to do more of.

Another interest is technology of course, and so I ensure that my work either involves writing about fitness and technology *or* working on apps, websites, and other online projects.

Likewise, I love spending time with my family and friends and being there for them—so I ensure I'm able to drop everything when I need to if my wife needs to be picked up from work, or if I want to meet a friend for lunch. I have side projects that I am highly enthusiastic about, like my blog, so I spend one day a week working purely on that (it brings in a little passive income, so it pays for itself). I make sure this is possible by working that little bit extra the other days.

I also make sure I have time for writing books like this one, and for learning: I'll be taking a fitness training course soon so that I have a qualification to demonstrate my knowledge in that area. I'm growing my career in a way that is dictated entirely by me.

I like focusing deeply on my work, and I like working in coffee shops—so I try to stay away from work that ties me down and keeps me in the house/office. I've had to compromise a little on that though, in order to take on some opportunities that will ultimately benefit my career. But this way *my* decision.

Likewise, I've had to compromise a little in other areas to ensure that I have enough steady income to afford the quality of life I want. I do keep a number of "boring adult" expenses down though (clothes, alcohol, etc.), so that I can invest more in tech and save enough money for a rainy day. Or a similarly wet kitchen floor, which is the challenge I'm currently facing as a homeowner thanks to a leaky pipe.

I even manage to travel more often than most friends. I can take my work with me on the go, and sometimes I go away for "working weekends" with a friend who also works online. I take smaller weekend trips, and that way I'm able to visit more countries. I also have the significant advantage of being friends with a pilot who can get me cheap flights to Europe. Last year, we picked a random destination at his airline and flew to Dortmund, Germany for a Christmassy weekend! We called it "travel roulette"!

This is all a huge juggle, but I have a system that works for me and that is *just* flexible enough to support things going wrong, or interruptions to my usual workflow. While there are times that I am stressed, I also have plenty of time to relax with my wife, read good books, and play on my Nintendo Switch. And while there are days I find myself writing about plumbing, I am constantly working on numerous big projects that I find highly rewarding. And I'm seeing constant progress in my career that spurs me on to keep going.

It's a constant process of refinement though, and of adapting to changes in your lifestyle. Your advantage is that you *can* refine and adapt. You can reduce your hours or increase them at *any* point. You can increase your rates, or switch industries. No one is going to stop you.

Find what you love and do more of that *right now*. And I can almost guarantee you that this does *not* require you to be a high-flying CEO.

Your Job Isn't the Be-All and End-All

Overcoming this flawed thinking means coming to two realizations:

- You don't need to get all of your career satisfaction from your job.

- Your salary doesn't dictate your income, let alone your wealth.

Most of us feel as though we need to be traditionally successful because that's what we always aimed for and that's what our parents and teachers wanted for us. We want to be able to feel as though we're successful and as though we've "made it." Maybe we want to be intellectually challenged, or to create something we can be proud of.

But then why does that sense of accomplishment and forward momentum need to come from your work? What if you were to take on a job that would just pay the bills, and then use your spare time to pursue something more meaningful? Maybe you could write a novel, maybe you could work on art, maybe you could compete in some kind of sport?

This comes down to that whole "what do you do?" question that gets asked so often at parties: you shouldn't define yourself by your job. Income shouldn't be your one barometer for success. And it certainly shouldn't be how you define your identity.

A lot of people want to be rich, or at least financially successful. This is something else that many of us have been taught to desire. So, we climb the ladder in our organization, again taking on more and more responsibility and sacrificing more and more of our freedom.

But your income alone is *not* the sole determinant of your wealth, as we have already seen. In just the same way as we calculated the income of our business while filing tax returns, we can do a similar calculation for our own personal wealth. That means

Income – Overheads = Wealth

So, if your salary is high but your overheads are also high, then you might actually earn *less* than someone who has a low income and low expenses. If you need more money, you don't necessarily need to work more. You can just spend less. Or look for other ways to bring in cash.

You can earn more by running side hustles, by selling items, by investing more wisely, and so on. Your aim is to be comfortable and to support the lifestyle you want, and once you realize that your job isn't the only way to do that, the world is your oyster.

Lifestyle Design and the Gig Economy

Lifestyle design is a powerful idea, but its potential goes through the roof once we combine this notion with the gig economy!

After all, if you're working for no fixed amount and you can choose how much work to take on at any given point . . . if you're completely location independent and you can choose precisely what *kind* of work you want to do

...well, then, the options are truly limitless. And the lines between your work and your lifestyle will become significantly more blurred.

Here are some examples.

Your Personal Turnover

When you're self-employed, you start to think of your money in an entirely different way. You realize that time and money really *are* interchangeable. My friends always find it funny how I often won't be bothered to take faulty items back to the store, or to complain about bad service. Why? Because in the time it would take me to do that, I can easily earn the same amount of money or more!

Likewise, I'll often take the train places instead of driving because I can work on the train and thereby end up finishing the journey in profit rather than at a deficit.

Let's say that you decide you want to take the day off. We've established that you're not going to get vacation pay, but you do still have a bunch of other options:

- Work an hour extra each day of the week to make up for that time
- Sell something larger and use that time to take the day off
- Reduce your expenses for that week

Sometimes I will see something I'd really like to buy, but know it is a bit of an indulgence. In order to afford it guilt-free, then, I will simply work an extra hour or two that night and thereby gain the money back!

Or conversely, I might decide *not* to buy something I would normally invest in and then to instead finish work a little early. Money, time, *stuff* ... it's all one interchangeable currency!

Long-Term Profits

Want to get rich but don't want to spend your life working? Another quick and easy option is to drastically reduce your expenses. For example, move to a smaller home in a less expensive area and thereby massively increase your disposable income. You could do that for just a few years and then invest in a big, beautiful home with the money you save.

In fact, you could even move abroad where the same income might allow you to live like a king! If you're self-employed, you are "location independent" and that means you can create the ultimate ratio of income-to-living expense!

Work You Love

Being self-employed means that you should be able to do more work that you love, and end up feeling far more rewarded as a result. This should always be one of the ultimate goals of anyone entering the gig economy. Not only will doing work that you love help you to work faster and more efficiently (thus meaning you earn more money), but it will also mean that you won't resent the time that you do spend working for others.

You know what they say: if you love what you do, then you'll never work a day in your life!

And then of course there's the fact that you don't have to do *one thing* at all. As we discussed in Chapter 1, you can provide 20 different services and ensure that every single day is completely different from the last!

Unlimited Possibilities

I'm having trouble choosing which options to describe here because there are literally *unlimited* possibilities in terms of how you want to design your lifestyle.

For instance, maybe you don't need more money but you *would* like to move nearer to your friends. Again, working online as part of the gig economy means you can live *anywhere*. Want to move to your old hometown and meet up with your friends for lunch? You got it! Heck, you could visit your mom every day and make her front room your office.

If you want more spare time, then you can work 16-hour days two and a half days of the week and then have the rest of the time to do whatever you want!

Lifestyle Design—Making It Work for You

As you just read, the idea of lifestyle design has a lot of potential to make you happier, healthier, and wealthier. So now the next question is how you're going to take this attractive-yet-abstract concept and turn it into a concrete set of goals that you can actually work toward by leveraging the possibilities of the gig economy.

Goal Setting

So, step one would be to imagine the perfect life that you want to achieve. If you had no limitations, then where would you live? What would your house look like? How would you spend your time?

What things matter to you most? Would you like to travel and experience the world? Do you want to do creative, meaningful work, or do you want to spend more time with your family in a beautiful, comfortable home?

Start with a kind of vision—an abstract picture of the life you want—and then narrow this down to a more concrete set of goals. These could be

- Travel to X number of countries per year
- Work no more than five hours a day
- Take a three-hour lunch break
- Contribute to a top-selling mobile app
- Continue to build your portfolio so that you can increase your hourly rate
- Earn over $100,000 a year
- Work only on projects you truly enjoy
- Buy a five-bedroom house

(I'm suggesting you pick one or two of these . . . not all of them!)

Once you've got an idea of the kind of lifestyle you want, then you can start to think about different business models that would allow you to get there. How much time off would you need? How much would you need to earn?

Budgeting

The next step is budgeting. Budgeting becomes very important if you truly want to benefit from lifestyle design. And here's why . . .

Most likely, wherever you are located and whatever your current lifestyle, you will require a certain amount of income per month to maintain that way of life. Once you know how much that is, then you can set some more concrete goals for yourself again.

So, if you know that you need $150 per day to live in your current home and enjoy your current way of life, and your goal is to work no more than five hours a day, then your objective becomes simple: establish some gigs that will let you earn that amount, in that amount of time. OR look at other aspects of your lifestyle that you can change in order to need less money to live on.

Maybe you could remove an expense. (Stop paying for Netflix, for instance, and you can finish half an hour earlier on one day of the month perhaps. Cancel your gym membership and train from home and maybe you can work an hour less!)

Budgeting is also very important for a whole host of other reasons. It will allow you to avoid getting into financial trouble as a household, for instance, by making sure that you have enough money to live and an emergency fund for unexpected expenses. At the same time, it will ensure you can keep saving toward any goals and so forth.

Obviously, being self-employed means that your income is going to be somewhat variable,[1] and that's why the aim should be to create a budget based on a sensible "minimum" income that you're going to aim to earn every day and every month. (Setting a daily target can also be easier to track and motivate yourself toward.)

Financial Modeling

Create a spreadsheet that includes all of your income (revenue streams) using conservative estimates, and all of your expenses/overheads. That means business expenses *and* personal ones. If all has gone well, then you should be left with some excess cash at the end of the month, and if you multiply this by a certain number of months, then you can calculate how long it would take you to save toward something such as a holiday.

This is called financial modeling—creating "models" of your accounts and then calculating projections into the future.

You can also use this same spreadsheet to try out alternative futures and possibilities. What if you were to cut one of those expenses? How would this impact your monthly profits? How would that affect your savings in five months' time? Financial modeling this way gives you a kind of crystal ball for looking into alternate potential futures.

Make sure that your spreadsheet uses your income *after tax* to calculate your finances. AND make sure that it includes a whole lot of extra budget to deal with things that could potentially go wrong. You should definitely have a buffer in your daily budget *and* you should definitely have a "rainy day fund."

While financial modeling is very useful, it will typically fail to account for the unknown unknowns. In other words, you need to prepare for the furnace breaking, the car brakes needing replacing (this cost my wife and me £340 the

---

[1]As we saw in Chapter 7, even when your clients are incredibly stable, you will still be at the mercy of external factors like changing fees and exchange rates.

other day), and all the other things that could go wrong. You can try testing these scenarios, or even try to calculate a rough average for your "unexpected costs" and split this across the year. There's always an element of guesswork however.

You can use this budget as well to test out different numbers of days off. That way you can see how many days off you can afford while still moving toward your goals and stashing some savings. Or you can see what other factors you might need to tweak to be able to take off *more* time.

You can also use similar modeling to see how you might be able to invest more money into aspects of your business (such as marketing) and then calculate how that might impact your profits over time.

Optimizations

In Chapter 5, we looked at several ways you could work more efficiently: either by improving your own concentration and focus, or by looking at "process fixes" in order to streamline your workflow.

Whatever the case, these can then help you to continue earning the same amount of money in less time—thereby helping you to either work less or earn more in the same amount of time. Either way, when you aren't tied to your desk for a set number of hours, being able to work faster and more efficiently will start to benefit your private life too.

In short, if you know how much you need to earn (including the buffer), and you can do that in half an hour ... well, then, you only need to work for half an hour! Find ways to cut this down and you will find it's much easier to write the budget that will allow you to live the lifestyle you're going for.

The Right Kinds of Clients

Of course, all of this feeds back into finding the right kinds of client for the work style that you have chosen. Gigging means you can negotiate the precise type of work you want to do—not only in the grand scheme, but also when discussing work with each *individual* client.

So, you need to think about the type of lifestyle that you've imagined for yourself and your family, and then look at the kind of work that will fit with that. Do you want to work on short-term projects through an agency that will give you steady and reliable work/income? Or would you rather work on longer-term projects and have more flexibility over the way you divide your time (in which case, you're going to need to be a lot more disciplined)?

Do you want to get into a nice routine that fits around your family and friends? In that case, finding recurring work might make sense. Or, do you thrive on the freedom and unpredictable nature of doing different jobs nearly every other day?

If you plan on traveling a lot, then you will probably want to stay away from clients that require you to have lots of Skype calls at specific times, or to be on Slack.

And again, this doesn't have to mean picking the *one kind* of work that is best for you. You will very likely find that a mix of long-term clients with set hours, one-off clients, and haphazard clients is ultimately what gives you the right balance of freedom and security.

Using your own vision for your lifestyle and your budget, you'll find that it's a lot easier to look at the terms of a contract, or the payment methods offered by a client, and then decide if this is right for you.

Create Rules

Whatever you end up designing as your work-life balance, however much work you choose to take on, and whatever hours you choose to work for, it is also now important that you come up with *some* kind of structure in order to make sure you can survive this way and that you are working toward the lifestyle you envisage for yourself.

This might seem to somewhat negate the benefits of being able to work how and when you want. But the difference here is that the rules are rules that *you* are introducing. And were I to get really philosophical, I might say something about discipline being necessary for true freedom.

No one is mandating when you must work, or where. But if you don't make these rules yourself, then it's all too easy to give yourself breaks all over the place and end up falling behind or letting clients down.

Want to break your working day into two halves and have a three-hour lunch break? That's fine. But make this a rule and stick to it.

Want to alter the amount you work based on your current income and outlays? Fine: but you still need to be disciplined once you've done this and create that minimum earnings target in order to ensure you're always bringing home enough to live on.

In other words, due to the lack of hard and fast rules, it is now up to you to regulate *yourself* and to introduce some discipline into your routine. You need to be your own manager, and you'll find that you can occasionally be a difficult employee! These rules should be in service of achieving the lifestyle you want though, and therefore they are ultimately going to give you *more* freedom in the long term.

More Rules

Rules can also regard prioritizing things in your life outside of work. For instance, I have a rule that if a friend or family member needs me, that will trump even the most important project for a client. Likewise, I have a rule that I will never *not* go to the gym because I have a busy day. That might sound a little reckless (I'm sure my clients won't be thrilled to read this), but ultimately if I want to stay in shape, I believe that's the way it has to be. Remember: I work to support the lifestyle I want, so it only follows that said lifestyle should take priority! As soon as this changes, something has gone wrong with my management.

As I mentioned before though, I also have a rule that I will *always* earn at least $150 per day. Rules like this simply help to avoid stressful decision making and provide a useful compass when navigating a sea of work and opportunities. If I fail to earn that money, then I will need to find a way to make it back.

I recommend writing your rules down somewhere. The same goes for daily to-do lists, which can help to provide a little structure for the day, week, or month ahead (organizing these into "must-dos" and "should-dos" is also useful).

The best analogy to draw here is getting into shape. If you want to build more muscle or burn more fat, then you should have an idea of where you want to be. What do you want to look like? How are you going to measure progress? What type of training will you use to get there?

But while the vision is what will motivate you and guide you, that should *not* be your focus. Focus on a long-term goal like "lose 20 pounds in one year" and you'll find it's all too easy to make excuses or put things off. If you don't train today, you can always train tomorrow. You've got ages before you need to reach that target anyway ...

And you may find you've been working hard the last week and you're no closer to your goal. Pretty demotivating! And very tempting to give up.

Before you know it, a year has passed and you've actually *gained* weight! The goal was simply too distant and too intangible.

The best way to reach a goal like this then is to use that "vision" to inform the smaller steps you'll take every day. Those become micro goals, and those are *all* you are going to focus on. For instance, your goal is now to

- Work out three times a week
- Eat no more than 2,000 calories per day

These goals are immediate, achievable, and simple. You can pass or fail them on a daily basis, and if they go wrong today, you can simply try again tomorrow. There are no excuses to be made and you know precisely what it is you need to do. But if you focus on them and get them right 90% of the time, the 20 lbs will take care of itself!

That's precisely what we're doing here: we're focusing on an inspiring end goal (traveling lots, being rich, spending more time with family), but we're also creating immediate rules that we need to follow in order to support that, or work toward it.

Work-Life Balance and Safeguarding Your Spare Time

In this chapter, we have been discussing the huge amount of potential freedom that comes from the lack of separation between your personal life and your job. When the two are more closely merged, you can begin to play around with the variables to create the lifestyle you really want.

But this cuts both ways and it can *also* be a highly negative thing. In other words, if you *aren't* able to work highly efficiently and you overrun, then what's to stop you from working later? Likewise, when you always have the option to earn more money, how do you avoid talking yourself into working longer hours, which is ultimately only going to cause you to end up being more tired tomorrow and getting less done?

If you allow this to happen—if you work into your evenings—then you will only create a vicious cycle where you get further and further out of sync and your work starts to fall in quality. This is only an option in desperate circumstances. So how do you prevent it from happening?

The answer of course is once again discipline. It is knowing that you need to create a separation between your work life and your private life—and it's taking responsibility for this separation as your own boss. Taking into account everything that we've just said with regard to creating a work-life balance where you are "working to live" and not the other way around, you can hopefully see the futility in working ridiculously long hours to achieve that!

It can help to create a number of contingency plans. For instance, if you can't complete all your work today, then could you maybe wake up a few hours earlier than normal tomorrow and finish it then? Likewise, maybe you could create a different arrangement with your clients to give yourself a little bit more buffer. Maybe you could outsource that bit of extra work?

Best of all, try to create your *own* set of deadlines and bring those a little forward from your actual deadlines. In other words, if you have a big project due on Friday, create your own deadline to finish it on Thursday and then treat it as though that were the actual deadline—no excuses! By doing this, you ensure that even if you should fall behind, you won't end up working late in a desperate panic.

But failing all this, be willing to use the tips in Chapter 6 to explain to your clients that work is coming late. Don't let it happen often—and see this as a sign that you need to alter the balance *somewhere*.

Fitting in with Others

Here's an aspect of being an online freelancer that often gets overlooked: other people.

As we've seen, working online as a freelancer means being able to take on *any* kind of work. It means being completely free from commutes, office hours, or rules. By being able to pick and choose jobs, you can ultimately make the lifestyle you want.

But unfortunately, employers are not the only ones that traditionally impose structure and restrictions on us.

Just as guilty are our friends and family. In particular, if you are in a relationship or if you have a family, then you will find that you have to somewhat fit around them. Maybe you need to wake up when your wife/husband goes to work. Maybe you need to take the kids to and from school.

Maybe your partner is unreasonably demanding that you spend at least *some* time with them in the evenings!

Again, to use a fitness analogy, it is always much easier to lose weight if your partner is also on the same diet. Eating nothing but crackers and water for dinner when your partner wants to enjoy a romantic meal out is going to cause conflict.

Even if you're single, you will still have this issue to a somewhat lesser extent. If you want to meet friends for dinner, you need to be available when they're available. And if you want to go to the bank, you're going to have to do it during the day.

In some ways, you'll find your flexibility is an asset. That bank thing for instance is actually easier because you can go during hours when everyone else is at work—no lines for the teller! And the same goes for getting your hair cut, going to the gym, posting mail, and so on.

As for the rest of it, you're going to have to decide how jealously you want to guard your self-imposed regimen vs. how keen you are to work around the schedules of friends and family. What's most important is that you don't resent or blame your family for preventing you from living the completely free lifestyle that you want to: be true to yourself and explain to them why it is that you are so keen to adapt this divergent lifestyle (that is what it is, to be frank).

Moreover, you might explain why your lifestyle is actually able to *benefit* them. For instance, my wife loves that I'm able to pick her up from work. And she loves that I am home to receive packages.

But accept that there will be *some* compromise if you want to be in a relationship and maintain friendships—as is always the case. Seeing as having some kind of structure is important for us, we can view this as a useful starting point. I've built my current workflow around the time my wife starts and finishes work. Previously, I had plenty of time to work with as I'd drop her at the train station at 7:30 a.m. and pick her up from there at 5:30 p.m. When we moved in together, this was very good for me, as it prevented me from sleeping in until 11 a.m. as I had previously been known to do and it allowed me to complete enough work to dedicate Mondays to side projects.

Now my wife is pregnant and I'm driving her directly to and from work so she doesn't have to take the train. This leaves me with fewer hours to work, but it is a compromise I'm willing to make—family comes first. I just have to readdress my budget, my clients, and my rates in order to make it work. For the most part, I have accomplished this. I even work in a coffee shop in town near her office on some days now, so that I only have to make the journey there and back once!

Things might be different for you, but explain your position to people you know and love, and take them into account when designing your own lifestyle.

Danger: Running Errands and Meeting Up

One thing you will find when becoming a freelancer is that people struggle to understand your availability or lack thereof.

While I'm committed to using my freedom and flexibility to help around the house, I do sometimes find I take on too much as a result. It only makes sense that it should be me who waits in for the plumber, who takes the parcel to the post office, who picks up Mum's birthday card in town during the day. But these errands start to add up, and they represent interruptions to your flow.

Likewise, this is also true of meeting friends for lunch. This becomes difficult because sometimes you will *want* to meet friends for lunch or take days off to spend with them. You'll move things around, work a bit extra, or take the hit financially (after checking in with your budget) in order to make that work.

But if you do that *once*, then you set a precedent. And now it's going to be hard to explain to friends that "no, you can't just drop in." Even if you tell them repeatedly that it's not always possible, you'll still have people telling you they have the day off and thought you might like to hang out.

If you're being strict, then you might make the rule that you shouldn't do once something that you can't afford to do often—better not to create those expectations and patterns.

But in order to maintain your flexibility and freedom, you alternatively just need to learn how to say "no" when someone makes the suggestion. A tip to make that easier: tell them you have an important Skype meeting, or a deadline. Those are concepts that they can understand.

Don't feel pressured into meeting friends or running errands when you don't really have the time: it's ultimately going to cause more stress than it's worth and, once again, foster resentment. Just make sure that this is accounted for in your larger budget.

Becoming a Digital Nomad

Becoming a digital nomad is for many the ultimate expression of lifestyle design. It is the concept followed through to its logical conclusion.

A digital nomad is someone who takes full advantage of their lack of location dependence or time restrictions in order to travel the world and live a life full of adventure and experience.

Let's say that you are completing programming jobs on Freelancer for a living, alongside maintaining websites for a few steady clients, and earning some money from an online programming course you set up on Udemy or Teachable.

You now don't need anything to earn a living other than a laptop and an Internet connection. Seeing as you can take a laptop with you anywhere in a backpack, and seeing as you can find Internet connections and power in pretty much any bar, café, airport, or co-working space, that means you can travel the world *indefinitely*. To many, this is the dream and the way that life should be lived. You're only alive once, so why not see as much of the world as possible? Have as many experiences as you can? Many people will go away for years at a time, some planning to settle down with a more stable job and lifestyle in the future, others planning to keep up the nomadic lifestyle indefinitely.

And something that might surprise you is that you often don't need as much money as you think in order to keep traveling. Sites like AirbnB (www. airbnb.com) and CouchSurfing (www.couchsurfing.com) make finding accommodation incredibly cheap. In many ways, AirbnB actually represents an alternative permutation of the gig economy, allowing people to rent out their accommodation to others on a one-off basis. CouchSurfing, meanwhile, is a site that lets its members invite other users to sleep on their sofas or in their spare rooms in exchange for receiving the same privileges when they are traveling. This is *free* accommodation and an example of the "sharing economy," a close cousin of the gig economy.

Budget airlines and cheap rail passes for backpackers are also increasingly common, and if you do have to fork out for a hostel one night, it usually won't cost much. It's very easy to find places to stay via apps these days too, meaning that you often don't need to secure accommodation prior to landing in that random town or city.

Travel light, choose cheaper destinations and activities, and there's no reason that you need to earn more than $50 to $60 a day in order to fund your lifestyle. Roughing it and never knowing where you are going to end up is all part of the adventure!

Is a Digital Nomad Lifestyle for You?

There's a chance that right now, your eyes are glazing over with the possibilities. Maybe you've always wanted to see the world and just hadn't realized that your coding skills or online coaching services were your ticket out of here!

But on the other hand, you might be experiencing the precise *opposite* reaction. Maybe the idea of sleeping on couches and in hostels is absolutely repugnant to you. Maybe you can't think of anything worse!

Whether or not the digital nomad lifestyle is for you is going to depend very much on who you are. But like every other aspect of lifestyle design, it's worth keeping in mind that there is more than one way to make this work for you.

For instance, if you're earning a little more income or have some savings, then you can always travel with a slightly higher quality of accommodation. There's nothing to stop you from booking a hotel for a few weeks at a time somewhere beautiful—and hotels actually lend themselves particularly well to working online. And of course if you were a travel writer or otherwise combined your work and travel, you may be able to write off some of your travel costs as expenses!

Even then though, some people are going to find it hard to be away from home for such extensive periods of time. They might get homesick or miss friends. Ultimately, only you can decide if the benefits outweigh the negatives.

If creature comforts aren't your main concern, then you may instead be more worried about the logistical challenges and how this might affect your career. Working on the move *of course* creates new issues—and you're likely to find yourself relying on World Time Buddy even more now! Not only that, but there are certain types of work that you simply can't complete when you work on the move. For instance, YouTubers will be able to travel vlog just fine, but you'll struggle if your videos involve high production values with lighting rigs and shotgun mics. Likewise, programming is of course easy enough as long as you have a powerful enough laptop. If you need to work with serious horsepower in order to develop AAA games though, then you'll find things get more difficult.

And of course, it's a risk doing any kind of work that 100% relies on an Internet connection!

The Compromise Solution

I feel there is one more compromise option that addresses many of these concerns. As I alluded to earlier, there is no reason to travel consistently when you can instead just travel more.

Instead of going away indefinitely, why not just endeavor to take several short trips throughout the year? You can still earn money on those trips, which therefore means you're able to go on more such adventures. You don't have to worry about leave, and you can work as you fly to offset the cost of travel. If you're fortune enough to know someone who lives abroad, then there's no reason you can't visit them for a week or so at no expense to yourself other than flights!

And because you can travel at unusual times of year, your flights will cost significantly less too.

Again, the only real issue here is fitting in around others. If you have a partner who works in a traditional job, then they may take issue with you constantly jet-setting around the world. Again, this is something to discuss and work around.

Tip   One more consideration is to travel more in your local area. If you want to take more advantage of your freedom but don't want to keep flying abroad, then why not just visit nearby towns and cities, or visit different spots to work in? You can work in public parks with great views, you can find cool rooftop bars, or you can work on the train to a new city. When I lived in London, one of my favorite places to work was the British Library. More recently, I've enjoyed working outdoors in the Cotswolds, which is a very beautiful area about 40 minutes away from my current location. On a day when I have a little less work (usually a Friday), working in a little café by a stream or sitting under a tree is fantastic for the soul.

Tips and Challenges for Digital Nomads

If you *do* like the sound of becoming a full-fledged digital nomad, then here are a few tips that will help you to make the lifestyle work for you.

Tech and Gadgets

The right tech and gadgets will make *all* the difference to your ability to work easily on the move. That of course starts with a light-yet-powerful computer that you can use to complete the work you're being asked to do. There's a trade-off here between power and performance, and where you land on that spectrum is going to depend on the type of work you need to do (do you need a powerful GPU, for instance, or perhaps digital drawing tools like a stylus?). There are more and more high-powered computers that fit into a small chassis these days, with the Microsoft Surface line of products being particularly well-suited to an on-the-go lifestyle.

Another point to consider here is battery life. Because if you're working in the middle of nowhere and your battery runs out, you will have no way to stay productive. To that end, it makes sense to carry a power brick that you can use to add some extra juice. It's also a good idea to have some kind of backup device that you can use in an emergency. I use an Android phone with a folding keyboard, or a pocketable computer called the GPD Pocket.

Similarly, you should make sure there's always a way to get online. The best way to handle that these days is with a mobile device that supports Internet tethering (most phones will do this) and the right mobile data plan. That way, you can use your smartphone to connect your PC to the Web and start uploading files again and answering e-mails.

Travel Light

If your hope is to travel the world while working, then it is highly advisable that you keep things light. This is really a topic for an entirely different book, but to keep it brief, carrying less makes adventure significantly easier. Some useful pointers:

- Get a microfiber towel, an incredible small and light towel that dries almost instantly.

- Carry a Kindle, not a pile of paperbacks (older-generation Kindles can also be useful for emergency Internet connections as they used to come with a built-in "beta" browser).

- Roll clothes into thin tubes and stuff into the sides of your bag.

- Speaking of which, the right bag will make a world of difference to your convenience - especially as a smaller bag can be brought on the flight as hand luggage and won't need to be checked in.

Take Advantage of the Many Helpful Sites and Tools Online

Nomad List (https://nomadlist.com) is a crowdsourced database of cities that you can use to find out more information about your next destination. There are many online communities where you can find other nomads to chat with (and meet up with), and plenty more online resources and databases for getting useful info. Coworker (www.coworker.com), for example, makes it easy to find co-working spaces near you.

The Problem of Stuff and a Base

If you choose to embrace the digital nomad lifestyle, then you can get by on a relatively minor budget as discussed. Stay in hostels and Airbnbs, or crash on people's couches. Visit affordable countries, and travel by car or rail. It's actually cheaper than the cost of living in one place a lot of the time!

Problem is that you will still technically need to live in that "one place." In other words, you will probably have possessions that you need to keep, and you will probably need to keep these in a property somewhere—or at the very least a storage unit. Likewise, you'll want somewhere to stay when you come back from your travels. If you're very lucky and your parents are willing to provide this, then you might not have to worry. Otherwise though, your costs may be *fairly* high.

The key here is to be more minimal in terms of your lifestyle. The less "stuff" you have, the easier it is to up and go when the spirit takes you. And living a more minimal lifestyle is generally very beneficial when it comes to writing that budget and getting to do the things you love doing. Many of us spend so much money on "stuff" that we ultimately do not need and won't help us to get closer toward our goals.

Again, it's a topic for another book. But try to stop buying things based on emotions and instead think about how much they will actually benefit you. Why are you buying new books and computer games if you haven't read/played all the ones you currently own? Would a widescreen TV that you pay off over the next two months really make you happier? When you could instead work for ten minutes less on Fridays?

Work-Life Balance

We've discussed how being a freelancer immediately makes you more responsible for your own work-life balance. It falls to you now to ensure that you aren't working late into the night just because you can.

The same problem arises when traveling. You need to work to afford the lifestyle, but you also need to make sure you are seeing the sites, enjoying the nightlife, and having adventures. Otherwise, what's the point?

Personally, I find this a little easier because, to me, the real value of traveling and visiting other countries comes from drinking in the atmosphere. Running around landmarks and taking photos to say you've been there—often just because they're the "best known" parts of the country—can sometimes actually *detract* from this experience. I love being in my own head, and being inspired by my surroundings—so working is actually part of the experience for me.

This is also why I prefer creative types of work. If you're churning out boring code or writing dull marketing posts, then you will feel as though you're missing out on the moment. But if you are able to write about something you find inspiring, or if you're able to solve problems and create unique apps and web tools, then suddenly there is great value in being inspired by your surroundings.

In fact, being in a "rich environment" is considered to be a "flow trigger." When we see new sights and sounds, we activate less-often-used networks in our brain, which can potentially give way to creative insights and breakthroughs.

The sense of "awe" that comes from an amazing view of the Grand Canyon occurs because the scene you are seeing is *so* different that it causes huge activation in your brain, which is followed by cascading brain-derived neurotrophic factor (BDNF) and dopamine. In the most extreme examples of awe, we reevaluate our place in the world—so blown away are we by what we're seeing—and this makes the brain *far* more malleable.

Seeing new things and having new experiences is actually one of the very best ways to maintain a healthy and plastic brain. And you should seek to do this as often as possible, whether that means traveling or just seeking out new activities and opportunities in your spare time.

One of my favorite memories is of sitting in a bar in Croatia with a friend who also works online, and typing away at around 1 a.m. We were drinking a few beers (not enough to severely damage the quality of said work), and listening to some awesome music that I discovered there for the first time (the artist Schiller, as I would later learn). There was no one else in the bar (I felt bad for the bartenders, who obviously wanted to go home), the place was lit with neon lights, and just outside we could see people passing by as they came in and out of clubs, and watch the rain dancing on the cobbled streets.

I similarly enjoyed working by a waterfall on that same holiday—Croatia has Wi-Fi everywhere!

The point is, you can tie the travel and the writing *together* if you are so inclined. Otherwise, the advice is the same as it is for those working from their own homes: work out precisely how much you need to earn and create a budget. Then find ways to work faster and quicker, so that you can clock off once you've reached that threshold and start enjoying the adventure. Think about the best times to work, and maybe try shifting that around during the week in order to experience the locations at different times of day.

Chapter Summary

While some people will choose to enter the gig economy working a regular 9-5 schedule, others will find that the freedom and flexibility that comes from choosing when and how you work is one of the big appeals of going this route to begin with. If that's how you feel, then this chapter may be the one that brings it all together for you. If not, then hopefully you've still seen some new options that wouldn't have been available to you before (such as traveling more, or earning passive income on the side).

But this is only the start. The gig economy, the sharing economy, the laptop lifestyle ... these are all changes to our lifestyle that result from the relentless march of technology. That's only going to continue as more and more people start adopting alternative ways to live and work using the Internet. In the next chapter, then, we're going to look at the changes that are likely to come for the gig economy as a whole, and for your own freelance business in particular. By preparing ourselves for the future, we can ensure we're able to thrive as we move forward.

Looking Forward

Using the freedom that entering the gig economy provides, we've found ways to create the perfect lifestyle for ourselves. We can work how, where, and when we like, and we can progress our career in any direction we choose, eventually becoming an online "superstar," capable of charging big fees to complete high-caliber work.

Now it's time to look forward. How are you going to develop your career from this point forward? And what future forces might impact the way you live and work?

Scaling Your Business

Were you to set up another type of business with employees and conventional physical assets, then your goal at this point would be to start *scaling* that operation in order to earn more.

For most companies, that would mean finding ways to sell more products and services, while spending less time and money to produce them. That might mean implementing automation and force multipliers, then investing more money into marketing.

So, let's say you have a business buying and selling clothes. You find a wholesaler, buy 50 jeans in a bulk order, and then sell them on via eBay and your own website for a profit. This yields a 150% profit. What next? You keep some of that profit and then you invest the rest into buying 100 jeans. You know they sell well, so the risk is minimal. You do the same thing over and over, investing in more jeans each time, until eventually you begin to expand your product range and you create a more fully comprehensive e-commerce site. Scaling.

© Adam Sinicki 2019
A. Sinicki, *Thriving in the Gig Economy*, https://doi.org/10.1007/978-1-4842-4090-8_9

Suppose that you next invest in some advertising and branding and now have an online clothes store. You are selling so many items of clothes that you need to hire some people to help you sell them. Then you invest in a warehouse. Then you invest in ten warehouses and TV ads. Further scaling.

This is an example of the trajectory, roughly, of most successful businesses. Up and up!

But if you're providing a service as a freelancer, then how can you possibly scale your production? You can't keep doubling your output: you're only human, after all.

We've discussed one method in Chapter 5—by working more quickly and efficiently via the "transhuman business model"—but this is, ultimately, limited to what you can accomplish in a day. Likewise, we've seen that you can charge more for your work over time, but that's still going to have a cap on it: there's only so much you can realistically charge on a regular basis for your programming skills.

So, does that mean you *can't* scale your gigs? Does that mean that you're never going to go global and become a millionaire by working in this manner?

Well, that depends . . .

Methods for Scaling

Here are some of the best methods you can use to scale a service-based business.

Hiring

One option when it comes to scaling your business is to start hiring people to help with your workload. If you have more and more orders coming in and you're not able to keep up with them, then you could hire someone to handle some of that work for you, pay them a certain amount per day, and then make sure there's a bit of profit for you to skim off the top.

This is scaling because you can repeat the process over and over in order to continuously expand your business operations. The downside is that it brings with it a lot more administration and complication. If you are hiring someone, you're going to need to sort out a lot of paperwork, take on more expenses, etc. Not only that, but to make sure you have work to assign to them, you're going to have to work extra hard to keep a steady stream of orders. This means aggressive marketing and juggling of tasks, which in turn requires even more investment and might also require the hiring of yet more people.

And where will these people work? You may find you quickly need an office to rent. And insurance.

Quickly this can get out of hand, which is fine if your ambition is to be a big CEO, but is far removed from the gigging we started out with!

Service Arbitrage

Hiring someone to handle your increasing workload is an awkward fit because it is a strategy from the old way of doing things. In the digital economy, we do things a little differently!

Specifically, what makes a lot more sense is to start offering gigs! In other words, look for people who are doing the same thing you're doing but charging less, and then outsource some of your work to them.

Depending on how far you want to take this, this strategy can ultimately replace your entire business model. Simply:

1. Look for a client willing to pay $500 for an app.

2. Look for a service provider willing to create that app for $400, without taking credit.

3. Manage the communication and keep the $100.

This is called "service arbitrage." Of course, the amount of time it takes to manage that communication is going to be a fraction of the time it would take to actually build the app yourself, which means you can take on countless more jobs and countless more freelancers, multiplying the amount over and over.

Finding people willing to provide the work for less is, of course, the main challenge. This is often easier than you might think though. Use the same sites that we looked at for advertising, but now from the perspective of the buyer. Consider their experience and qualifications, look for examples of the work they've completed, and read their reviews (more on this in the next chapter). Often, finding a good coder who charges less will mean looking at someone from a country where living expenses are lower, or a student who is doing this as a hobby.

Alternatively, you could look for a "white label" service, a company that will provide a service without asking for any recognition. For instance, you can find white label web design companies that build websites *precisely* for this kind of purpose. You can stick your logo all over it (hence the metaphorical blank or "white" label), and they wholly expect you to sell it on for more money. They're happy with the arrangement because they get a steady flow of work at a price that works for them, and it works for you because you can sell their work on for a profit.

Likewise, we've mentioned how you can use other services—such as a VAS—in order to help you find clients and streamline those other aspects of the work. If you're a web developer, then you might outsource *specifically* the parts of the job you don't like: you handle the Drupal and hire someone else to design the logo.

You can take this as far as you want. Either keep hiring others as an option in your back pocket for when you're stretched or you want to avoid doing a particular part of the job yourself, or go all in and remove yourself completely from the creative work and instead simply become a middleman.

Do keep in mind that the latter option isn't *quite* as stress-free as you might imagine though. Inevitably things will go wrong: services will let you down with late work or poor quality, clients will be difficult, and the sheer amount of e-mails you'll be bouncing around can get hard to manage. If you've built a list of clients that regularly hire you for work because they've grown used to your reliability and quality, then they might notice a drop in that quality and look elsewhere. Some clients may explicitly object to subcontracting.

I tried this for a while with a website called IWantYourWords (specifically I would buy unused content that people had lying around on their computers and then find buyers for it), but ultimately, I opted to give that up and return to actually doing the work myself (the site is now defunct). The idea was effective in theory, but the amount of admin involved was quite overwhelming and I didn't find the experience overly enjoyable.

Teaming Up

Or, why not take the spirit of sharing and gigging even further and create a situation where no one is "in charge" as such? If you want to expand your business, take on more clients, and avoid being overrun, then another option is to team up with someone else! Sell them on the merits of the kind of work you're doing and then encourage them to work alongside you.

If you're a coder, then you can become *two* coders. Then you can simply divide the work between you. Or, if you're a coder, you could look for a designer to handle your user experience (UX). You can now benefit from the unique skills that both of you bring to the table, and you can that way take on a more diverse range of clients and projects. Or why not find someone who is good at marketing to help you sell whatever B2C product or service (e.g., coaching or proofreading) that you're selling?

And actually, this opens up a whole *host* of new possibilities and opportunities. Maybe you don't want to quit your 9-to-5 job just yet but would like to expand your growing business. Then why not divvy up a full-time job's worth of stuff to do between several of you?

Likewise, if you're working full time, you can call in friends and other professionals to work occasional weekends or evenings and let them keep the income. There's no requirement for them to "commit" permanently, or to match you in terms of hours. If I get overloaded, or if we need a little more household income, my wife will often pick up a little of the slack for me.

They say not to mix friends and business, and of course there are some risks here. Then there's the simple fact that you no longer have total control over your business.

But there's also something very fun about being "in it together" with a friend. This also works if you want to set up forms of passive income or create other, more conventional business models. If you want to grow a website or YouTube channel, for instance, finding a few passionate people to help you do it can make a huge difference.

My advice is to try and keep it pretty casual at first. If you have made no strict commitments to one another, then there is no reason for either of you to be upset or offended. If this grows into a serious business with the two of you, then you can look at creating much more defined roles.

Note as well that this is another scenario where using collaboration and project management tools will come in handy. Only now you get to decide how and when you contact one another.

Productization

Another option if you want to scale your business is to *productize* it. That means taking whatever it is that you sell as a service and finding ways to turn it into a product.

We've already looked at ways you can do this. For instance, if you are currently selling web design services, then you could productize this concept by creating a CMS (content management system) that can be installed by anyone with a single click. This way, you have removed yourself from the equation. pNow you are selling the same end result, but with no need to be as actively involved in the process. You can still offer to set it up if you wish or to customize that base software. *Or* you can sell the installation files on their own.

And if this business model sounds familiar, it's *exactly* the thought process that Matt Mullenweg and Mike Little used when they built WordPress.

WordPress is essentially software as a service (SaaS). Other examples of this include things like Asana, Slack, Feedly, Salesforce, Copyscape, or Hootsuite. All of these are web apps that act as tools to help customers and clients achieve more. Such tools can generate revenue through monthly subscription fees or other models, and this way you can automate your own services. This is a brilliant option available to programmers in particular—though the tool you build could work in any industry. Don't have coding chops? Think about how you could productize your current service this way, then find yourself a programmer.

Franchising

Another typical method that bigger businesses might use to scale up is to franchise themselves. This means that they "loan out" their brand and their methods to other entrepreneurs and small businesses. One well-known example is KFC (a.k.a. Kentucky Fried Chicken). KFC franchisees pay a license in order to use the secret recipe and the KFC name, and this then al-but-guarantees a certain amount of custom. Meanwhile, KFC profits from the thousands of stores around the country using their branding!

While you won't be able to do this overnight, there is a chance that if you are exceedingly good at your job, you may eventually get to the point where your name alone carries clout - think of someone like Chase Jarvis. If you build recognition for your brand (and ideally you use a more marketable trading name), then you might find that people will pay to use your logo when they sell their services. It's not a strategy that is terribly common on the Web, but this chapter is all about charting new territory!

Growing Personally

I've already touched on how you can increase the amount you're able to charge by constantly adding to your portfolio and your résumé. This way, you can gradually increase the quality of the gigs you receive *and* the amount that you charge.

But building up a portfolio is only one way to do this. Another way to go about it is to focus on developing your own skills and acquiring qualifications. Want to write about a different topic? Then why not get a quick qualification in that subject?

Want to offer a different type of coding? Then do an online course in PHP, or in Unity development. Or get a book.

You can easily add to your own repertoire of skills using a number of on- and offline programs, many of which offer legitimate qualifications at the end of them!

Working online gives the freedom and the time to stay in education and to build up a *mega* résumé that will be hard for people to ignore. You can then bring in higher-paid work and even charge huge fees per hour as a consultant.

Introducing: The Digital Polymath

Not does working online allow you to build a huge resume, but the Web itself also makes it more possible than ever before for to learn huge amounts of information. The rise of the gig economy is one huge repercussion of the Web and our always-on communication, but I suspect that the "digital polymath" might be one more.

A polymath, or "homo universalis," is someone who dabbles in a wide range of different subjects, skills, and areas of expertise. The prototypical example that we hear about most often in this context is Leonardo da Vinci: painter, scientist, inventor, writer, astronomer, botanist . . . the list goes on. Da Vinci would have a LinkedIn page to make the rest of us weep!

But during da Vinci's time—the Renaissance era—it was much more common for someone to have multiple areas of expertise like this. Those in a position of luxury would often spend their time painting, reading, writing, and even conducting their own experiments. Anyone could make a significant contribution to almost *any* field.

So where have the polymaths gone? What changed?

For one, we now have far more comforts and forms of entertainment. With computer games, Netflix, and television always beckoning, it's much easier for us to simply crash out and relax when we finish our working days. Then there's the fact that most of us work harder and for longer. There is less poverty, but that also means that there are fewer aristocrats able to spend their days idly reading and creating. Most of us get home from work completely exhausted and completely spent. Unfortunately, that work is not often creative or challenging in a manner sufficient to help us keep expanding our minds.[1]

And then there's the fact that every field has developed to the point that it has. In the earlier days of physics, you could read a few books and generally be brought up to speed. Today, becoming an expert in any scientific, artistic, or other field can take a lifetime of study. Several doctorates later and you *may* stand a chance of making a contribution to the very specific field of "gaze direction in primates." We have been forced to specialize.

But the Internet changes *all* of this.

For starters, the vast majority of us now have access to all the world's information. We can learn any subject as easily as we can type a well-phrased

---

[1]There are reasons that this is actually incredibly unhealthy for our brains. The reason that the adult brain is so much less plastic than a child's brain is likely due to the fact that the child is constantly learning and discovering (and so producing more BDNF and plasticity-promoting neurotransmitters), while adults have largely fallen into routines that include very little by way of learning and discovery.

question into Google. And the amazing thing is that many more of us really are expanding our horizons as a result. Many of us will watch TED talks and YouTube documentaries, take online courses, and use sites like Skillshare (www.skillshare.com). Listen to the way that some YouTubers talk about computer games or films, and you'll realize there is a level of understanding and appreciation here that was absent before—understanding and appreciation that can undoubtedly be applied to other fields.

Then there's the cloud and automation which can pick up the slack and help us achieve more. And the best place to see how this can impact the way we work is in the world of game development. Go back to the '80s and you'd find that anyone could create a successful computer game like Arkanoid. Games used very simple graphics, because the ZX Spectrums and Tatung Einsteins that ran them were only capable of very simple graphics. The games were necessarily short because the amount of stage that a Spectrum cassette could hold was roughly equivalent to 2MB.

Every game was an indie game!

Then we saw the advent of 3D graphics. We saw games gain orchestral soundtracks, cutscenes dubbed by professional actors, and levels that spanned the equivalent of miles. In games like Shenmue you could search every drawer in Ryu's house! There was no possible way that an individual could handle the sheer volume or complexity of the work necessary to compete.

But then the indie game came back. Partly this was due to a renewed interest in original games that took risks that big studios were unwilling to entertain. But partly, it was due to the fact that indie developers gained access to tools like Unreal Engine and Unity[2]. These tools and others like them provided developers with ready-made game engines that included all the physics and complex calculations required to power a 2D or even 3D game. At the same time, they gave developers access to stores where they could find useful assets like 3D models, animations, special effects, and more. 3D models can now also be downloaded for free from community websites. If you need music, then you could ask a willing creator to make something with FL Studio (www.image-line.com/flstudio/). Or you could outsource the process and get someone to make it for you on Fiverr. Not sure how to scale a bitmap? Just ask someone on Stack Overflow for the quick answer.

In other words, outsourcing, crowdsourcing, automation, open source software, and powerful tools can all now take the place of a huge team. That means that a single programmer with a vision can once again build something amazing. The more skills you develop and the broader your knowledge, the more you'll be able to accomplish this way.

---

[2]Be sure to check out my other book published by Apress: *Learn Unity for Android Game Development* (2017).

And this is also true for freelancers. One person really can build an incredible website, edit a professional-looking video, and manage an entire online marketing campaign.

The same is true in many other fields, which is to say that you no longer *need* complete knowledge of a field in order to make a valuable contribution or to create something amazing. You can work with others online, you can use tools, and you can pick and choose the skills you need to develop.

And working in the gig economy will meanwhile give you the time *and* the incentive to develop these skills and to become a digital polymath. This is not only a very valuable and noble pursuit in itself that can help you to contribute far more to society and gain a far greater understanding and appreciation of the world you live in, but it is also quickly becoming a *necessity* if you wish to thrive in the gig economy ... or even traditional employment!

The people in traditional employment that are the most expensive and that end up enjoying the highest salaries are those who receive investment from their companies: the ones who get sent on management courses, who are taught new skills, who earn new qualifications, and who are asked to head up important projects and departments. All these things help those people to create amazing résumés that let them move into higher-paid work, or charge more for what they can do already. This is more important than ever at a time when salaries often aren't increasing at even the rate of inflation. You need to do something *else* in order to stand out and get ahead. And that goes double for those of us that are self-employed.

Accelerated Learning and Online Resources

How exactly do you go about developing the skills to become a digital polymath?

The first tip is to make sure that you know the resources you have available to you.

I already mentioned Skillshare, which is a sharing-economy take on the idea of online courses. Anyone can create classes, and anyone can take them. Then there are other sites such as Udemy (www.udemy.com), Udacity (www.udacity.com), Code Institute (www.codeinstitute.com), Teachable (https://teachable.com), Codecademy (www.codecademy.com), Coursera (www.coursera.org), Treehouse (https://teamtreehouse.com), and others. Many of these are coding-based websites, but for non-techies there are plenty more resources out there. YouTube is likewise a surprisingly useful resource, with lots of completely free tutorials that will walk you through everything from video editing, to website creation, to electronic engineering. If you want to gain this information even faster, try watching those videos on 2x speed (click the gear icon below the video, click Speed, and choose 2). You can pull the same trick with audio books from Audible (www.audible.com). Audiobooks and podcasts are perfect for multitasking, by the way, as they allow you to listen and learn in the car, while jogging, or when chopping veggies. If I've been asked to write about a subject I don't know, then I will often watch a YouTube video or listen to a podcast while I'm driving or cooking, so that I've got plenty of ideas to work with when I sit down the next day.

And if you prefer learning from books, then you can of course find a huge number of excellent resources at Apress.com!

If you're interested, then consider looking into accelerated learning techniques. These are techniques used to help you learn complex subjects much more quickly, often by changing the order in which you learn individual elements, or breaking up your time spent learning.

For instance, the AnkiApp flashcards app (www.ankiapp.com), which began life on Linux but has since made the journey to many more platforms, is a fantastic tool for learning pretty much anything you can think of. This is a simple flashcards app but one that utilizes two strategies that have been demonstrated to enhance learning in several studies: active recall, which is required to retrieve the knowledge you have learned, and spaced learning, which involves taking strategically timed breaks in order to enhance the value of repeating the same tests. The best part is that you can easily download ready-made "stacks" of flashcards provided by the community that enable you to learn pretty much any subject you can possibly think of!

There are also plenty of books on the subject of quickly absorbing information. Tim Ferriss describes the DiSSS method, for instance, in his book *The 4-Hour Chef*. This is an acronym for Deconstruction, Interviewing, Selection, Sequencing, Stakes, and basically provides a framework for learning in a particular order. One of the most interesting suggestions here is to start at what would normally be considered the "end" when learning and then work backward. So you might learn how to get some in check when playing chess, or how to lead when dancing and then work backwards from that point.

In his book *The First 20 Hours*, Josh Kaufman explains the importance of framing your learning by having a goal or an ambition in mind. I always advise people NOT to try and "learn Java" but instead to learn how to make a calculator in Java. Or a notepad app. Or a simple game. As any programmer reading this will know, you never completely master a programming language but rather just learn the amount that you need and then look up the rest as it comes. Having that end goal in mind helps to motivate, structure, and guide your learning, which in turn makes you ultimately much more successful.

Or how about the Feynman technique? Named for physicist and author Richard Feynman, this technique involves gaining true depth of knowledge by making sure you are able to explain the topic in simple terms. If you can't, then you identify where you are stumbling and you revisit. This forces you to engage with the information, to relate it to your own life, and to build connections with *existing* knowledge (which also enhances memory). This is one of the reasons that I find writing about a subject to be *so* beneficial when it comes to learning it—a perk of the job for me!

Using different modalities and sensory learning can help a lot, and is made all the easier thanks to YouTube and the Web. My university experience became much easier once I discovered I could learn topics like neuroscience from YouTube!

If you combine these strategies with the immense resource that is the Internet, if you learn how to correctly phrase a Google search, and if you develop your speed-reading skills and your ability to grasp the key lessons from a book quickly (you haven't read *everything* in this book up to this point, have you?), then you will find that you can gain new knowledge and skills *immensely* quickly. *Matrix*-style.

Oh, and all this also means that I reject the argument that you don't have enough marketable skills to enter the gig economy: as we've seen, it is perfectly possible to simply *acquire* such skills! In fact, while this is something I probably *shouldn't* be proud of, I was once hired to write an e-book on Python *before* I actually knew how to code in Python. I used the techniques just described in order to learn to the point where I was able to teach other people! And I did this in short enough a time that the gig was still profitable for me.

Don't worry if this seems impossible right now; you'll find that, just like anything else, learning new skills online is something that you will get better at with time. It is a skill in itself, after all: a skill that unlocks *all other skills*.

The Other Side of the Coin: Hiring and Working with Freelancers

Expanding your own skill set is one option for continuing your growth going forward. Another is to leverage the help of others and to outsource.

If you intend on getting into the world of "service arbitrage," then you will find yourself in an interesting position: getting to view the gig economy from the perspective of those who are hiring. This is a completely different ballgame and actually something that can be a useful learning experience in itself if it teaches you to better understand what it is that your clients are looking for and the challenges they face.

At one point, I tried buying and selling copywriting in order to effectively outsource the bulk of my own work (a successful experiment, but one that ultimately proved to be a little soul destroying). What I found when trying to hire writers, though, was just *why* I had been so successful providing this service against the competition.

In my experience, 99% of online copywriters would fall into one of two camps:

- Those who would charge very low rates but often speak poor English and/or people just trying to make a quick buck with no real interest or understanding for the topics they were asked to cover

- Students, entrepreneurs, and others that would start out very well but ultimately get bored. Flaky types who would hand in work late, or fail to communicate at all.

What I also recognized during this time was just *how important* it was to hire writers that understood (and ideally loved) the topics they were covering. This experience allowed me to hone and refine the service that *I* was offering, thereby increasing my wage and enabling me to better understand my position when negotiating pay and terms. I would highly recommend this, if only as a thought experiment in your own industry. Just take a look around and imagine that you are trying to hire someone. Which ads jump out at you? What problems do you see? Where do you look first?

Hiring Freelancers for Businesses and Entrepeneurs

While most people reading this book will be interested in entering the gig economy as freelancers, there is also a good chance that some people are reading this from that alternative perspective: learning about a marketplace from which they can hire professionals. And of course, there's always the chance that if things go well as a freelancer, you might expand your operations to the point where you do need to start hiring.

Here are a few tips to help you find the right people to work with.

Look at Previous Experience

This is the most important consideration. How long have they been working? Are they willing to show you examples of their previous work? What skills and traits do their previous projects demonstrate? Do they have accolades or recommendations from previous clients?

Make a Small Order

In this book, I recommended against freelancers doing "sample work" for free. However, there is nothing wrong with putting in a small order to a freelancer first to find out if you can work together. Order something that is representative of the kind of work you're going to be looking for but that won't cost you much and won't take the freelancer long. This way, you'll quickly see if they're at least capable of delivering the kind of work you need.

Consider Communication

Communication is very important in any business interaction, but this is even truer when you're working with someone online. When you start discussing your project, you will likely get a kind of "vibe" from the person you're speaking with. Either they'll put you instantly at ease and you'll feel like they are listening to what you're saying, *or* they'll leave you wondering if you're going to get anything even resembling what you're looking for. Go with your gut instinct; it is correct more often than not.

If possible, speak with the freelancer directly. Meet them in person if you can (this limits your choice but is a big advantage, especially for projects like large coding jobs) or have a Skype call if not. You can learn a lot more about a person on a call than you can from some e-mails. That said, keep in mind what I've advised in this book about communication overhead. If your order is small, then it is unfair to expect your freelancer to find time to call you (especially if they're working on the move), and a call is not a great use of your time either. For a massive project, aim to still keep calls brief; friendly but to the point. Respect their time, and you'll find they are much more likely to stick with you!

Trust Your Freelancer's Expertise

One of the most frustrating feelings as a freelancer is when a client won't listen to reason: when they order jobs that won't help them achieve their goals and might even hurt their organization. Freelancers want their clients to do well, because that reflects well on them.

And that's why it can be very frustrating when a client wants an article with 10% keyword density (meaning that every other word is a keyword and the content is unreadable), or when they want to continuously make tweaks to a web design to the point that it is completely different from what the designer originally delivered.

Freelancers get it: it's your website and your brand. But why hire a web developer at all if you won't listen to their recommendations regarding what will look good and be effective? Experienced web designers know what they're talking about, typically have designed *hundreds* of websites before, and have valuable tips and insights that can help your brand to look amazing. Remember: you aren't designing this website for you; you're designing it for your customers. And unless you're a professional designer too, chances are that the person you're hiring has a better idea of how to do this. In fact, they *benefit* from being emotionally removed from the project.

Respect Their Job Description

One more thing: don't ask your SEO writer to "collect a list of e-mail addresses from potential business partners." That is not their job description, and it's actually very insulting. Hire freelancers to complete work that they specialize in, don't get them performing menial tasks that fall outside their expertise.

Hash Out Details

During initial communication, know what are you looking for. It's important to make sure you both know precisely what to expect in terms of turn-around times, revisions, updates, and so forth. If the provider is forthcoming with this information, then you won't need to chase them up. If they're not, then make sure to ask precisely when you can expect to get your work, what tools they use, what will happen if you don't like the work you're given, and so on.

You Get What You Pay For

While there are exceptions to every rule, a general rule to follow is that you will get what you pay for. Don't expect to work with a consummate professional that will be absolutely dedicated to your project if they're charging the equivalent of $3 per hour!

Great Talent is Hard to Find

Finally, recognize that great talent that is professional and committed to your work is hard to find. In other words, if you are fortunate enough to land upon someone who is going to go the extra mile to finish your projects, and who always delivers on time . . . if you manage to find someone whose working style gels with your own . . . don't let them go! A high-quality service provider can be a huge asset to your business, so make sure you treat them well and, if possible, try to fold them into your workflow as much as you can. Be good to them, and they will be loyal to you.

Exit Strategy

As you grow and improve your business, you might consider scaling in order to increase your income exponentially. Failing that though, you might consider another option: selling up and moving on.

Having a destination in mind like this for your business trajectory is what's known as having an "exit strategy." Here, of course, the strategy is *selling* as a way to exit your business.

This might give you pause for thought though. How do you sell a business that doesn't have any tangible assets? (Or even financial assets if you're a sole proprietor?)

The answer is to focus on what you *can* sell. Here are some examples:

- A client list
- A list of freelancers
- Your trading name/company name/intellectual property
- Any tools you have built
- Your website/YouTube channel/social media presence

In short, you can sell off anything that might be of use to someone else trying to set up their own business. If you're a coder and you own a company called Coding For You (that you own the trademark for), with a series of social media accounts that collectively have millions of followers, a thriving website and blog, and a massive list of repeat clients, then that is going to potentially fetch a decent amount of money. On the other hand though, if you have one or two direct clients who hire you because of your personal skills—and you trade under your own name—then you'll struggle to sell. This is something to consider as you build your business if this is your eventual exit strategy, and even if it is only one of several options you are considering.

This is also why gradually removing yourself from your own operations as you scale up is such a smart move.

If you're interested in calculating the value of your business, then there are a few different methods you can use:

- Calculate the total sum of all tangible and intangible assets
- Use the traditional (and somewhat inappropriate) method of calculating your net profit per year and multiplying by five
- Calculate the value of a website by looking at the number of inbound links, the amount of content, the niche, and the ranking
- Calculate the value of a list of clients by roughly assuming that one lead = $1
- Use online tools that aim to calculate the value of a website

None of these methods is perfect at the best of times, and they become particularly unhelpful when you're trying to calculate the value of a sole proprietor business. It is hard to measure just how important *you* are to the operation, and of course you aren't going to be a part of the company anymore!

Another alternative method is to look for an investor who is willing to buy the business and take you on as the manager and employee. This might be helpful if you're looking for a cash injection and want to minimize risk (while sacrificing some control, of course).

Passive Income for Tech Entrepreneurs (and Others)

If you want to increase your financial independence even further, give yourself even more freedom, *and* make your business all the more resilient, then another strategy you can use is to set up sources of passive income.

Passive income is essentially income that you earn passively—that is, without working. Passive income is money that trickles in even when you're sleeping or traveling the world, making it very useful for the lifestyle design options we discussed in Chapter 8. This doesn't mean "money for nothing," but rather it tends to mean earning money today for work that you did days, months, or weeks ago; working hard today so that you can profit tomorrow.

How might you earn a passive income? Some examples include

- Create a website with advertising on it. You'll be paid each time a visitor views or clicks an ad, even when you're sleeping.

- Create a YouTube channel with advertising.

- Publish a book. This will result in a one-off payment, similar to but different from working for clients, but it will also yield a recurring income as you earn royalties from book sales. Plus, it is VERY good for your résumé and LinkedIn profile. People tend to assume you are an expert if you have written a book.

- Sell a digital product. This might mean selling an e-book from a website landing page or on Kindle, or it might mean selling a WordPress plug-in, or a Unity prefab. You could sell motion graphics for After Effects, or you could sell music via Bandcamp.

- Sell a mobile app, piece of software, or computer game.

- Create an online course to teach other people coding, web design, SEO, working online, or any other topic that interests you.

- Create a SaaS offering, such as an online tool.

Creating passive revenue streams will serve as the perfect accompaniment to the gigging lifestyle. For one, it means that you *can* take days off and still earn some money. At the same time, it means that even when you have no new clients biting, you'll still be earning *something* (and have something to work on).

As we've seen, your overall wealth and "value" isn't tied precisely to your "salary," and this is another perfect example of that: a passive income stream could perfectly offset the decision to work a little less!

Selling an e-book via a sales funnel, selling a mobile app, or creating a YouTube channel/website should be a lot easier for you if you have the experience of working with clients to provide the same services for them. In other words, you have the "inside scoop" and you know precisely what makes a successful product online. So, there is nothing stopping you from accomplishing that same thing for yourself.

This is a tip in general: pay close attention to the business models employed by the people who hire you. This might provide some valuable insight!

Even a relatively small website with a few ads on it could bring in $50 per month, which might not be huge bucks, but it's still very welcome!

Selling Leftover Materials

It's also often easy to set up passive income streams using only materials that you're *already* creating. This way, you are often selling the tools you've created and materials to other creators via a B2B distribution platform of some sort.

Let's say for instance that you are tasked with creating some kind of web design or logo design that utilizes a 3D model. Once you've made that 3D model, you can arrange it as part of your image and take a "snapshot" that will become the design element for the client. But at the same time, you can then *reuse* that model by uploading it to a site like TurboSquid (www.turbosquid. com) or 3DExport (https://3dexport.com). Likewise, you can use an image of the model from a different angle, perhaps with some different colors, and make that into another client's logo design, where relevant.

It's important that you clear this with the clients first and make sure they know that you will be recycling an element that you used to create their image (though it won't necessarily be recognizable). Usually, there is no real reason why they should mind.[3]

---

[3]Another completely different way to sell 3D models is to use a 3D printer (or online service like Shapeways.com) to turn those models into physical sculptures that people can buy!

Maybe you've been hired to create a video for a client to help them sell a product. In this scenario, you might end up creating filters and presets that you can use to make the video look more professional. In this scenario, there is absolutely *no* reason that you can't use those creations in future work to save yourself time, or even sell them on sites like VideoHive (`https://videohive.net`, part of Envato Market).

As a programmer, it is a huge mistake if you aren't reusing portable classes, libraries, and methods that you've written to perform useful jobs. And if you think in a modular manner *as* you create the solutions, you'll have more reusable tools to sell *or* to make future work faster.

Likewise, you can sell

- WordPress themes
- WordPress plug-ins
- Code libraries
- Classes and methods
- Photos (on Shutterstock and iStock)
- Video footage (Shutterstock)
- Unity prefabs

If you've written blog posts for a client and you clear it with them first, you could even put some of those articles into a PDF and sell them on the Kindle Store as an e-book. A client wants exclusive copyright and isn't willing to play ball? Then suggest splitting the revenue, or alternatively giving them a discounted rate in exchange for giving you the rights to reuse the content offline.[4]

Alternatively, why not write into the contracts for your clients that they will have exclusive copyright for the next two years? Most will think nothing of that, but it means that in two years' time, you can start selling those e-books and apps for yourself!

Finally, keep in mind that you can also use content this way that has been rejected, or that never gets completed. If you've written half of an app for someone who eventually decided they would go with another developer (it happens), then why not use that as the starting point for your next gig? Or why not see if you can turn that app into something of your own that you can sell?

---

[4]The value in content for webmasters and business owners comes from it being "unique." Google will not index and rank content that is not unique, and this can be checked via a tool called Copyscape (`www.copyscape.com`). However, if the content is on the Kindle Store and in PDF format, then Google can't reach it, and therefore the content is still "unique" for all intents and purposes.

Essentially, this comes down to efficiency and looking for opportunities. But if you're savvy and you remain on the lookout, you can find ways to gain *additional,* recurring profit from a vast number of your gigs. And if you do this, then you'll bring in a small amount of additional income that will help to provide a safety net and give you more leverage when charging your clients.

Better than that though, it could eventually grow into a *large* additional income that may allow you to pick and choose only the very best gigs. And at this point, you may find you're able to gain even more freedom in the way you design your workflow and lifestyle. Maybe you could give up gigging entirely and live purely off passive income?

This is another "exit strategy": using the gig economy to grow passive income streams until you can stop working *altogether.* And as far-fetched as it might sound, there are actually plenty of people who make a full-time living from selling apps, e-books, courses, and more—so that they can travel the world, volunteer, or generally live the life they want to live!

Gigging vs. Passive Income

You might now find yourself with another question: if it is possible to make a living entirely from passive income, then why set out to do anything *but* that in the first place?

What advantage does gigging have over creating products yourself to sell?

A few actually . . .

First, gigging is a strategy you can use to generate money almost immediately, and in a far more reliable fashion. Conversely, creating a website or successful app that is able to generate an ongoing income is something that can take years and years of work—and that has no guarantee of success. You may find that after working for years on an app, you only ever make 20 sales. You could build a blog that still only has 100 visitors a day after years of promotion.

Meanwhile, gigging means finding work, completing it, and very often getting paid *that night.* This is why using gigs to "bootstrap" other projects is actually often the best strategy of all.

Bootstrapping

One of the massive advantages when it comes to working online in the gig economy, from my perspective, is the opportunity to work on side projects. Not only can working on side projects help you to further your career and hone your skills, but it could also end up leading to even bigger opportunities.

If you're looking for side projects that will help you to fund your lifestyle and provide more side income to make your business more resilient, then some excellent examples include

- Online courses (teach people how to program on sites like Udemy, Skillshare, or Teachable)

- E-books (sell them from your own website and landing page, or through distribution platforms like Kindle)

- Apps

But maybe it's not just about the income? Maybe you want to bootstrap a project that you've dreamed about for years? Maybe you want to build a website? Maybe you want to write the next great American novel? Perhaps you're an inventor!

So, you may choose to look at your "side hustles" not purely as ways to earn extra money and gain more financial security but as being focuses in themselves and opportunities to earn even more income than you could do through gigs.

In this case, gigging still plays a very important role. Specifically, gigging gives you the ability to spend more time focusing on those projects than you would otherwise be able to afford.

This is "bootstrapping," which refers to one's ability to pull themselves up "by their bootstraps." In other words, you're funding your project or business idea by investing in yourself, and you're working to bring in that money. You might gig four days of the week, for instance, so that you can spend time and money on day five to work on other projects. Maybe it's that project that will ultimately be where you make it big, but gigging gives you the flexibility to make that happen.

And remember: you don't need to get your sense of purpose *from* the work that brings in the same money. If you never turn that passion project into a money maker, it doesn't matter!

The Future of the Gig Economy

There is no shortage of people willing to declare that the future of work is online. It is commonly said that more and more people will soon work from home, and that a lot of conventional jobs will become obsolete as robots and programs step in to do the work for us.

Right at the very start of this book, we discussed some of the reasons that companies choose to hire freelancers over taking on staff. One major reason is that it reduces their overheads, their admin, and their risk. Another is that it enables them to choose from a *far* larger and more distributed pool of talent.

These forces will continue to persuade businesses, and soon, more and more companies are likely to turn to online entrepreneurs rather than going through traditional channels to hire their staff.

Other factors will also contribute to the trend of using freelancers. Collaboration tools and freelancing platforms will inevitably improve, for instance. In the future, I highly suspect that we will collaborate in *virtual reality* offices where we can sit right next to a team member in another country and discuss ideas with them as though they were right there. Even better though, we'll be able to draw on the air in front of us to share and explain our ideas, and tap into cloud computing to utilize a literally *limitless* amount of processing power. And when it's time to focus, we'll rocket to a beautiful location free from all distractions.

Speaking of VR, what about the impact that VR training and remote operation could have? Imagine being able to learn a complex skill using virtual reality—something that NASA, DARPA, and other organizations are already implementing. And what if you could then control a robot *via* a similar VR tool in order to operate a forklift, fly a drone, conduct an orchestra, or even carry out complex surgery? The number of jobs that *can't* be learned and handled online is only going to shrink going forward.

At the same time, the capabilities of individuals will greatly increase as a result of better tools and learning resources, just as we discussed earlier in the context of the gaming industry.

It's now more affordable than ever to invest in a high-quality camera—most of us already have one built into our smartphone. Tools like Adobe Creative Cloud make professional-quality video editing possible for everyone. Why hire a studio when an individual can create an ad that looks just as professional?

Google and Microsoft are providing individual coders with access to cloud computing, machine learning, and powerful APIs. A single web developer can create something incredibly by using open source tools like WordPress or Drupal, and by leveraging tools like Adobe Illustrator.

We're seeing start-ups increasingly overtaking larger businesses thanks to their improved agility and speed. Where it takes a big organization *months* to implement new systems, individuals and start-ups can adapt on an almost daily basis. David is repeatedly taking on Goliath and wining, with the Internet acting as the great equalizer, leveling the playing field at every step.

And there are social and economic factors too. People are living longer and are more likely to work for multiple employers across multiple different industries. We no longer live in a time where it is normal to take on a single job and work that job for a lifetime.

If it has already become commonplace to switch jobs every few years; how long before we ultimately conclude that it's better not to be tied to one job *at all*?

Then there's automation. Automation *is* going to drive this trend even further. It is predicted that as we move forward, programs and robots might replace hundreds of millions of jobs. This doesn't just mean manufacturing jobs either: it means anything that *doesn't* require human creativity and empathy. Data analysts, checkout assistants, fraud investigators, and many more will lose their jobs to the rise of the machines.

Gigging vs. Sharing

The sharing economy also has close ties with the gig economy. The idea of exchanging a service for cash directly, or for another service, is all about decentralizing markets: removing the need for big organizations that maintain monopolies and force things to be done in a certain way. By providing a service directly, you remove the middleman. Prices can be driven down, and industries are disrupted. The companies that survive this will be those that are able to adapt by outsourcing, and by listening to consumer demand.

Traditional taxi firms and hotels have struggled against the likes of Uber and Airbnb because they simply aren't able to offer the same value and convenience. An individual has no overheads. If they already have a car parked in the driveway or space in their holiday home that isn't being used, then *any* money they receive will be additional to their current income.

Nor are larger companies able to adapt as quickly to changing technologies and markets. Governments are stepping in to try and level the playing field - making it harder for companies like Uber so that traditional taxi firms stand a chance, but it is too late: Pandora's box has been opened and we've all had a taste for just how affordable and easy travel can be. And the same thing is happening in business, only not everyone has noticed yet.

We are in what many people are calling the "Fourth Industrial Revolution." Technology is developing at a pace that is forcing businesses to adapt. We've seen the fall of physical CDs in the music industry, we're seeing shops close on main street, and countless companies are investing big money to try and replace their own staff with programs and machines. If you think Uber is disruptive for the taxi firms, just wait until driverless cars become commonplace!

What happens when we all own 3D printers in our homes, capable of manufacturing furniture, ornaments, electronics, and more? Why buy something from Ikea and pay for transport, storage, branding, and countless other overheads, when instead you can simply buy an STL file from someone online (or swap it for a bit of code) and print it out yourself at home? Apart from anything else, think how much more unique our decorating will become!

Again, we'll be cutting out the middleman. At this point, the only thing of any real value will be the 3D designs that we download online. Only creativity and inventiveness will hold any value.

Not even the brightest futurist could tell you precisely how all this will play out. At this rate, we might even reach the singularity before we all have a chance to adapt! All I can tell you is that you are in the right place right now. That developing your skills and learning to provide direct services of your own, learning to thrive in the gig economy, is the very best shot you have at future-proofing your career prospects.

Future-proofing Yourself

Learning to sell skills online is one crucial step, but there are other forces also at play here that will determine the *types* of work that we will be able to sell.

Specifically, creative work is likely to be increasingly in demand, while anything that could easily be automated is likely to fall out of favor. The simple fact of the matter is that companies are looking not only to replace their employees with freelancers, but also to replace the need for anyone to do the work *at all*. That's where automation will come in.

There is a chance that some of us will be the Blu-ray discs of the jobs market. That is to say that we will replace the traditionally employed (just as Blu-ray did indeed replace DVD), but not before automation has had a chance to jump in and replace us (just like streaming replaced Blu-ray before it really fulfilled its promise).

The threat that our rising breed faces will come from tools designed to replace the need for us to work at all. This isn't just a threat for the gig economy, but even more so for traditional jobs. As machine learning improves and computing power grows, more and more jobs will soon be able to be carried out by computer programs, leaving less and less space for the rest of us.

It might sound bleak that so many jobs are going to be lost to more-capable machines. But my hope is that someday we will reach the point where the economy can run itself as computers and machines run "algo-businesses," manufacture cars, drive taxis, and handle customer service calls. Governments will need to introduce universal basic incomes[5] for the rest of us to live off. Again, the only work that will have *any* value will be creative. People will write books, paint works of art, and create cool new apps because they want to. The only economy that will remain will be the sharing economy. And the only

---

[5]A strategy that is already being tested in several countries, such as the Netherlands.

way to provide value will be to offer what makes us uniquely human. We will work because we want to.

Of course, the machines might have already burned the Earth to the ground before this utopia has a chance to transpire. And if not, that would only come after a significant period of difficulty as many of us are left without work and with no provisions yet in place to manage the crisis.

The best thing we can do to protect ourselves meanwhile is to make sure we offer the kind of work that is very hard to replace. And that means creative work. Manual labor can easily be handled by a machine. So too can any kind of rote activity such as data entry or analysis, or even anything that involves simple interactions with members of the public. All the things that we discussed could be sidestepped through process fixing or automating in previous chapters.

But true creativity is still something that will elude AI for a while. If not indefinitely.[6]

How do we define creative work though? You might expect that programming would be the *first* job to fall to the rise of the machines—as you're literally speaking their language. In fact, though, coding is for the most part a *highly* creative process. It's about problem solving and coming up with novel ways of doing things. Not only that, but someone has to actually *write* the programs that are replacing the jobs!

Creative work includes problem solving, ideation, and creating novel and unique works. At its most fundamental, creativity is often described neurologically as being the unique combination of disparate ideas. And this is another reason that learning a wide range of subjects and skills is *so* valuable.

So, programming, writing content, design, consultancy, marketing, and anything that involves a deep understanding of human psychology is likely to be safe. Play to these strengths and develop these aspects of your game and you'll remain in high demand. Why do you think I focused on psychology, programming, digital marketing, writing, and personal training?

And at the same time, learn about the very tools that are threatening you. Learn how to utilize machine learning and the power of the cloud with tools like Google's AutoML (https://cloud.google.com/automl/). This type of work is going to be in increasingly high demand going forward. People who can work with big data and AI are increasingly in demand, and that's likely to continue exponentially going forward. You can charge a LOT if you know how to build apps that utilize computer vision, voice recognition, or learning.

---

[6]It has also been suggested that jobs that require empathy and sympathy, from day care, to nursing, to counselling, will also remain relevant.

One of the smartest things you can do right now is to look for ways to make your own job obsolete. Beat them to it!

Your job as a service provider is to keep learning and growing, to anticipate and adapt to a changing marketplace. While some of the changes that are coming our way pose big risks, they also offer huge advantages. Work smart and you can thrive.

Returning to Traditional Employment

There is one other "exit strategy" that you might at some point be forced to contend with: heading *back* to the world of being an employee after a hiatus. This is something that can pose a challenge, as you will now have an apparent gap in your résumé from a traditional employment standpoint, and will potentially come across as someone who is ultimately looking for a way out. My generation (millennials) has a bit of a bad reputation in that regard!

Fortunately, employers have become a lot more sympathetic to our plight on the whole. These days, it is increasingly common for people to take time out of their careers for a whole host of different reasons: including travel, mental health, and more. The key is to look for forward-thinking employers that view this as a form of self-development, and to know how to frame it in that way.

Find a good reason to explain why you took the time out, and emphasize the positives that came from it. Working for yourself teaches a lot of things that employers are looking for, from discipline and self-motivation, to the ability to work toward deadlines and targets. Try to anticipate the concerns that they will have (you are going to leave the position as soon as another self-employment opportunity comes up) and explain them away (it was an idea you just needed to explore, but it wasn't for you).

Another tip is to keep this possibility in mind as you're taking on work and accepting it. We've talked at length about the importance of building your personal brand and how this is something that the traditionally employed equally need to consider. Well here is the proof: the very same portfolio-building efforts that will help you to ultimately charge more and more as a freelancer will likewise help you to get work in traditional employment.

This is especially true if you also know how to present the skills and experiences you're collecting. Here are some examples of things that would look excellent on your résumé:

- Use of collaboration tools and project management software, such as Asana, Slack, and Basecamp

- Overseeing the creation of top-selling online course

- Working with a team of other programmers on a large app project

- Being published on prominent online media outlets, including [INSERT WEBSITE TITLES HERE]

- Building a personal blog with over 1,000 daily hits

- Managing relationships with over 500 clients

- Hiring and working with freelancers, employees, and agencies to complete large projects within deadline

Make it clear that you weren't just sitting on your hands during this time, but actually running a business and gaining invaluable expertise and skills along the way.

If you're struggling looking for work, then you can also consider the opportunities that your gigging has created. Maybe you could discuss working full-time for one of your current clients. Maybe you could look at a compromise situation, where you work as an independent contractor, for example. Maybe you could transition to a part-time contract with one client, and then look for a part-time job on the side.

Maybe you don't need to think of this as an either-or scenario at all, but rather as a fluid spectrum that you can transition in and out of at any time you choose. At any point in your career, you can be employed, self-employed, both, or anything in-between!

Chapter Summary

This chapter has been all about looking ahead and deciding what the next step is. That means not only looking at ways you can grow your business and increase your earnings as a result, but also ways that you can eventually divorce yourself from it so that you can retire to that tropical island.

Failing that, we've looked at some of the possible futures that are coming our way, and at how freelancers can prepare themselves for that.

In the next chapter we're going to rewind a bit. You have the theory now and you have your entire trajectory mapped out. All that is left is lift-off: launching yourself into the gig economy and exploring those new possibilities!

No more theory, it's time to take action.

Setting Sail: Making the Gig Economy Work for You

Okay, that's enough theory and enough speculation.

You are aware of the gig economy works, you know the pros and cons, and you are aware of all the minute details regarding setting yourself up legally, using common tools and sites, and dealing with clients.

All that's left is to put all this into practice and take the leap into the gig economy. This might be easier said than done if you're currently feeling overworked or overwhelmed, or if you have too many responsibilities to want to take that risk.

This chapter is about getting over those obstacles and actually making it happen.

© Adam Sinicki 2019
A. Sinicki, *Thriving in the Gig Economy*, https://doi.org/10.1007/978-1-4842-4090-8_10

Action Plan: Entering the Gig Economy

I hope all the lifestyle design strategies I provided in Chapter 8 are very aspirational and exciting, but I also realize they are a little abstract. Before you can start designing your perfect lifestyle around the job opportunities available to you, you first need to simply *start selling* something.

So how do you go from scratch to becoming a successful member of the gig economy? Here are the steps to take.

1. **Decide what you're going to do.**

   Take a look at your skills. Take a look at the market and what there is demand for (this might just mean perusing forums and freelancing sites). Take a look at what you can learn easily. Think about the contacts that you already have, and any routes to market that are open for you. And importantly: think about the kind of work you'd actually enjoy and be happy doing on a daily basis. You might also want to keep in mind what your longer-term goals are and where you are heading with your business. If you are using the gig economy to build your résumé and get rich, or if you are using it to launch a personal project, then those things can help to keep you motivated.

   Think too about everything we discussed in Chapter 8 on lifestyle design. How much work do you want to do? What are your priorities? What does your ideal day of work look like, and what types of opportunities are out there that can make that happen? Does the kind of work you're considering facilitate that? And how can you repackage it so that it will?

2. **Think about your terms and packaging.**

   Selling writing or coding in itself is not a service. Your service will rather be defined by the details of precisely *how* you are selling these things. What is your turn-around time going to be? How will you deliver the work? Will you offer packages? Do you want to be paid by the hour or by the word or line of code?

I don't want you to waste months in the planning stages here though. This is something you can think about in your spare time, but it's also something that you can tweak and iterate upon in the meantime. Just grab a basic working business model and go. This should take no more than half a day to decide. Like I say, you can change it later!

3. **Find some spare time.**

   Try and find some spare time that you can use to do part-time work. Unless you're feeling particularly bold, the aim here is not to quit your job and then hope that you make enough money to live on. Instead, the aim is to generate some healthy income that you will be able to use as you test your business model *before* you take the leap. That means finding some time in your current schedule that you can complete the work, whether that's one weekend a month, a couple of spare evenings, or during vacation time.

4. **Set up accounts.**

   Now build your LinkedIn account, making sure to squeeze every last drop out of your skills and experience to make yourself look as appealing as possible. If there's anything extra you can do quickly that will help to round out your profile, do that. Remember to make this as targeted to the type of work you want to do as possible.

   While there are some limitations to using freelancing sites like Freelancer, PeoplePerHour, and Fiverr, they can still provide some great opportunities and they're low maintenance. In other words, there's no reason *not* to set up your accounts.

5. **Get proactive, write ads.**

   A mistake would be to wait for the work to come in from freelancing sites. Instead, respond to job listings that others have posted and put your name forward. Better yet, advertise yourself on webmaster/coding forums, sites that list professionals in your niche, and anywhere else that your target audience will be likely to be. Finally, try e-mailing or contacting companies directly through websites. Does a business look like it needs a new website? Are they looking for content writers? Is there an agency that might benefit from another app developer? Or an indie games company you admire that you can offer your skills to?

   Make sure that you are selling yourself in a compelling manner with a well-written, persuasive script. Think hard about your pricing, and consider changing it, or offering packages and discounts in the future.

6. **Complete work, get paid.**

   I would advise against investing a lot more time and effort into marketing yourself at this point until you've started to get *some* work coming in. The temptation here is to distract yourself by spending lots of time building websites and reading books on business, rather than actually just getting your hands dirty and getting stuck in. The more time you invest now, the more crushing it can be when things don't work out right away and the more likely you'll be to give up. Don't kid yourself into thinking that you need anything fancy to start finding work—you just need the right e-mail to land in the right inbox. Until you've proven this model can work, you shouldn't waste your resources and energy on anything else.

   For now, you're going to focus on completing work for clients and getting paid for it. Prove to yourself that you can sustain this on a regular basis and spend some time refining the way you communicate, charge, and manage your time. Don't try and launch the perfect business out the gate: evolve it with time. As you go, keep a note of your clients' contact details. Even one-off clients can be remarketed to at later dates.

7. **Register your business.**

You don't need to register your business before you begin looking for work, but once you have been earning a little income for a month or more, it's time to declare that cash and set up your business. As a sole proprietor, that just means registering your income. You'll do this by heading over to the relevant government web page and then following the instructions. Ninety-nine percent of people reading this will be best served by registering as a sole proprietor to begin with. It's up to you whether you want to trade under your own name or choose a trading name.

8. **Build platforms.**

You don't want to rely on these sources of work forever, though, so once you have established yourself and demonstrated that you can find and complete work, it's time to build your own platforms. That means creating a website to act as a portfolio and portal (and that you can then later advertise through PPC, or promote via content marketing), and it means creating social media accounts that provide value to the readers and demonstrate your knowledge and expertise. This is part of the long game. Don't expect to be able to monetize a blog or YouTube channel overnight: it takes years to build thousands of followers. But once you get there, you'll have the ability to sell your services for *considerably* more.

9. **Develop.**

Now all that is left to do is to take your business big time. That probably means eventually quitting your day job so that you can focus 100% on your new business, or at least going part time in your current job.

At the same time, you should start hunting out bigger and bigger clients, while building on that résumé. Put yourself out there and chase after the kinds of jobs that will turn you into that "superstar."

Further your own education, seek out new qualifications and experience, and build your platform. Once you're a well-known tech blogger with hundreds of thousands of subscribers who has worked on massive best-selling projects, you'll be able to charge enough to live whatever kind of lifestyle you're hoping for. So, seek out those opportunities to impress and grow.[1]

This is ultimately all you need to do to build your business. Of course, the day-to-day details are going to vary depending on precisely what kinds of skills you're selling, but that's the general gist.

The take-home here is that the most important step is to *just start*. Don't make excuses, don't procrastinate. By the end of this week, you should already have money in your account.

How to Transition to the Gig Economy (Fear Setting)

Now you are aware of to set up your own online business, and you have a pretty comprehensive list of options to get you started.

So, the question is: why *haven't* you started?

If you're like a lot of people, you might now feel a little resistance to go out there and start selling yourself. Maybe you want to read just *one more book* about it first. Maybe you need to make sure you've completed X qualification before you can start? Maybe you just have too many responsibilities to take this risk right now? Maybe you need to wait for a quieter time in your personal life, or in your current career?

The truth of the matter, though, is that there is never a perfect time to start a business; just like there is never a perfect time to get married, buy a house, or have a kid. If you're waiting for the perfect moment to enter the gig economy, then it's not going to happen.

And truth be told, you're probably blowing your fears out of proportion anyway. This is a low-risk decision and one that you should feel confident to make. We've already seen that you don't need to quit your day job in order to make this work: you can easily start gigging on the side and then go full time *only once* you're absolutely sure that the business model works. Companies do this all the time when selling products. They will sell a beta version, or they

---

[1] A personal tip: write a book! It fits perfectly around a freelance schedule, and it is fantastic for raising your authority.

will sell exclusively to a very small audience before investing in it completely—they call it "verifying the market."

So, there is no real risk. If anything, this could be a fun hobby/experiment to try for a few evenings.

Then why do you still get that knot in your stomach when you think about it?

Unfortunately, this is just human nature. It's that risk aversion that we talked about earlier. You're convincing yourself that you aren't ready to take such a big step. And in truth, that's probably going to be your biggest obstacle when it comes to unshackling yourself from the desk.

Step one to building your business is to *start*. And step two is to *be consistent*. You'll learn on the job. It's the precise same as getting into shape. You can read theory and "prepare" yourself until you're blue in the face. I've had friends tell me they haven't yet started their workout because they need to "read some more fitness books." Or because they need to "wait for a quieter time in their life." But nothing will happen until they drop and start doing push-ups. In both scenarios, learning on the job is preferable by far.[2]

So how do you convince yourself that it's okay to try (and potentially fail)? We can take some pointers from a school of psychology called cognitive behavioral psychology, or CBT (psychology graduate, remember?).

CBT is a psychotherapeutic approach that has you focus on your thoughts and how these influence your behavior. In this case, you're going focus on the beliefs that you might hold about going freelance, which focus you accomplish by employing a little mindfulness: being consciously aware of what's going on in your own head.

Ask yourself: "What I am afraid of?" "What is causing that mental block that is preventing me from just *getting started?*" "What narrative am I telling myself?"

Here are some likely fears:

- You'll lose your current job and end up with no way of going back.

- Therefore, you will find yourself with no income, potentially having to sell your home, or becoming unable to support your family.

---

[2]Fun fact: Even the act of telling people about your new workout plan, or your new business idea, is often just a form of procrastination. And it may be that by telling someone, you are able to make that business or that workout a part of your identity and thereby get some kind of "release" from that discussion. Don't talk, just do.

- You will discover that you aren't good enough, and thereby damage your own self-esteem.

- You'll discover that you can't do it, and thereby lose the "idea" of someday giving up your job.

- You'll run into tax difficulties and end up being fined.

- Your workload will snowball and you'll end up with too much to handle.

- People will scoff at you and think that you're being stupid, telling you that you should "get a real job" (urgh).

While these might seem like insurmountable problems in the short term, the reality is often that you are actually blowing them out of proportion in your mind. In truth, you can probably mitigate all of these problems or come up with contingency plans. Many of them might be completely unfounded to begin with.

Write down your own challenges and problems, then go through each one and analyze just how based in reality it is. For example:

- *You'll lose your current job and end up with no way of going back.* You don't have to quit your current job right away, and if you do, you can probably find another one (or even go back to your old one) fairly quickly.

- *Therefore, you will find yourself with no income, potentially having to sell your home, or being unable to support your family.* Most of us have enough to live on for a few months. Most of us have parents or family who are able to support us in the most pressing of times. Many of us can get by on the salary of our partner. If these things aren't true for you, then consider again that you can probably find other work fairly quickly, or even take out loans, or go on the dole.

- *You will discover that you aren't good enough, and thereby damage your own self-esteem.* There is only one way to find out. And besides, the point is that this is a learning curve, and you will get better only by doing.

- *You'll discover that you can't do it, and thereby lose the "idea" of someday giving up your job.* This is but one attempt at branching out and starting your own business. Most of the "successful" people we read about failed multiple times before they eventually landed on their big idea.

- *You'll run into tax difficulties and end up being fined.* As long as you try to meet the requirements, the worst-case scenario is normally that you'll be asked to pay back what you owe if you get this wrong. And getting it right is not as hard as you might think.

- *Your workload will snowball and you'll end up with too much to handle.* If this happens, you can simply refuse some of the work. That's the beauty of being self-employed! In fact, this is a very good problem to have. Another option is to subcontract the work. Worst-case scenario, you can book some vacation time from your day job—or from your other clients—to focus on what's outstanding. You don't have to give much notice or get permission for this: after all, you are self-employed!

- *People will scoff at you and think that you're being stupid, telling you that you should "get a real job" (urgh).* So? Anyway, most people are far more likely to be *impressed* with you for taking a chance.

This is called "thought challenging" and it's part of a larger process known as "cognitive restructuring." The ultimate aim? To replace your negative thoughts with positive ones that will lead to positive action. Tim Ferriss, who I've acknowledged a few times previously, describes something similar that he refers to as "fear setting."

Better yet, why not go one step further and use the next crucial aspect of cognitive restructuring: hypothesis testing. This means that you *test* those fears and negative beliefs by actually doing the thing you're afraid of in a small, controlled manner.

At the same time, you can also do the reverse and focus on the reasons that you *need* to take action. That means focusing on your current sense of dissatisfaction, or your fear of being stuck in a rut for the rest of your days. This emotion can be a powerful motivating force that will get you to get up and take action.

Likewise, try to focus on the end goal, on the reason that you really want to make the change. Focus on your "why" (to quote Simon Sinek's excellent TED talk). Focus on the vision and picture yourself in five years' time if all goes well.

Remember: motivation is driven by emotion, not logic. So, picture what it could be like to have financial independence and freedom from a manager or set hours. Imagine the things that could be possible with a flexible job, whether that means working on some kind of dream project or means traveling the world with your laptop.

The Power of "The Little Investigation"

The most important thing you can do to allay your fears is to take a "little investigation."

Take one tiny step in the right direction—or better yet, just *glance at it*. Think of this as "breaking the seal" as it were. Often, the biggest psychological hurdle is just starting: it seems so massive and yet abstract. It seems like you need to dedicate all this time and mental energy to it.

So, don't think about the long term. Just investigate the steps you might need to take: whether that means playfully writing out your ad just for fun, or whether it means taking a look at the government website to see how you would go about registering your business. There's no obligation or requirement to actually *do anything*. You're just looking out of interest as a thought experiment.

But once you've gotten a better idea of the size and scope of the problem, you'll find it's much easier to lose yourself in it. You might find that while taking a look, you make a note of some sort, or perhaps open up an online account. Before you know it, you'll have completely lost yourself in it: that small bit of momentum will carry you forward until it's an unstoppable force.

Recently I decided to set up a Patreon account to receive donations for my YouTube channel. I'd been putting it off for ages (there are always more pressing things to do) until I decided to just take a look. Before I knew it, the whole thing was set up. This likewise recently worked for me boarding my loft, and it will work for you setting up your online business.

Just *take a little investigation*, and before you know it, you'll wake up a sole proprietor.

The Dream Scenario

While I believe that it is possible for anyone to safely transition into the gig economy, I also acknowledge that it isn't always easy—and that it's harder for some people than others. The ideal scenario in which to start working online, then, would be while living at home with parents or while still in school. If you are in a position where you don't yet have the financial responsibilities that come with adulthood, or if you are in a position where you have a safety net, then there is nothing to stop you going "all in," taking risks, and building the business you want.

If you're already married with kids, this dream scenario is but a dream. BUT if you're reading this as someone who still lives with parents and you like the sound of working online even a little, then I would *urge* you to take action right now and get started. You'll never have a better opportunity to pursue risky propositions and test your limits.

Going Part Time

To reiterate: you don't need to give up your day job in order to become a functioning member of the gig economy. Just as valid an option is to start working gigs on the side, on top of what you're currently doing, and thereby start testing the waters and ensuring that your business model works as a viable way to earn a living.

But what's more is that you need *never* become a full-time member of the gig economy. The amazing thing about the gig economy is that it adapts to fill the space that you have in your current lifestyle. We've discussed this already in Chapter 8, but it's worth repeating: you certainly have the option to work as a freelancer on top of a part-time job. And this can be a great option if it means you reduce some of the pressure of running your own business. It also means that people who need that social interaction and that routine can get the best of both worlds: by working a part-time job that they enjoy as a personal trainer, as a checkout assistant, or as anything else they're interested in.

This is also a great option for those in stable relationships. If one of you is bringing home a full-time income and you have at least a part-time income guaranteed yourself, then you can afford to take more risks in your self-employed work. At the same time, you still have that potential to eventually expand to full-time freelancing and realize the sense of satisfaction that comes from owning a business of your own. Note that you still need to pay tax this way, however.

Side Income

Another option for using the gig economy to your advantage is to use it as a way to earn a side income—to create a "side hustle," which is an increasingly trendy option. The same goes for finding ways to earn passive income.

This is another way that you can experiment with the gig economy in a completely pressure-free manner. Essentially, you will treat your time working in the gig economy as a "hobby that pays." You can do this work in the evenings or on the occasional weekend. Focus on producing work you find rewarding, whether that means coding physics every now and then for an indie game company, for example, or writing articles for big websites. If you get a little extra money, then you can treat yourself and your partner to a nice meal out, you can go on a small trip, or you can invest in a nice laptop. Or you could save it as a backup fund in case you decide to become a full-time freelancer.

Financial Support

Finally, one more possibility is to use the gig economy—and this book—as a kind of "emergency funds" machine. If your furnace breaks, your car battery dies, or you lose some money on a bad investment, having the gig economy at your fingertips ultimately means you have the option to dedicate a couple of hours and earn $20, $30, $50. Just set aside half a Saturday, and you can earn some more money!

Likewise, if you should see something that you want to buy but can't really justify, just work a couple of hours and then buy it guilt-free!

While I tried to make joining the gig economy full time sound as undaunting as possible in this chapter, I am well aware that it does take a little courage. But the gig economy is not just for the bold: this is a tool for anyone and everyone.

Between Jobs

One last way that you can use the gig economy as a "resource" in this sense is by using it to tide you over between jobs. If you've been let go, if you're currently looking for work, or if you're unable to work for whatever reason, the gig economy is there for you!

In fact, this can be a very useful tool for those that want to change careers. For instance, if you can't stand another minute in your current job, then why not leave and do some freelancing until you find something better? OR freelance and use that as a way to give yourself the flexibility to start another career. I always think that this is the perfect option for struggling actors, for instance, or for people that want to volunteer at organizations in order to build skills and experience. This works doubly well if you also gain relevant experience *from* the gigs you're working.

Funding

Speaking of emergency funds ... funding is something that some people reading this will need to consider.

For the most part, selling your own services online is a process that has zero overhead. That's part of the appeal and it's part of what makes it so flexible and useful for so many people. But with that said, there are some situations where you will need some kind of funding: if you wish to buy or rent your own office (or you need to), if you plan on investing in an advertising campaign to bring in more clients, or if you need specific equipment.

Alternatively, taking out a loan of some sort is another option if you *do* want to go with the scarier option of giving up your job and going full time right away. This way, you will have a little cash to act as your fallback and to live off of while you build toward a more stable income.

In these scenarios, you might need to make an initial investment and work for a set amount of time before you reach breakeven (the point at which you've paid back any and all initial expense). So how do you get this money?

One option is PayPal Working Capital. This is a loan system that works by charging a set fee determined by how quickly you choose to pay back the amount. While the interest is actually pretty bad once you calculate it, it does have some other benefits. One is that you pay back the loan as a percentage *out* of your PayPal income. For example, you might pay 10% on any money that comes in. That means that if your clients dry up, you won't need to pay as much (or any) back. What's more is that a PayPal loan won't affect your credit score and the banks don't even need to know about it (it won't show up on statements either). This means it won't affect your ability to, for example, take out a mortgage. That's a considerable advantage in our line of work, seeing as lenders don't tend to trust freelancers at the best of times! Note that the amount you can borrow is dependent on your sales history with PayPal, so this option is better suited to those that have been working smaller gigs for a while already.

PayPal Working Capital also isn't the best option in terms of your APR in most cases (unless you spend a long time paying it back). But it has a number of other benefits for those of us in the gig economy. The fact that it comes out of your PayPal income and doesn't have any late payment fees or traditional APR (meaning the amount you're paying back will never increase) makes a PayPal loan a very "safe" option and very convenient.

Other options include taking out a business loan, looking for a small business grant from your government, asking "the bank of Mom and Dad," or even setting up a Kickstarter campaign (www.kickstarter.com). Kickstarter is a crowdfunding site, meaning it is a place where you can get funding to launch a project that people want to see succeed—usually in return for some kind of reward (such as a free gift, called a perk) or accolade (such as acknowledgement in the credits, or a special thank you e-mail). There are other crowdfunding sites that do this too, such as Indiegogo (www.indiegogo.com). Note that this won't be relevant for 99.99% of people reading this, as the audience needs to want the thing you're building or producing badly enough to be willing to pay lots of money for it, and needs to see that you require their help in order to make it a reality. The only scenario where that's likely in our case is if we're providing a very exclusive and exciting B2C service.

Finally, if you can find a client that trusts your abilities and you intend to work with them for a long period, then you can discuss the possibility of getting an advance on payment. In other words, get paid a large amount up front that you then work off.

As mentioned, most freelancers won't find that they need this kind of investment to begin offering their services. I highly recommend that you avoid taking out a loan unless it is absolutely essential for the running of your business. If you *do* need a loan, though, then make sure that you don't ask for any more than you need, and that you aim to pay that amount off as quickly as you can.

Likewise, try to make sure that you have contingency plans in place for all outcomes. That means you should know precisely how you plan on paying back the amount once you start earning (and ensure that the payback scheme suits this plan); and it means you should know precisely how you will pay it back if you don't earn a single penny from your business venture. The aim here is not to get into debt!

Do keep in mind though that any interest you do pay back will be tax deductible, and that these funding options are useful to hold in reserve as your business grows too—as you might find that you can use them to advertise later on, to pay for branding and other features, or to acquire new tech and resources.

Don't overcomplicate things early on though. Remember from the steps presented earlier in this chapter that the first thing you need to do is to *start offering and providing work*. Worry about growing later on, after you have a working business model.

Final Tips Recap

With that overview of funding taken care of, we're almost ready to part ways. I hope that at this point you're starting to feel confident that you can go ahead and start providing services on the Web.

Before you go though, let's just recap some of the most important and valuable tips that you should take from this text.

The Balance of Power

First, recognize that there is a balance of power in any relationship with any client. How that balance plays out will go a long way toward determining how easy your life ends up being. In other words, whether you end up working extra hard as a dogsbody, or whether you end up being able to pick and choose the work you want to do.

Subtle things you do, and small aspects of your communication, will decide this. Have you made yourself indispensable and proven your worth? Or are you constantly apologizing for late work?

Do you agree to unreasonable demands? Do you let the client contact you at every time of day? Are you willing to work for a pittance?

Small aspects of your language can also have this effect. Make sure that you don't ask permission. Make sure that your clients know that you consider yourself to be valuable—never enter into a business relationship where you are desperate for the client to offer you work.

Communication Overhead

In a similar manner, you should always keep in mind the communication overhead when discussing projects with clients, and you should make sure you're happy with the "cost" in this regard.

Every minute that you spend chatting on Skype, or answering an e-mail, is a minute that you haven't spent working. And a minute that you're not getting paid for.

A lot of clients will be overly fussy. Some are just trying to make themselves feel more professional. Whatever the reason, you will meet plenty who want to have long, drawn-out discussions. Make sure that you avoid this wherever possible and learn to just knuckle down and get the work done.

Becoming a Superstar

One of the most valuable tips I can share is to make sure you are always thinking about your résumé and your portfolio as you work and grow. The more prolific and qualified you can become, the more people are going to be willing to hire you and pay you well. When taking on work, then, don't think primarily about the monetary reward, but place more stock in the opportunities that could come from it and whether it may be able to one day help you charge more for your work.

Being Specific

While building your portfolio, qualifications, and a varied skill set are all very important, it's usually better to be more specific when advertising your services. Try to make yourself seem like the very best machine learning expert, security consultant, fitness writer, real estate web developer, or whatever your niche is, not a Jack of all trades.

Work-Life Balance

Estalishing a healthy work-life balance is what attracts many people to the freelance lifestyle in the first place, and protecting that work-life balance is incredibly important.

Thus, it is really rather important that you ensure you keep this as your priority and don't allow work to run away with you. Protect your free time, and make sure you are designing your work to fit around the lifestyle you want—not the other way around.

If your work evolves into something you no longer enjoy, look at ways you can change that.

The Options

On that note, make sure you are aware of all the options available to you as a professional within the gig economy. In other words, keep in mind that you don't necessarily have to be a full-time freelancer, but are equally entitled to

- Work in the gig economy part time, and do another job part time

- Do odd jobs when you need/want a little extra cash

- Use the gig economy to support another objective—to bootstrap another business idea, to find your dream job, or to gain additional skills and expertise

Resilience

If you want to build a resilient business as a service provider, then the following are some important tips:

- Find a wide variety of different types of client. Ideally, that means looking for someone that will pay for work whenever you provide it, or at least someone that will be around for a long time. It also means finding a good mixture of long and short-term clients.

- If you can, create some form of passive income.

Increasing Your Wages

If you want to increase your income as someone who is self-employed, it can sometimes be tricky negotiating a better wage. One option is to try increasing your asking price so incrementally that the client doesn't notice (which works especially well if you charge in some kind of unit, such as per line of code). Another strategy is to break your service down into different types of package that the clients can choose from. Also effective is to try looking for higher paid work and securing that (maybe taking "vacation" from your current clients to test that they are long-term), enabling you to then start a bidding war of sorts.

A Few More Rapid-Fire Tips

- Work in coffee shops if you struggle working from home.

- If you don't want to be a digital nomad, you can try traveling in short stints.

- Blog, build a social media platform, and/or create a YouTube channel. Creating an audience gives you more clout, more advertising power, and more charging power.

- Don't let anything go to waste. How can you reuse those classes from your code? How can you reuse those Premiere presets?

- Think about ways to productize your business.

- Cut the communication overhead.

- Fill your office with inspiring things (such as a personal hero, or an example of fantastic work that you would like to aspire to) to stay more motivated, and try watching short clips and films that put you in a productive mood.

- If you struggle to get started with work, or even with getting over the fear of setting up your online business, "take a little investigation."

Consistency

The most important tip of all though is consistency. I've tried to provide as much advice, commentary, and information as possible to help you make the best decisions when it comes to growing your business. I've tried to explain how this can be a perfect route to creating your dream lifestyle, and how you can use it to grow your portfolio and résumé to the point where you're a titan of your industry.

But all that is secondary. What you mustn't do is use any of this as an excuse not to get started in the first place. You mustn't let it put you off, or become overly daunting.

Check the start of this chapter again. The steps involved in getting started aren't that difficult or complex; in fact, they're very easy. All you need to do is place that ad, and then start delivering on the work you've promised once the requests start coming in.

And then what's more important than *all of the other stuff* is that you are consistent. Put in the hours. Don't hand in work late. Be the best there is at what you do.

After all, we are what we repeatedly do. If you want to run an online business selling tech services, then that's what you need to do. Starting now. No excuses: get writing that ad!

And if that sounds scary? If that is still too massive a task?

Then just have a look—just launch a Little Investigation into it.

Good luck!

Index

A

Advertising, 47–48

Asana website, 114–115

B

Black Hat World, 32

Bonusly website, 118

Brain-derived neurotrophic factor
    (BDNF), 172

Business (nitty-gritty details), 123
    accounting process
        company account, 146
        paperless, 145
        pay day preparation, 146
        PayPal, 144
        spreadsheet, 145
        use of, 147–148
    agreement, 130
    billing (see PayPal)
    contracts
        key points, 130
        ownership, 132
        payment plan, 133
        scope and responsibilities, 132
        signatures and termination, 133
        types of, 131
        warranties, 133
        writing contracts, 132
    financial trials (self-employment)
        leave/holiday, 149
        loans/lease/finance, 149

        pensions, 148
        sick pay, 148–149
    invoice
        benefits of, 127
        currency, 129
        key details, 127
        sample invoice, 128
    monthly payment, 130
    tax (see Tax returns)

C

Collaboration tools
    advantage, 114
    Asana, 114
    Bonusly, 118
    challenges of, 121
    DocuSign, 117
    disadvantages, 114
    Dropbox, 117
    GitHub, 119
    Google Calendar, 117
    Google Drive, 116
    SharePoint, 118
    Skype, 120
    Slack, 115
    Tettra, 117
    workflow tools, 120
    Zoom, 120

Communication
    art of
        agencies, 113
        clients, 111
        e-mails, 109

© Adam Sinicki 2019

A. Sinicki, *Thriving in the Gig Economy*, https://doi.org/10.1007/978-1-4842-4090-8

Communication (*cont.*)
    engagement, 110
    right tone, 109
    social engineering and advice, 111
    suggestion, 112
  clients, 107–108
  complaints, 106
  definition, 100
  downward spiral, 104
  e-mails
    batching, 102
    charging, 103
    explaining, 102
    order forms, 101
    overhead, 101
  mistakes, 107
  prioritize, 105
  realistic deadlines, 105
  revisions, 106
  temptation, 104
  wiggle room, 106

Consistency, 217

Content management systems
  (CMSs), 15

Content marketing, 35

Cookie-cutter projects, 90

D, E

Deliver client work
  advantages and disadvantages, 76–77
  attentional control, 78
  automation, 93
  cookie-cutter projects, 90
  dorsal attention, 78
  executive attention, 78
  flow states, 77
  heartrate variance, 78
  jobs, 91
  on time, 75
  optimum performance
    exercise, 88
    general physical preparedness, 88
    meditation, 88
    nootropics, 89
    passion, 89
    pruning process, 87
    sleep, 86–87
    strategies, 90
    transhuman business model, 86
    wetware, 86
  outsourcing, 92–93
  productive
    candle problem, 85
    cognitive bias, 85
    feedback loops, 81
    functional fixedness, 85
    goals, 82
    intrinsic motivation, 80
    pertinent and interesting, 79
    priming and inspiration, 81
    removing distraction, 82
    right environment, 82
    scheduled breaks, 84
    separating creativity and
      flow, 84–85
    states, 78–79
  risks, 94
    hardware, 96–97
    process fix, 95–96
    process fixes, 95–96
    WordPress, 95
  stress and flow, 78
  tunnel vision, 79
  waste, 91

Digital Point Forums website, 32

DocuSign website, 117

Dropbox, 117

F

Fiverr website, 24

Forums, 32–33

Freelance details
  admin and fiddly stuff, 9
  benefits of, 3
  business and personal development, 7
  coders, 20
  communication overhead, 5
  discipline, 8
  freedom of location, 4
  future-proofing, 7
  potential downsides, 10
  problems, 8
  productive, 6
  risk, 9

scaling method (see Scaling method)
set your own fee, 5
stability, 6
team performances, 9
time flexibility, 4
websites
    conventional, 25
    digital marketing, 28
    experience and proof, 27
    experiment, 29
    liquid, 26
    listing skills, 27
    overview/introduction, 28
    profile photo, 26
    sell online, 25
    start small, 26
    video adding, 26
    winning bids, 29
work online/work short-term, 5

G, H, I, J, K

Gig economy, 201
    action plan, 202–206
    advantages of, 3
    automation, 196
    balance of power, 214
    benefits of, 2
    capabilities of, 195
    collaboration tools, 195
    communication overhead, 215
    definition, 2
    dream scenario, 210
    financial support, 212
    funding, 212
    future of, 194
    future-proofing, 197–199
    gigging *vs.* sharing, 196
    Google and Microsoft, 195
    Google's AutoML, 198
    jobs, 212
    lifestyle design (see Lifestyle design)
    little investigation, 210
    options, 216
    overview of, 214
    PayPal, 213
    resilience business, 216
    resource, 212
    side income, 211
    social and economic factors, 195

specific option, 215
superstar, 215
tech professionals and entrepreneurs, 1
transition, 206–209
VR training and remote operation, 195
wages increase, 216
work-life balance, 215
zero-hour contracts, 2
GitHub, 119
Google Calendar, 117
Google Drive, 116

L

Lifestyle design
    budgeting, 159
    career, 152
    clients, 161
    digital nomad
        advantage of, 171
        AirbnB, 167
        challenges, 169
        compromise solution, 169
        concepts of, 167
        flow trigger, 172
        lifestyle, 168
        rich environment, 172
        sharing economy, 167
        stuff and base, 171
        tech and gadgets, 170
        travel light, 170
        work-life balance, 171
    financial modeling, 160
    gig economy, 156
        long-term profits, 157
        personal turnover, 157
        working process, 158
    goal setting, 158
    income-overheads-wealth, 156
    optimizations, 161
    realizations, 155
    rules creation, 162–164
    sequence, 151
    spare time (work-life balance), 164
        benefit of, 166
        contingency plans, 164
        danger, 166
        fitness analogy, 165
        online freelancer, 165

Lifestyle design (*cont.*)
    traditional employment, 151
    trap, 153–155
LinkedIn, 33

M

Money
    career, 68
    complex morality (freelance work), 67
    finding clients, 70–71
    friends/work, 72
    fulfilling, 68
    gigging life, 72
    guidelines, 68
    over-correct, 72
    skill set, 70
    superstar developer and editor, 70
    video blog (vlog), 70

N

Networking, 49
Non disclosure agreements (NDAs), 131
Non-tech-related jobs, 17–18

O

Optical character recognition (OCR), 145

P, Q

PayPal account
    accounting process, 144
    Bitcoin, 126
    blockchain, 126
    features of, 125
    fees, 125
    gig economy, 213
    online transaction, 124
    payment method, 125–126
    TransferWise, 125
    workflow, 124

PeoplePerHour sites, 23

Persuasive techniques
    address concerns and pain
        points, 43–44
    engaging and holding attention, 42–43
    jargon/buzzwords, 41

SEO writing services, 45–47
teach, 44
value proposition, 44–45
WORST business websites, 42

R

Rates and gigs
    benchmarking, 54
    charging, 51
        bulk orders and long-term deals, 67
        factors, 62
        free samples, 64
        options, 65
        packages, 66–67
        per job *vs.* per hour, 64–65
        up front *vs.* on delivery, 62–63
    clear and comprehensive comments, 55
    communication, 55
    dry spells, 55
    existing clients, 56
    imposter syndrome, 54
    incremental fake, 58
    long-term clients, 56
    maintenance, 56
    multiple prices, 55
    negotiation techniques, 59
    participant, 58
    personal reasons, 57
    possible agreement, 60
    shopping around, 57
    test out, 57
    worth option, 53

Rent-a-coder, 25

S

Scaling method
    conventional physical assets, 175
    employees, 175
    exit strategy, 188, 190
    franchising, 180
    freelancers
        businesses, 186
        client's expertise, 187
        communication, 187
        hash out details, 188
        job description, 188
        online copywriters, 186

pay for, 188
previous experience, 186
service arbitrage, 185
small order, 186
talent, 188
growing personal
accelerated learning, 183
AnkiApp flashcards app, 184
digital polymath, 181
Feynman technique, 184
homo universalis, 181
Matrix-style, 185
online courses, 183
Skillshare, 182
traditional employment, 183
hiring, 176
methods, 176
passive income
bootstrapping, 193–194
earning money, 190
gigging *vs.* passive income, 193
inside scoop, 191
selling leftover materials, 191–192
tech entrepreneurs, 190
productization, 179
service arbitrage, 177
teaming up, 178
white label service, 177

Search engine optimization (SEO), 8

Sell online
combining jobs, 19
content marketing, 16
3D modeling, 16
find work, 21
contests, 24
Fiverr, 24
Freelancer, 24
freelancing sites, 21–22
PeoplePerHour, 23
Rent-a-coder, 25
Stack Overflow, 25
Toptal, 25
upwork, 22–23
internet marketing and SEO, 16
IT skill, 15
package skills, 19
programming, 14

tech job, 16
tech skills, 14
video editing, 17
virtual assistant service, 17
web design, 15

SharePoint, 118

Skype, 120

Slack, 115

Social media, 40

Software as a service (SaaS), 179

Sole trader *vs.* not a sole trader
company name, 144
independent contractor, 143
limited/incorporated, 142
meaning, 141
sensitive, 144

Stack Overflow, 25, 33

T

Tax Residency Certificate (TRC), 131

Tax returns, 133
advantage of, 138
claiming expenses, 137
entertaining clients, 138
equipment, 139
expenses, 139
loans and bank charges, 140
marketing, 140
mileage, 140
premises, 140
services, 140
software, 139
sole trader *vs.* not a sole trader, 141
supplies, 140
VAT, 141
working process, 134–136

Tettra, 117

Toptal, 25

Traditional employment, 199–200

Turn-around time (TAT), 106

U

Unique selling point (USP), 55

V

Value-added tax (VAT), 141
Virtual assistance service
        (VAS), 17, 92

W, X

Warrior Forum, 32
Website
    Asana, 114–115
    Bonusly, 118
    brand creation, 37
    content marketing, 35
    creation, 31, 34
    Digital Point Forums, 32
    DocuSign, 117

Fiverr, 24
freelance (see Freelance details)
landing page, 34
SEO basics, 37–39
steps of, 36
WordPress, 36
WORST business, 42
Zoom, 120
WordPress, 36

Y

YouTube, 39

Z

Zoom website, 120

CPSIA information can be obtained
at www.ICGtesting.com
Printed in the USA
LVHW040131131118
596842LV00007B/68/P

9 781484 240892